"Companies have had to, mistakenly, choose between delivering customer delight or increased revenue—assessing that delivering the former is expensive and delays the latter. With patterns gleaned from 50 real-world case studies, Akin delivers a clear roadmap for how to deliver customer delight AND increase revenue! In fact, one cannot live without the other."

Avinash Kaushik, *Author:* Web Analytics: An Hour A Day; Web Analytics 2.0; *Global Lead, Strategic Analytics, Google*

"Akin's deep expertise in digital intelligence shines through as he delivers practical tools to help you understand your customers better."

June Dershewitz, *Digital Analytics Association Board Chair*

"There's no lack of customer data for Marketers and CX professionals. But much like the famous line 'water, water everywhere and not a drop to drink' in Samuel Taylor Coleridge's poem, that doesn't mean all that data is useful or usable. Akin Arikan's book provides the key to unlock insights from digital experiences so that business leaders can make improvements to increase customer loyalty and drive value to the enterprise. Highly recommended."

Bob Thompson, *Founder/CEO of CustomerThink and Author of* Hooked on Customers: The Five Habits of Legendary Customer-Centric Companies

"At Human37 most of our clients are complementing their traditional analytics solution with experience analytics to get comprehensive and actionable insights so they can fine-tune all the details of the experiences they offer on all of their digital assets."

Julien De Visscher, *Managing Director, Human37*

"At Wunderman Thompson, our clients prioritize delivering the best possible brand experiences. This book illustrates that at the core of any great brand experience, is great data."

Josh Archer, *VP Analytics, Wunderman Thompson*

T0293222

Customer Experience Analytics

An unprecedented guide to user experience (UX) analytics, this book closes a mission-critical skill gap and enables business professionals in a digital-first world to make smart, effective, and quick decisions based on experience analytics.

Despite two decades of web metrics, customer experience has largely remained a black box. UX analytics tools help businesses to see themselves and their customers with a new lens, but decision-makers have had to depend on skilled analysts to interpret data from these tools, causing delays and confusion. No more: this book shows a wide range of professionals how to use UX analytics to improve the customer experience and increase revenue, and teaches the C-SUITE method for applying UX analytics to any digital optimization challenge. It provides 50 case studies and 30 cheat sheets to make this a daily reference, and includes ten mindmaps, one for each role discussed, from senior leaders to product managers to e-commerce specialists.

Managers across industries will regularly consult this book to help them guide their teams, and entry- to mid-level professionals in marketing, e-commerce, sales, product management, and more will turn to these pages to improve their websites and apps.

Akin Arikan has over 20 years of experience working with customers in the field of digital intelligence and is an award-winning industry speaker, a published author on multichannel marketing, a frequent contributor to magazines, and a blogger. Akin is a director of product at Contentsquare, a popular customer experience analytics and optimization solution, and a guest lecturer on the first-of-its-kind Cross-Channel Management certificate program at the University of St. Gallen.

Customer Experience Analytics

How Customers Can Better
Guide Your Web and App Design
Decisions

Akin Arikan

Foreword by Thomas H. Davenport

Routledge
Taylor & Francis Group

NEW YORK AND LONDON

Designed cover image: © Getty/ Preto_perola.

First published 2023
by Routledge
605 Third Avenue, New York, NY 10158

and by Routledge
4 Park Square, Milton Park, Abingdon, Oxon, OX14 4RN

Routledge is an imprint of the Taylor & Francis Group, an informa business

© 2023 Akin Arikan

The right of Akin Arikan to be identified as author of this work has been asserted in accordance with sections 77 and 78 of the Copyright, Designs and Patents Act 1988.

All rights reserved. No part of this book may be reprinted or reproduced or utilised in any form or by any electronic, mechanical, or other means, now known or hereafter invented, including photocopying and recording, or in any information storage or retrieval system, without permission in writing from the publishers.

Trademark notice: Product or corporate names may be trademarks or registered trademarks, and are used only for identification and explanation without intent to infringe.

Library of Congress Cataloging-in-Publication Data
Names: Arikan, Akin, 1969 – author.
Title: Customer experience analytics: how customers can better guide your web and app design decisions / Akin Arikan.
Description: 1st Edition. | New York, NY : Routledge, [2023] |
Includes bibliographical references and index. |
Summary: "An unprecedented guide to user experience (UX) analytics, this
Identifiers: LCCN 2022036762 (print) | LCCN 2022036763 (ebook) |
ISBN 9781032370774 (hardback) | ISBN 9781032370767 (paperback) |
ISBN 9781003335191 (ebook)
Subjects: LCSH: Consumer satisfaction. |
User interfaces (Computer systems)–Design. | Consumer behavior.
Classification: LCC HF5415.335 A75 2023 (print) |
LCC HF5415.335 (ebook) | DDC 658.8/343–dc23/eng/20220818
LC record available at https://lccn.loc.gov/2022036762
LC ebook record available at https://lccn.loc.gov/2022036763

ISBN: 9781032370774 (hbk)
ISBN: 9781032370767 (pbk)
ISBN: 9781003335191 (ebk)

DOI: 10.4324/b23273

Typeset in Sabon
by Newgen Publishing UK

Contents

Acknowledgments   ix
Foreword   xi

Introduction: The Experience Imperative—Experience
or Bust!   1

PART I
Experience Analytics Essentials for Closing
Blindspots and Connecting the Dots   9

1   What Ingredients Make for a Good Experience?   11

2   Where Are the Blindspots in the Traditional Digital
    Intelligence Ecosystem?   22

3   A Map of Digital Experience Analytics and Metrics   39
    3A Experience Analysis 47
    3B Automated Experience Insights 71
    3C Impact Quantification, Customer Insights, and
        Segmentation 87

4   Connect the Dots Between Experience and the Digital
    Intelligence Ecosystem   95

PART II
**Solve Everyday Business Challenges Faster with
Experience Analytics** 105

5 Solve Common Challenges at the Top of the Funnel   107
   5A Solve Marketing Acquisition Challenges 109
   5B Solve Brand Marketing and Content Challenges 127

6 Solve Common Challenges at the Middle of the Funnel   145
   6A Solve Ecommerce and Ebusiness Sales Challenges 146
   6B Solve Visual Merchandising Challenges 168

7 Solve Common Challenges at the Bottom of the Funnel   180
   7A Solve Customer Feedback Management Challenges 181
   7B Solve Operations, Triage, and Technical Performance
      Challenges 194

8 Solve Common Challenges at the Flip Side of the
   Funnel   215
   8A Solve Customer Experience, Service, and Support
      Challenges 217
   8B Solve Customer Marketing Challenges 230

9 Solve Challenges Across the Entire Customer Journey   246
   9A Solve Product and UX/CX Challenges 247
   9B Solve Conversion Rate Optimization and Analytics
      Challenges 266

PART III
See Into the Future with Experience Analytics   289

10 Target and Personalize Marketing Experiences
    Based on Digital Body Language   291

11 Extend Experience Analytics to New Channels   305

    Table of C-Suites and Case Studies   314
    Index   321

Acknowledgments

This book would not have been possible without the work of hundreds of individuals over more than a decade.

The first thank you in order of priority goes to all the Digital Experience Analytics practitioners at the 50 case study companies covered in this book. But chronologically, I owe the first thank you to the people who invented Digital Customer Experience Analytics, founding and growing software companies for session replay, heatmaps, experience scoring, and more. I received my training in Experience Analytics from them.

Their thousands of staff are the people that innovate new Experience Analytics possibilities every day. They serve the needs of hundreds of thousands of Experience Analytics practitioners, who in turn make the Internet a better place.

I want to thank my teammates who make it fun and family-like to get up and go to work every day. More specifically, some of the sections in this book draw on the expertise and writings of subject-matter expert colleagues of mine. Excerpts of their content are included here with permission, for example:

- Natacha Madeuf, Matt Christie, Antonin Mathez for Digital Accessibility;
- Katie Leask, the Content, and BI teams for the Digital Experience Benchmark;
- Nelly McCarthy, Katie Wallshein, and Rachel Herlihy for metrics definitions;
- Boris Shapiro on Web Performance Monitoring;
- Customer Success team colleagues who partnered with the companies covered in this book and documented their successes;
- Marketing team colleagues who documented many of the published case studies included in this book;
- Lucie Buisson, James McCormick, Michael Rose, and Nicole Mazanitis for enabling me to publish this book.

Ana Grace, who worked at GoDaddy at the time, is the original thought leader behind the theme of this book, that is: "Let customers show you the way to create better experiences." It's as simple as it is brilliant for describing the value of Experience Analytics.

A big thank you to Tom Davenport for writing the foreword to this book. With his strategy books, Tom set the North Star for my entire generation of data-driven workers.

I want to thank my editors at Routledge, Taylor & Francis, as well as my Technical Editors that revised the content based on their industry experience, especially Callie Miaoulis, Cynthis Goh, Dustin Chamberlain, Manuel Cornu, Matt Berry, and Tanya Terzieva.

Finally, thank you to coffee. Without coffee, I could not have gotten up long before sunrise every day for two years to indulge in putting together this book. It's been a labor of love.

But it takes a village.

Foreword

For the last 20 years or so I have been researching how organizations gather and make sense of the increasing amounts of data at their disposal. Despite a lot of progress in this regard, there are some very common mistakes that companies and their advisors make in the realm of customer data and analytics. I'll describe these mistakes first, and then point out how Akin Arikan largely avoids them in this book.

Focusing on only one type of data—Companies, consultants and authors seeking to understand customers often focus only on a single type of data, be it internal transactional, external, digital, sensor, image, and so on. It's understandable that they do so, given the challenge of managing structured and unstructured data in all its many forms. However, to really make sense of any business domain—and the most important one, your customers—requires using all the data available. One of the great things about the current environment is that we have so many data types to choose from. We should choose as many as possible!

Addressing only one customer channel—New channels to interface with customers have come along at regular intervals over the past few decades, be they direct mail, call centers, the web, social media, and so on. Each new channel understandably brings considerable enthusiasm for employing it with customers, improving their use of it, and making sense of the data coming through it. But each channel provides only a partial view of how customers interact with a company, since most customers employ multiple ways of communicating with companies. Better to employ a multichannel approach whenever possible (which, not surprisingly, this book does, given that the author previously wrote a book on multichannel marketing!).

Dealing with only one business function—Many authors and companies focus their attention on one business function, be it sales, finance, or supply chain. But if your primary interest is in creating more loyal and satisfied customers, there are several different functions that serve them—including marketing, sales, customer service, and various aspects of operations. You really can't ignore any function that customers deal with.

Pushing for a single metric—Those who want to know how customers are feeling about a company tend to argue for a particular metric. Most recently, for example, the "Net Promoter Score" has been advocated for this purpose. Now Fred Reicheld, its creator, is a friend of mine, and I do believe it is a useful metric. But I don't really agree that any single metric is the "ultimate question" (as his book on NPS is titled). There are many different aspects of the customer experience, and they need to be assessed by multiple metrics.

Advocating only one analytical method—Even most enthusiasts for analytics typically focus their enthusiasm and efforts on only one type of analytical thinking and investigation. I'm somewhat guilty of this myself, having advocated for predictive and prescriptive analytics for many years, and now for AI. But I try to remember that all types of analytics, customer-oriented and otherwise, can be useful, including simply counting stuff and displaying it in a bar chart.

The good news, as I already suggested, is that Arikan and this book avoids most or all of these mistakes. That's only appropriate, because "customer experience" is a broad term that should encompass all the interactions a customer has with an organization. To address such a broad concept through any particular narrow lens doesn't make any sense, though many have attempted it anyway.

Throughout the book there is an admirably broad focus on multiple data types, multiple channels, multiple analytics foci, multiple metrics, and so forth. I really like the term "digital intelligence ecosystem" that is central to Arikan's approach, because it suggests an array of related inter-action types that customers pursue. Multiple analytical techniques are discussed and promoted, including web analytics, A/B testing, application performance monitoring, voice of the customer tools, journey mapping, and more. Each of these has something to bring to the understanding of the customer experience, but each alone is not enough to make sense of our complex world.

Admittedly, this book is primarily about the digital customer experience. That might be perceived to be somewhat narrow. However, it's undeniably true that the customer experience is increasingly a digital experience at least in part, so I don't begrudge that focus. And the book does discuss non-digital customer experiences like visiting a store, calling a helpline, and so on.

In case you're not yet persuaded to read beyond this foreword, the book has many other virtues. It has plenty of examples and case studies. It deals with past technologies like web analytics, current ones like AI, and even (mostly) future ones like augmented reality and smart cities. Throughout it addresses the core questions of the customer experience, such as:

- To what content was the customer exposed?
- How much did they consume of the content, and what difference did it make?
- What problems did the customer have in navigating through the available information?
- What particular journey did they take, and was it a good one?

The book is also admirably down to earth, with lots of helpful frameworks and management tools. However, I don't want to suggest that it will be easy for any company to create a digital intelligence eco-system that gives you intimate knowledge of your customers' needs and desires. Despite a growing amount of software that helps you understand your customers' experiences, a good bit of detective work is still required. But with this book you at least have a detailed guide to the investigation!

Thomas H. Davenport
Distinguished Professor, Babson College
Fellow, MIT Initiative on the Digital Economy
Author of Competing on Analytics and The AI Advantage

Introduction

The Experience Imperative—
Experience or Bust!

Why Experience? Why Read This Book?

Meet my colleague, Lisa. She's a professional, a manager, head of household, and a busy city slicker. She is in tune with the times. She's on her digital screens more than ten hours a day. Do you want Lisa as a customer? Better not make her eyes bleed with a bad or bland digital experience!

She doesn't have a second to waste on sites and apps that are slow, confusing, broken, or dull. You can't make her work too hard to achieve her goals. There is only so much disposable energy and attention span left at the end of her day. Her head already hurts most of the time, so don't give her another headache (e.g. see Figure 0.1)!

If you do not maximize the moment by making Lisa's experience seamless, inspiring, and rewarding, she will be gone before you get a second chance. However, tens of other sites and apps are next in line to give it a go after you.

Life Is Digital

Does Lisa seem familiar? That's right! Most of us are a bit like Lisa today. With Smartphones, Smart TVs, Smart Homes, Smart everything, everywhere, all the time, we now stand with one foot in the real world and one foot in the digital world. Although, if you look at our kids, you might be forgiven to think that they are only dipping one toe into the real world anymore, while the rest of their lives are firmly digital.

Wherever we go, as we shop, travel, talk, or type, digital is by our side. Almost everything we plan and do involves some digital component. We're on digital when we buy something, when we study, travel somewhere, communicate, enjoy some downtime, fix everyday ailments, fix the dishwasher, or exercise for fitness. Heck, even our quality of sleep is measured digitally.

DOI: 10.4324/b23273-1

Figure 0.1 Why this book exists.

Business Is "Digital-First"

The pandemic of 2020 has accelerated this trend to a "digital-first" economy further, prompting "10 years' growth in 3 months" for ecommerce, according to a study published by McKinsey in 2020.[1] That shift in 2020 wasn't a one-time spike, however. Instead, it was a permanent change to a new normal. The pandemic is slowly starting to get under control as of this writing, but the growth of ecommerce is continuing.

Yet, an even more significant shift to digital is still on the horizon if Asia and the UK are a tell-tale of what's to come: As eMarketer reported at the end of 2020, in a global historic first, ecommerce has reached over 50% of total retail sales in China, and around 30% in S. Korea and the UK (while the US is still far behind at 15–20%).[2]

Visit this book's supplemental materials online to view growth charts for ecommerce across a variety of regions.

https://ExperienceAnalytics.live/Figures

Select Ecommerce Growth for the Introduction chapter.

Stage	Example	Differentiation and pricing power
Extract Commodities	Coffee beans	Lowest
Make Goods	Coffee	Low
Deliver Services	Brewed coffee	Medium
Stage Experiences	Starbucks	High

Figure 0.2 An example of the shift to the Experience Economy.
Source: Based on B. Joseph Pine II and James H. Gilmore, The Experience Economy. And based on an example from Runtriz published on HospitalityNet.

Our Jobs Are Becoming "Digital-First"

In our professional lives, as the people tasked with creating and improving these digital experiences, our work is meaningful beyond just business optimization. We are the people that are making the (digital) world a better place.

Competing in a digital-first economy is no small feat. Suddenly, traditional business advantages such as local store proximity represent less of an advantage, or sometimes no advantage at all. Businesses don't want to compete in the race to the bottom on pricing, either.

So, that leaves businesses with a few strategies. They can compete on brand perception, unique product offerings, and in most cases, also by engaging customers by providing better experiences. It's what has been dubbed the *Experience* Economy.[3] It follows the earlier agrarian economy, the industrial economy, and the most recent service economy (see Figure 0.2).

How Will I Know What's Missing in the Experiences We Provide?

"OK, smartypants," you probably say. But we have been working for decades to make our digital experiences the best we can. "We're not stupid." So, how can we tell where our experiences are missing something? And, how can we design better ones?

The truth is, we probably can't always tell by ourselves. But our customers can show us. They can show us how to create a better site and app through their behavior. Their behavior on the site and app holds all the clues in the world. What is it that they are looking for? How do they wish to interact with you? How do they make decisions? Are we succeeding with them? So, we need to have a look.

Customer is king—yet, we cannot see our digital customer.

The problem is, until the advent of Digital Experience Analytics, there hasn't been a systematic, proactive, and quantifiable way to take a look at where and why we are succeeding or failing at the goal of providing our digital customers with a good experience. When business managers could see their customers with their own eyes for thousands of years and understand their wants and needs, they cannot do so on digital channels.

Despite two decades of Digital Analytics tools, customer experience has largely remained a black box. Meanwhile, the 2021 Digital Happiness Pulse survey[4] by Contentsquare found that only 15% of consumers say that shopping online makes them feel happy, while the majority agree that they have more satisfying in-store experiences.

Digital Customer Experience Analytics tools were supposed to help close this gap by providing behavioral insights via session replays, heatmaps, journey analysis, and frustration scoring. They give the digital team a new lens on their customers and businesses. But until recently, the people tasked with managing digital experiences have primarily had to rely on blackbelt analysts. The analysts needed to interpret Experience Analytics data and hypothesize what the data means to improve experiences.

It's as if business managers could not hope to know their customers directly but had to ask an intermediary to write them letters about what customers want and need. Due to this process's inherent delays and shortcomings, most decisions have still been made based on gut feel.

That gap in data and skills may have been acceptable before the shift to digital in 2020, but now it no longer is. Experience metrics are now as mission-critical for the management of any business in the digital-first world as eyes and ears have always been critical for running a business offline.

This book aims to help everyone in the digital team close the know-how gap and train their digital eyes and ears to take advantage of experience metrics (Figure 0.3).

Who Should Read This Book?

This book is for everybody in the digital team at B2C and B2B companies. As my colleagues at Contentsquare always say, the digital customer experience is too important to be the job of only analysts or technical roles. Ultimately, nobody can succeed in business if they don't know their customers. So, this book is for both people in business-oriented roles and those in more technical and analytical functions.

For example, readers in business roles that will gain value include the CDO, VP Digital, VP Ecommerce/Merchandising, Marketing, and Digital Content and Customer Experience (CX). Readers in more technical and analytical roles that will benefit from the book include leaders in Product Management, User Experience (UX), Analytics, Experimentation, Ecommerce Operations, and the Performance / Support teams.

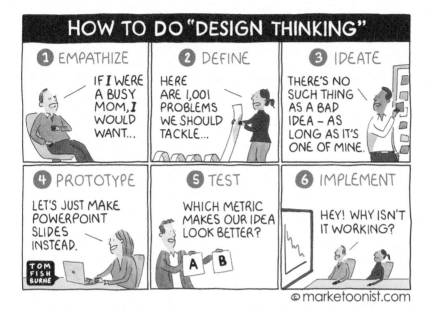

Figure 0.3 Without data, it's just a guessing game.

What You Will Learn

With this book, the reader will train their new eyes to see and understand their customers on digital channels. You will know how to make better decisions for improving customer experience and revenue by letting customers show you the way.

This book is focused on behavioral Customer Experience Analytics data and metrics rather than survey data or customer feedback. Behavior-based data is sometimes referred to as quantitative experience data vs. qualitative in the case of user research. The latter is covered by many dedicated and scientific books already. So this book will only touch on them as far as it is necessary for understanding the many great connection points for using both types of experience insights together.

What This Book Covers

Part I covers "the what" of behavioral Customer Experience Analytics metrics and visualizations for websites and apps, that is, what are the essential metrics, and how do they go beyond traditional digital analytics? Where are the connection points for using both together?

Part II covers "the how" of Experience Analytics, that is, how users in various roles apply metrics for everyday decision-making across all stages of the customer lifecycle, from the top to the bottom of the funnel. Practical examples, case studies, and cheat sheets, not just "theory."

Part III is an outlook on emerging trends and the future of Experience Analytics. The future is already visible today but not yet widely adopted.

Privacy is a Critical Part of the Experience

For decades already, customer-centric marketing has sought to maximize moments for customers by understanding them as individuals. Toward that goal, CRM marketers worked to build as rich data profiles of customers as possible. That's great for customers that have opted in and given their permission to market. However, brands first need to earn customers' trust.

For that, experiences need to be excellent even before we can get permission. As a result, we need data that informs better decisions without compromising customers' privacy. We'll cover how Experience Analytics achieves that with a privacy-by-design approach and anonymous data in the book.

About the Screenshots

Throughout the book, screenshots have been used for illustration purposes. Following the precedent set by other books on analytics, the screenshots were created using the Experience Analytics tools that will be most familiar to users based on their market share. Therefore, unless marked otherwise, the screenshots are from the most commonly used digital Customer Experience Analytics products on the market today, namely Hotjar for SMB users and Contentsquare for enterprise users.

However, this was not to suggest that similar reports could not be created with other comparable products. Everything covered in this book will be useful to the reader, regardless of which Experience Analytics tools you are using. Check in your digital Customer Experience Analytics provider's documentation how you can create the closest equivalent reports. In full disclosure, this author works at Contentsquare, so their products were also most easily accessible to me.

How to Contact the Author

I would be grateful for feedback from you about this book or about books you'd like to see in the future. You can reach me by writing to akin@MultichannelMetrics.com. For more information and to join

ongoing discussions, please visit the accompanying website at https://
ExperienceAnalytics.live.

Notes

1 McKinsey, The quickening, 2020 www.mckinsey.com/business-functions/
   strategy-and-corporate-finance/our-insights/five-fifty-the-quickening
2 eMarketer, In global historic first, ecommerce in China will account for more
   than 50% of retail sales, Feb. 2021, www.emarketer.com/content/global-histo
   ric-first-ecommerce-china-will-account-more-than-50-of-retail-sales
3 Wikipedia, Experience Economy https://en.wikipedia.org/wiki/Experience_
   Economy
4 Based on Contentsquare, Digital Happiness Pulse survey, 2021 https://
   contentsquare.com/digital-happiness/

Experience Analytics Essentials for Closing Blindspots and Connecting the Dots

A Fresh Pair of Eyes Is Needed to See Your Digital Business Today

So, what's all the hype about with Digital Customer Experience Analytics? In this first part of the book, we get to know the new breed of Experience Analytics and how they close gaps in the traditional digital intelligence ecosystem. Experience Analytics are not meant to replace traditional analytics, however. On the contrary, they are better when used together. So we will also review the many connection points.

Chapter 1: What Ingredients Make for a Good Experience?
Chapter 2: Where are the Blindspots in the Traditional Digital Intelligence Ecosystem?
Chapter 3: A Map of The Essential Experience Analytics and Metrics
Chapter 4: Connect the Dots Between Experience Analytics and the Digital Intelligence Ecosystem

DOI: 10.4324/b23273-2

What Ingredients Make for a Good Experience?

There are already many digital analytics tools in place at most modern businesses. So, why is there still a gap of insights in the midst of all of them? The saying goes: "We are data rich but insights poor." That's where experience metrics come to our rescue. But before we can understand the gaps that Experience Analytics should be filling, we need to be clear on what we mean by *experience* and what makes up a good experience.

Experience Defined: The "Three Cs"

You know when you're having "an experience," good or bad. But how do we define it? Let's start with the "Three Cs": Content, Context, and Customer at the highest level. A digital experience comes together when a customer interacts with given content in a given context.

Context

The same customer can have a different experience interacting with the same content if the context is different. For example,

- On a slow mobile connection in the subway vs. on a fast 5G connection.
- When the user is in a research mindset and looking for inspiration vs. when they are in a price comparison mindset or a quick buy mindset.
- When a parent is browsing during a peaceful moment of solitude while the kids are at school, vs. when their energetic kids surround them.

Context is always part of the experience, although most of it is impossible to capture in analytics. However, the same customers will often exhibit different intent and behavior browsing the same content. We can see that as different segments based on behavior. So while we can't always know why someone engages with the content in a quick purchase mode

DOI: 10.4324/b23273-3

vs. research mindset, we can capture the behavioral segments and opti-mize the experience for the most relevant ones.

Customer

The same content can leave some customers satisfied while others are struggling or confused in the same context.

- One typical example is customers from different countries with different browsing patterns. For example, studies by my colleagues at Contentsquare showed that customers from Germany were more likely to search for the Terms and Conditions details on a checkout page before proceeding to confirm the transactions, whereas customers from France and the USA were more interested in the visual content.[1]
- The behavior will differ depending on a customer's familiarity with the site or app, their customer status, past purchases and products they already own, what they are in the market for now, etc.
- Customer personas also differ, e.g., some have a greater tolerance for working around less than intuitive experiences (e.g., when you click and nothing happens for a few seconds) while others will get utterly confused, frustrated, or just bored.
- The customer's cross-channel behavior matters too, of course. It's one thing to come to the website because you are a happy customer that just opened a new investment account and deposited your hard-earned savings. It's another thing to return to the website or app because you are frustrated that the last stock you purchased just tanked.

The more we can include on our customers' profiles, the better we will make sense of their behaviors and experiences. Decades of customer-centric thinking and marketing practice have proven that relevancy and customer intimacy helps.

That said, in the digital world, our users cannot always be identi-fied. Brands first have to earn their trust and provide value in return for getting them to register. Yet, that means that upstream experiences need to be optimal before a customer would even consider authenticating. So, Experience Analytics has to provide insights even in the absence of customer details. That is why Experience Analytics has focused on pro-viding anonymous data, while any available additional customer detail is "cream on top."

Content

Within the "Three Cs," Content is just a placeholder for everything customers interact with on a digital channel. However, the word Content by itself is far from sufficient for making sense of the Content experience. That is where the "Seven Ps" come in that give color to content.

Content, Defined: The "Seven Ps"

In hindsight, it's hard to believe, but traditional digital analytics captures almost nothing about the content that customers interact with except page titles and URLs. That's why Content may have been a sufficient simplification as a concept during the dark ages of digital analytics, but it is far from enough in the age of experience.

A content experience is shaped by the "Seven Ps": Page, Promotions, Placements, Products, Pricing, Personalizations, and Performance. (Superior powers must have known something about the experience to have given all of these a name starting with the same letter.) With these dimensions added and captured in our data, we can make sense of experience. As an illustration, see Figure 1.1.

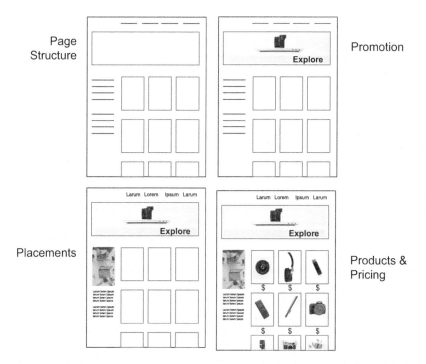

Figure 1.1 Five of the 7 "Ps," Page Structure, Promotion, Placement, Products, Pricing.

Page Structure

The first thing that comes to mind for UX and digital analysis is the page and its structure. Pages include areas of real estate, or "zones," for everything from branding to navigation and detailed textual and visual content. For example, think about interactive content such as forms to complete transactions and customer service tasks. The same content can be presented in different ways, so what is the best page structure that achieves a win-win for the user and the business?

Promotions

Sites and apps that market or sell something tend to promote brands, products, and marketing offers. Promotions can also be for calls to action such as registration and sign-up for loyalty programs. These promotions include signposts to guide the user in the directions that we're hoping will be relevant for them. They also have the actual promotional content, that is, what do you want your users to know and do? What are the most effective ways to phrase and design these promotions? For example, when we promote an offer for lipsticks, how many lipsticks are we selling as a result?

Placements

Most pages promote multiple content elements and multiple product promotions. So, what are the best placements and rankings of these elements on the page? You cannot put everything above the fold line on a page. So, what content is most attractive to users that you should prioritize to be visible at first glance? What content should be left for scrolling, and in what order? With modal windows that appear to nudge the customer in a given direction, what are the most effective ways and times to pop those up? What are the right signposts to include for our navigation menus, how many of them, and in what order?

Products

Not just ecommerce websites promote products, but also B2B, Financial services, and even healthcare, media products, and so on. What are the most effective products, categories, and brands to promote for a given page, customer, and stage in their journey? What is the most effective content for promoting those products? It's important to single out products for ecommerce websites and apps because later on, we will want to attribute carts and transactions back to the interactions with related product content earlier in the journeys.

Pricing

Price is also part of the experience. After all, everyone is familiar with "sticker shock." You may love everything about a product and promotion, but the price puts you off. The reason why some customers aren't converting may have nothing to do with the content but simply be because you are overpriced compared to the market. So, you would likely be seeing relatively few add-to-carts in that situation. However, if you spin off a bunch of A/B tests to improve add-to-carts by changing pages, promotions, placements, and so on, it will be an uphill battle. So, instead, what are the most effective prices that will increase add-to-carts and maintain your margins?

Personalization

Many pages by now include elements of personalization and automation, that is, product recommendations, personalized marketing offers, or simply a different version of the page for different customer segments. Personalized content aims to be relevant to the customer and change their behavior. So, if we didn't consider personalized content for experience analysis, it would be silly to interpret the data as if everybody saw the same content. Yet, as we will see later, this is easier said than done. For example, traditional heatmaps came from an era when content was more static.

Performance

Even the best-designed sites and apps will fail if the page speed is too slow to keep users engaged. Content is a balance between speed and everything else. So what areas of the site and app are performing slowly, and how is that impacting behavior and conversion?

Likewise, error messages are also a critical part of the content that makes up the experience when issues happen. Will the error message be clear enough for the customer to notice and understand? Will it help them recover and still accomplish their goals?

There are probably even more aspects that could be added to describe the many facets of content. (But if there are any others, I am sure that their names will probably also begin with the letter "P.")

What Is a Good Experience?

We know when we have one and when we don't. A customer interacting with content in a given context makes up the experience. My colleagues at Contentsquare describe a good experience from the perspective of the site and app user as follows.

Inspiring

Is the content engaging and inspiring to customers? Is it attractive and even exciting? Are the products the right ones, and for the right prices?

Rewarding

How easy is it for customers to accomplish their goals, for example, find and acquire the products they are looking for? Or achieve their customer service goals? Do they get the information that they came for? Can they open their account easily? How accessible is the site and app for all customers?

Seamless

Are customers having a smooth experience free of technical issues, frustrations, and perceived performance problems?

If these aspects of the experience are successful for a given customer in a given context, we've probably got a happy customer.

What Is the Business Case for Better Experiences?

From the perspective of the business, the benefits of digital happiness translate into better business outcomes, for example, supporting the following business key performance indicators (KPIs):

Increasing conversion and revenue
By improving customer journeys, e.g., lead registrations, account openings, or ecommerce.

Higher average order values and margins
By both improving cross-sell conversion rates and enhancing experiences so that customers are less likely to go comparison shopping for lower prices.

Improved customer loyalty and repeat purchases
By making the brand more sticky and giving customers fewer reasons to look at competing providers, reducing churn, and increasing repeat transactions.

Reach the total target audience
By making experience accessible for all including those with accessibility needs.

Lower customer service costs
By improving self-service customer journeys and reducing the need for live customer support (an average customer service call may cost on the order of $15 and a live chat approximately $5).

Lower effort for the business and cost
By reducing time to resolution of issues and guiding innovation to the enhancements that are most likely to move the needle on experience in a lasting way.

Faster time for resolution of issues
By narrowing down the root cause of problems and helping teams recreate the issues to understand how to fix them.

Improved customer satisfaction, brand equity, and word of mouth
By providing an inspiring, rewarding, and seamless digital experience that lives up to the brand's promise.

Why it Matters for the Business

Ultimately, even these hard metrics undersell the business case for a better experience. In a digital-first economy, the success of the digital channel is a life-or-death question for the business.

A Harvard Business Review (HBR) report cited research already in 2017 that "since the year 2000, 52 percent of companies in the Fortune 500 have either gone bankrupt, been acquired, or ceased to exist as a result of digital disruption. The collision of the physical and digital worlds has affected every dimension of society, commerce, enterprises, and individuals."[2]

Improving digital experiences and KPIs is vital for businesses to grow and stay viable. It would be easy to just throw money at the problem by running more advertising to increase traffic. But that cannot possibly scale. So, Experience Analytics need to help drive more business from the same traffic coming to the site or app.

Besides countless anecdotal case studies, a study by the Qualtrics XM Institute[3] showed the correlation between better customer experiences and purchases. For example, only 50% of customers are likely to purchase more from a company after they've had a poor customer experience.

> Visit this book's online supplemental materials for a link to the study by the Qualtrics XM Institute study from 2020, published by eMarketer
>
> https://ExperienceAnalytics.Live/figures
>
> Select the Qualtrics study for Chapter 1.

Likewise, the risks posed by bad experiences are well understood. It's not just to potentially lose a transaction but to lose a customer for good. For example, an international survey of Business and Customers conducted by Dimensional Research and [24]7.ai in 2020 found that 29% of Internet Users Worldwide had a recent customer support experience so bad that they decided never to do business with the company again.[4]

Miles to Go Before We Can Declare Success

Digital teams and analysts have already worked hard for decades to improve conversion rates and revenue. As a result, most websites and apps work pretty well today, most of the time, and for most of their users. So what's the problem?

A comparison of average conversion rates between digital stores and regular brick-and-mortar stores shows how much room for growth there still is.

- For example, in typical digital retail stores, conversion rates hover in the 2–5% range. They are even lower on mobile phones.
- Compare that to regular brick-and-mortar stores where typical conversion rates are much higher ranging from 20–80%.[5]

> Visit this book's online supplemental materials for a comparison of typical conversion rates on digital channels and brick-and-mortar stores.
>
> https://ExperienceAnalytics.Live/figures
>
> Select the Conversion Rates Benchmark for Chapter 1.

Competing on Experience and Analytics

If you now look back at the Three Cs, the Seven Ps, the elements of digital happiness, and the business case for better experiences, wow, Experience Analytics have a lot to live up to.

In their seminal 2007 book, *Competing on Analytics: The New Science of Winning*, Tom Davenport and Jeanne Harris[6] laid out a North Star for all data-driven business leaders. Namely, they described the phenomenon that many successful businesses use analytics as more than just a supporting tactic. They bank on analytics as a strategic skill on which the companies compete. That's exactly the role that Experience Analytics can play in the Experience Economy.

However, to fill that strategic role, analytics need to cover all ingredients of what makes for a good experience. And they need to be insightful for all steps in the customer journey. Additionally, as the authors of Competing on Analytics call out in their preface to the 2017 update of their book, it's not just a matter of more data and tools either. "Instead, it's how aggressively you exploit these resources, and how much you use them to create new and better approaches to doing business."

Fix the Potholes and Build New Peaks

In the early days, Experience Analytics was narrowly centered on just the seamlessness of experiences, that is, catching frictions, frustrations, and errors. Fixing these basics remains mission-critical today but barely scratches the surface of what Experience Analytics need to deliver for a business to succeed.

To use an analogy, in your brick-and-mortar stores, you would always fix broken cash registers proactively, but you would never think that this is sufficient for getting a sale and staying in business. It's just the bare minimum to open the store. Troubleshooting and innovation need to go hand in hand.

The faster and more agile the digital team is with updating experiences and launching new ones, the better for innovation. But at the same time, the more often it happens inadvertently that some of these enhancements cause unintended side effects. They introduce new confusions, frustrations, and even errors. Fixing these "potholes" faster by troubleshooting proactively and reacting to issue tickets more quickly will recover lost revenue faster, e.g. as seen in figure 1.2.

That frees up time and resources to use for innovating new ideas for revenue. The new revenue "peaks" built from investing in the right ideas, and getting them right more quickly, are a pure upside for the business.

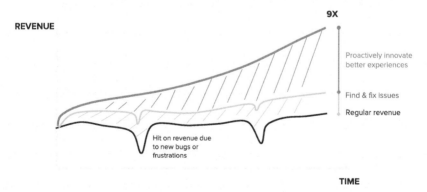

Figure 1.2 The revenue benefits of troubleshooting and innovating experiences compound over time.

They raise the baseline on conversions and revenue. Business benefits compound over time, as the graphic shows.

Troubleshoot Faster to Free Up Time for Innovation

A study by Stanford Professor Chip Heath found that companies tend to be off-balance in terms of how much time they are investing in troubleshooting vs. investing in innovation: "For every hour we spend fixing problems, we spend 15 minutes building peaks." Yet. "There are $9 of revenues for building peaks for every $1 resulting from fixing problems."[7]

In part, that is because troubleshooting is still taking too much time. After all the time invested in fixing existing experiences, there is not much capacity left for innovation.

However, that imbalance also echoes the origins of Experience Analytics, that is, their narrow focus on supporting troubleshooting use cases at the time. But, now that we know what makes up a good experience, it would be crazy if Experience Analytics stopped there. That would help us make experiences seamless but not inspiring and rewarding.

> Check out a video on the topic by Chip's brother Dan Heath on YouTube: "Build Peaks, Don't Fix Potholes." For a convenient link go to:
>
> https://ExperienceAnalytics.Live/figures
>
> Select Build peaks, don't fix potholes for chapter 1

So, with a clear picture of what we are shooting for, let's take a tour of the typical traditional digital intelligence ecosystem to understand where and why it is falling short.

Notes

1 The Global UX Map, Contentsquare, 2019.
2 Digital Transformation Is Racing Ahead and No Industry Is Immune, Harvard Business Review, 2017, https://hbr.org/sponsored/2017/07/digital-transformat ion-is-racing-ahead-and-no-industry-is-immune-2
3 Qualtrics XM Institute study, 2020, published by eMarketer, www.emarketer. com/chart/244852/us-consumers-who-very-likely-purchase-more-company-based-on-their-customer-experience-cx-by-select-industry-may-2020-of-resp ondents
4 eMarketer, Exploring the strategic value of customer experience, March 2021, https://www.insiderintelligence.com/content/exploring-strategic-value-of-customer-experience

5 Forbes, Retail Conversion Rate Secrets you never knew, July 2020, www.forbes.com/sites/patfitzpatrick/2020/07/23/retail-conversion-rate-secrets-you-never-knew/

6 Competing on Analytics: The New Science of Winning, 2007 by Thomas H. Davenport and Jeanne G. Harris. New update in 2017, amazon.com/Competing-Analytics-Updated-Introduction-Science/dp/1633693724

7 Chip Heath, Professor of Organizational Behavior, Graduate School of Business, Stanford University, forrester.com/what-it-means/ep19-defining-moments/

Chapter 2

Where Are the Blindspots in the Traditional Digital Intelligence Ecosystem?

Take a look at any modern website, lift the covers behind most mobile apps today, and you will find numerous digital intelligence tools deployed behind the scenes. The traditional digital intelligence ecosystem spans a variety of analytical tools that are a must-have for running any digital business, for example, Digital Analytics, A/B Testing, Personalization, Voice of Customer, Application Performance Monitoring, and so on.

You are undoubtedly familiar with many of these tools, even if you might not be a hands-on user. Many of these tools are the subject of dedicated books, for example, on Web Analytics and A/B testing. So, rather than squeezing a lengthy description of these analytics into this chapter, let me summarize where they shine.

With the help of these tools, businesses try to understand their customers and put together a picture of their digital experience. But even the combined data from all these tools leaves a blindspot in the middle that is so big that conclusions on customers' actual feelings and experience are mere guesswork. That makes it very challenging to manage the digital experience and compete on providing a differentiated digital channel.

That is the blindspot that Experience Analytics helps close so that digital teams can build a whole new muscle for managing experiences and steering their business.

Digital Analytics

Got to love them because, without Web Analytics, online businesses would never have made it this far. Known by their more modern name of Digital Analytics today, they are the very heart of tracking for any digital business, showing success from the perspective of traffic, business, and marketing acquisition.

Digital Analytics gave birth to a whole new profession back in the early 2000s, the digital analyst. Best practices of this profession are now served

DOI: 10.4324/b23273-4

by the Digital Analytics Association and confirmed via certifications and standard definitions. Digital Analytics know-how has also been accessible to practitioners via numerous dedicated books over the past 15 years.

Given that many businesses think of Digital Analytics as a treasure chest of data that is so deep that they seem to be only skimming the top 5% of it, how could anyone possibly suggest that businesses need even more information to succeed? How would anyone have time to look at even more data?

Well, it's because what's in the Digital Analytics treasure chest is, let's say, a lot of silver. So to get to the gold nuggets, we need to combine them with another ingredient. Traditionally, trained analysts are required to derive insights and actions. But when combined with experience metrics, it becomes clearer for everybody what the data are telling us about customers, what makes them tick, and what puts them off.

What We Love Traditional Digital Analytics For

Grossly oversimplifying, Digital Analytics is used for managing and monitoring the success of your digital business by tallying up:

- Traffic
- The success of investments in traffic acquisition via marketing efforts
- Progression of users through the site and app and the conversion funnel.

It will be easy to understand the value-add of Experience Analytics when we glance at a few typical Digital Analytics examples.

Marketing Acquisition Reports

If your company is like most digital businesses, you are probably spending the most significant portion of your budget on acquiring traffic via advertising and marketing initiatives. It's what fuels the entire digital funnel with traffic, and most businesses can never seem to get enough of it.

Marketing reporting in Digital Analytics is the vital pulse of your marketing campaigns. It is indispensable to understand which of these initiatives are working so you can allocate ad spend to the best channels.

Over the decades, marketing reporting in Digital Analytics has become an art and a science. Especially when it comes to attributing success and ROI to the typically multiple marketing touchpoints that attract and re-attract users to the site before they eventually convert into a customer. For example,

- Should all credit be given to the ad that attracted a user to the site for the first time?
- Or, to the last touchpoint triggering the session where a user finally completed the deal and converted?
- Or, should credit be shared among the ads and marketing initiatives that brought the user back multiple times until they finally converted?

This is called marketing attribution, and it is an excellent example of something that Experience Analytics tools typically don't provide at all.

Some Digital Analytics solutions go even further with marketing attribution by integrating directly with data from advertising channels. For example, no surprise, Google Analytics integrates very nicely with Google's advertising channel data (e.g. see Figure 2.1). So marketers can connect the dots between traffic and the marketing spend used for acquiring that traffic.

However, despite all this marketing reporting, bounce rates of ad-driven traffic (i.e., customers that see the ad's landing page and then leave the site immediately) remain frustratingly high on average. The average bounce rate across industries and devices was 50% based on the Digital Experience Benchmark by Contentsquare in 2022.[1]

Marketers are dying to know why so many customers are bouncing and how to reduce bounces to increase ROI. Yet, that requires additional information beyond the data available in traditional Digital Analytics.

It's a huge opportunity for marketers. For every 100 paid visitors to the site, if marketers could identify how to persuade just five additional visitors to stay instead of bounce, this would already mean a 10% improvement to their return on ad spend (ROAS), based on the average bounce rate above. To put that in perspective, it would be as significant

Figure 2.1 Google Analytics™, Attribution, Model comparison report in the Google Analytics, Demo Account.

Note: Google Analytics™ service is a trademark of Google LLC, https://analytics.goo gle.com/

as getting an ad budget that is 10% higher without actually needing to spend that additional money.

The only problem is, how? What A/B tests or changes to landing pages and journeys would permanently move the needle to achieve this? As we will see later, this is one of those critical insights that experience metrics provides.

Traffic Reports

Traffic reports and dashboards are what most people know Digital Analytics for. They sum up overall "foot traffic" to the site and to specific site sections and pages. It's often expressed as metrics such as unique users, sessions, and pageviews.

These metrics are helpful not only for summarizing the opportunity to convert site visitors into customers but also to gain a sense of the overall demand and popularity of your brand and offerings. For example, a car manufacturer can see trends for interest in various models, and a retailer can see demand for products and categories.

> For images of typical Web Analytics reports, visit this book's supplemental online materials.
>
> https://ExperienceAnalytics.Live/Figures
>
> Select web analytics examples for chapter 2.

However, content marketers also want to know which of their content and merchandising placements within those pages succeed at engaging and persuading site and app users. Without that information, Content Teams, Brand marketers, and Merchandisers cannot see whether their strategy is working and how to improve it.

Based on the Digital Experience Benchmark by Contentsquare in 2021, 45% of content on a website goes unseen by visitors on average during their session. That's just as bad as the adage saying 50% of marketing spend is wasted.

Yet, content creation costs are high. For example, on a luxury brand's site, brands invest massive effort and budget to create immersive digital experiences for engaging customers. Content creation costs can go into the tens of millions per year.

It is even more tricky to get it right on a small mobile screen. It comes with risks for page speed that can counteract the benefit of all the effort when pages are perceived to be too slow. You cannot succeed if you cannot measure what's working vs. what's not.

As we will see shortly, Experience Analytics helps here as well, enabling businesses to manage their investment in content for better engagement, persuasion, speed, and conversion. Said simply, Experience Analytics doesn't just capture customers' behaviors, but it captures it in context with the content elements they interact with.

Conversion and Progression Tracking

Ultimately, you don't care about traffic; you care about business results. So, Digital analysts wouldn't be earning their keep if they stopped at traffic reporting. Instead, their real mission is to increase conversion and revenue. They are assisted in this challenge by conversion rate metrics and iconic visuals such as the funnel report. This is where the money is in Digital Analytics!

For any conversion journey on the site or app, for example, a retail checkout or a mortgage application process, funnel reports measure progression and drop-off at each step of the journey (e.g. see Figure 2.2).

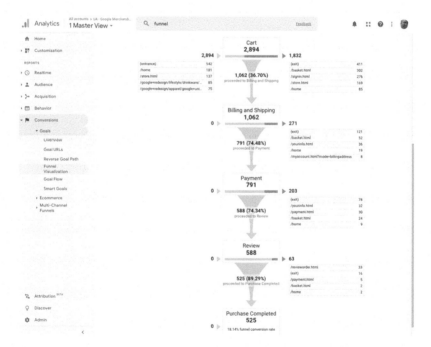

Figure 2.2 Google Analytics™ Funnel Visualization.

Note: Google Analytics™ service is a trademark of Google LLC, https://analytics.goo gle.com/

Source: Google Analytics, Demo Account

While probably the most iconic Web Analytics report of all time, funnel reporting triggers a series of next questions that business managers also need to answer.

- Why did some customers abandon the site at each step of the funnel? Did they run into confusion or frustrations? Were there errors or slow performance that hindered them? Or what is their intent?
- We can see in Digital Analytics what pages on the site users most frequently visit after they exit the funnel. However, that still leaves the question open on the most likely enhancements or A/B tests for improving funnel conversion.
- How did users browse within pages? What content elements did they see? Which of them were attractive? What helped persuade customers vs. confused or frustrated them?

While journeys such as retail checkout or a banking account application resemble a linear funnel, most journeys at earlier stages in the customer lifecycle are much less linear and much more complex.

Users may go in loops as they are searching for what it is that they came for. They may visit various page categories and leave and come back again. They try to make sense of the navigation menu of the site. Even checkouts include many side journeys, for example, for cross-sell / up-sell offers, shipping options, and so on.

Digital Analytics funnel and path reporting are a great start. Still, they trigger a long list of additional questions that need to be answered to understand journeys at every stage of the digital customer lifecycle.

Extending Traditional Digital Analytics to the In-Page Event Level

Proud and savvy analysts know how to stretch their Digital Analytics data to the max. Over the decades, tools such as Google Analytics 4 and Adobe Analytics have grown into incredibly powerful analysis solutions that enable users to augment the data for reporting in infinite ways.

Through their JavaScript tags for data collection, behavior information can be extended beyond the pageview level and down to the event level. An event can be anything worth tagging, for example, the click on a marketing banner or selecting a drop-down box. For an auto manufacturer's site, digital analysts might ask to add a tag to the selection options for engines that customers add to their car configuration.

This does extend the data available for digital analysts. It still requires pre-planning. There are also many additional questions that need to be answered.

1. Events beyond the pageview level need to be custom configured, e.g., with an on-click JavaScript event trigger.
2. If you didn't pre-plan and deploy the tag, the information may not be available when new questions arise. You cannot answer questions at that moment. You first have to get back in line with developers, add the tag, QA the site, and wait for new data.
3. After all of that effort, it's still only click-based data, but arguably most behavior on any web page or within an app screen is happening between clicks and taps. The click is only the last moment of engagement on the page after the user has experienced the page, scrolled, and seen various content elements. Without the additional information, we don't know why somebody clicked or didn't. What was their intent? Why did they not succeed, and why did they abandon the site or app instead?
4. JavaScript, API, functional errors, and performance issues are some of the root causes behind user frustrations. Yet, they are not typically captured and visible in Digital Analytics.
5. And finally, the reports on all this additional event-level data in Digital Analytics are typically tabular reports and charts. Yet, how can you put this behavior in context with the content itself to better visualize how customers saw and experienced your pages at the time of their sessions?

Digital Analytics is mission-critical. They provide insights and capabilities that go beyond Experience Analytics in many ways. However, their value goes so much further when Digital Analytics is combined with Experience Analytics.

Blindspots Will Kill a Business's Ability to Manage Experiences

As well-known Digital Analytics consultant and author Eric Peterson used to say in an adaptation of a famous line from the 1979 movie *Alien*,[2] "On the web, no one can hear you scream." Likewise, best-selling Digital Analytics author Avinash Kaushik used to lament the common issue that "visitors come to a web page, puke, and leave again." Yet, the problem is that Digital Analytics provides only part of the answers for helping with these frustrations.

Despite all the bar charts, trend charts, and click behavior numbers, nobody can still hear a customer's rage on a site. And despite two decades of Web Analytics, too many customers are still puking and leaving, as benchmarks on typical site and app conversion rates show. As we saw in the previous chapter, ecommerce conversion rates are still so much lower than those of brick and mortar stores.

Digital intelligence needs to go much further to live up to the expectations of a "digital-first" economy.

A/B Testing

Successful A/B tests are the stuff of legends and heroes. On sites and apps, A/B testing refers to the practice of trying out multiple versions of a page or journey in order to identify the one that will improve metrics, that is, typically conversion rates and sales.

Today, a digital business that isn't using A/B testing to improve its site and apps would not be considered serious. A/B testing and the tools supporting experimentation have long become a "must-have."

What We Love A/B Testing For

A/B testing is often described by its users as the basis for innovation and improvement in business. For example, *Always Be Testing* is the title of an iconic book on the subject by Bryan Eisenberg et al. from 2008.[3]

The success stories from experimentation that bubble to the top are very impressive. For example, Pizza Hut ran an A/B test to promote their deals better (see Figure 2.3). The Pizza Hut digital team A/B tested adding a call to action (CTA) to each of their deal cards.

Control: No CTA visible on the deal card
Variant: "Select" CTA visible on the deal card

When a customer clicked on the deal card CTA in the variant, it opened up the deal builder experience where they could select their choice of pizza, toppings, and drinks and then add that to their basket.

Very quickly it became clear that the variant was performing better by far. Extrapolating on the results, Pizza Hut anticipates an annualized uplift of $7.8 million in revenue.

So Then, What Else Could Anyone Wish For?

What's not to love about a great test? You are putting multiple experiences into a race against each other to see which one will perform best. If the test that you designed moves the needle for your key performance indicators, you will become a legend. It can be as exciting for us in the digital team, as maybe a Music Idol TV show race.

Unfortunately, the challenge is that after the first couple of A/B tests, identifying the most promising next tests to run that will move the needle becomes more difficult. So, the rest of the races can feel a lot more like

Control   # Variant

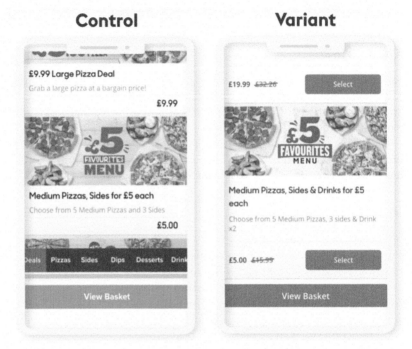

The "Select" CTA was added to the variant version on the right.

Figure 2.3 A/B test example at Pizza Hut.
Source: Case study, Contentsquare, 2021.

the pre-qualifier to the Music Idol show where probably untold numbers of hopefuls are applying and getting rejected. Many of these hopefuls should have never even submitted a bid.

But every A/B test takes significant effort to create and time to run. You have to get buy-in, create the content, set up the test, and then execute it. There needs to be a better way to inform test strategy with data in order to create uplift more often.

The run time to conduct an experiment until a winner has been identified with statistical significance can also vary widely.

- First, based on the volume of traffic to the experience in question, i.e., the lower the traffic, the longer the experiment needs to run.
- Secondly, depending on the amount of difference in results between test variations. The less impactful a test variation is, the longer the test has to run so you can tell whether a small improvement was just a fluke or statistically significant.

In practice, this means that many tests have to run for many weeks before a winner is crowned. Meanwhile, the company has multiple experiences running in parallel, some of which are less ideal for customers than others.

How Close A/B Testing Comes to Improving Experiences

Benchmark studies show that it usually takes multiple A/B tests before teams hit one that makes a difference. For example, a survey by VWO found that 1 in 7 tests is a winning test.[4] That's very effective on the one hand. On the other hand, it means that 6 out of 7 don't generate any meaningful improvement to the target metrics. But they all take time and effort to create. So any improvement to the ratio of winning tests will multiply the value from A/B testing. That's a killer opportunity for the team!

Testing can also be highly sensitive and political.

- If the CMO wants a giant hero banner at the top of a page for a fancy new marketing campaign, well good luck with trying to get buy-in for running a test with a more reasonably sized banner.
- Likewise, an improvement to navigation that improves traffic flow to some sections of the site or some product categories can at the same time shift traffic away from others. So, it becomes a hotly debated question whether this represents an improvement overall.

The key to overcoming these challenges is to close the gap in data that can inform test strategy. Once a company has tested the low-hanging fruit, what should be tested that is most likely to create uplift to targeted KPIs? Testing is much too valuable and important to leave to chance.

Without closing this gap, test strategies may often be driven by time-intensive user research and focus groups or be based on guesswork and dictated by the highest paid professional in the room (HIPPO). Not scalable. Not acceptable.

Thankfully, as we will see, Experience Analytics is widely adopted today as a more scalable and faster way to inform A/B test strategy for creating uplift more often. As the co-founder of Clicktale, Tal Schwartz, used to sum up:

- *Before testing*: What are the experiments that are most likely to generate uplift?
- *During testing*: Is my test working as intended or is there something I should be fixing quickly and restarting the test before weeks are lost?
- *After testing*: Why did a given test variation win and what were the biggest success factors so that I can create even better tests?

Personalization

Soon after the market for A/B testing solution vendors became crowded, the same vendors expanded their capabilities to enable personalization as an opportunity that is even bigger than A/B testing. Since every user comes to a site or app to accomplish different goals, it makes sense to personalize their experience as best as possible. Just like a store clerk in a physical store would engage every customer differently based on their intent. For the future of a digital-first world, this is not just a "nice to have" but absolutely strategic.

Why We Love Personalization

Targeted and individualized marketing communications are of course as old as marketing itself. It is commonly accepted that an experience will be better and lead to better outcomes if it is relevant. Campaign management and marketing automation have the purpose of making this idea scalable.

Why Is True Personalization Still Rare?

The vision with personalization is to go beyond merely recommending products and articles that a user is likely interested in based on their past clicks and taps. It is to truly recognize the user's intent and present them with experiences that best meet their interests. It is to make them feel that the business understands them as a person and serves them that way.

That's easier said than done! True personalization multiplies the investment needed in content creation and experience optimization. Instead of managing a single digital experience, all of a sudden you are creating and optimizing many permutations of that experience.

How Close Personalization Comes to Improving Experiences

Personalization tools are automatically serving content elements based on rules set by the digital team and based on machine learning about the content that is most effective for various users. These automations can draw on behavioral data and also draw on customer and user profile data as available, for example user location, time of day, pageviews, and so on. So, given this automation, what else could you possibly need to improve experiences?

Similar to A/B testing, personalization strategies need to be informed by data in order to succeed. A very basic example is product and article recommendations.

- Where are the best placements of content blocks with personalized content on the page?
- What should be the size and format of those personalized content blocks?
- How does personalized content change how users see and engage with the overall experience, i.e., not just their interaction with the content blocks that are personalized?
- What are different segments of customers that are behaving differently so that business users can derive their wants and needs and devise personalization strategies?
- Where personalization is based on rules, what rules should you put in place? And, where personalization is based on machine learning, how can you independently understand and validate why the personalization engine is promoting what it is promoting?

That is where experience metrics come in to help you ...

- Discover the segments of customers that behave differently on the site;
- Identify their intent;
- Inform the personalization strategies that are most likely to improve their experience;
- Show whether personalizations are effective at improving the overall experience and how customers see the site and app;
- Show how to improve engagement with personalized content by adjusting placement and layout;
- Identify why some customers may not be engaging with personalized content as hoped and how to improve personalization efforts.

Voice of Customer

"This was the worst experience. Your checkout is broken. I guess you don't want my money. I hope you lose your job. I am never coming back."

Oh boy!!! That's just the kind of comments that customer feedback management teams have to deal with sometimes. And they are grateful for it. For over a decade already, companies have been looking at their feedback and surveys as their first line of defense. If something breaks on the site or app, customer feedback is where the company may first hear about it. An absolute must-have today and a lifesaver for the business.

Why We Love Voice of Customer

The opportunity is to act on feedback quickly before other customers run into the same issues and frustrations. Digital customer feedback and surveys on websites are gathered by Voice of Customer tools that are considered mission-critical.

How Close Feedback Comes to Showing Experiences

Additional insights are needed for turning feedback into the goldmine that it can be. Namely, digital teams need to understand what steps and issues led up to the complaints so that they can take action for improving the situation. What was the context that caused somebody to get so frustrated?

As explicit as customers can be in their feedback, they are rarely descriptive enough to help the digital team understand what happened. Weeks and months can go by until some underlying issues are finally identified.

There is usually so much feedback. So which concerns should the team investigate further? It's hard to convince technical teams to troubleshoot an issue without evidence that the problem is real and not just an outlier that impacted only a few people that were confused. Meanwhile, tens of millions in annual revenue potential keep leaking from the conversion funnel while the issues remain unresolved.

Opportunities for Augmenting Voice of Customer Data for Experience Optimization

As customer feedback management teams have seen over the years, the following key questions can be better answered by combining feedback with Experience Analytics.

- What were the steps leading up to complaints?
- How can we step into the shoes of our customers and recreate the experiences they suffered through?
- How can we pinpoint what underlying root causes were to blame, e.g. errors, slow performance, or merely an experience that was confusing to a customer?
- How can we separate outliers from the issues that impact experience and business for many customers? How can we quantify how many others are experiencing the same frustrations even if they didn't complain? And what is the impact on revenue?
- Given that typically less than 1% of customers leave feedback on a site, how can we measure the experience for the other 99% of customers proactively?

Qualitative data from customer feedback and quantitative data from Experience Analytics go hand in hand.

Application Performance Monitoring

How does a travel website know which flights are available and which seats on those flights are still available? How does a retail website know which products are in stock at your local store? How does a banking app know how many millions you've got in your bank account and that you used a few of those hard-earned bucks to purchase this book?

It's all because modern websites and apps communicate with layers and layers of backend applications that do the actual work and hold the information needed. They typically communicate through APIs (Application Program Interfaces) to retrieve information and invoke actions (e.g. booking a ticket). These APIs can talk to backend systems that are operated by the company itself or they can talk to third-party systems, for example credit card payment services.

When any of those applications in the background become unavailable or exhibit unusually slow performance, it impacts the site and app's ability to function correctly and swiftly. So, no wonder that IT and Operations teams are always on the hunt to catch issues with uptime, performance, and errors on the digital channel and its underlying application stack to fix them quickly.

Why Application Performance Monitoring Is Mission Critical

How can anyone monitor so many background applications, servers, systems, and APIs, some owned, some operated by third parties? That task is made scalable for technical teams through Application Performance Monitoring (APM) tools. APMs provide everything from alerting to error reporting and detailed performance analysis. For example, a waterfall diagram shows the exact server requests and response communications that unfold in the seconds when a page on the site or in the app is loading and displaying.

> If you'd like to learn more about typical Application Performance Monitoring diagrams, visit this book's online supplemental materials.
>
> https://ExperienceAnalytics.Live/figures
>
> Select APM for Chapter 2.

When things go wrong, IT teams may often combine data from APMs with log analysis solutions such as Splunk that keep track of even further detail of the communications between backend systems, for example, the data passed back and forth. Those logs may ultimately hold the clue to what needs to be fixed.

Performance Impacts Conversion and SEO

Performance is a mission-critical part of the experience. Not just errors but also the slow performance of sites is highly correlated with journey abandonment and loss of conversions. Published statistics show the loss of revenue for every second of delay as users are waiting for the site or app to respond.

For example, Amazon reportedly found that every 100ms of latency cost them 1% in sales.[5] Meanwhile, Walmart was reported to see a 2% increase in conversions for every 1 second of improvement in load time.

Beyond the benefit for increasing conversions, in 2021, performance metrics started factoring into Google's algorithms for deciding how to rank sites in organic search listings, that is Search Engine Optimization (SEO). Google refers to this as Page Experience, which it measures via a set of Core Web Vital metrics.

The solution would be easy if we could just remove all images and rich interactive content from sites and apps to turn them into old-fashioned text-based HTML pages. This would remove most of the elements that need to be loaded and processed before the page is ready to use.

Just for fun, check out the CNN screenshot gallery from 2015:[6] "What your favorite websites looked like 20 years ago."
https://money.cnn.com/gallery/technology/2015/05/08/old-websites/

Just kidding of course. In fact, many brands are trying to provide an immersive, content-rich experience on their site to help convey some of that brand experience online that customers would normally experience in the brands' beautifully designed physical stores and branches. It's the same idea.

Opportunities for Augmenting APMs with Business Impact Data

Performance, usability, and content-rich experiences need to be balanced to be successful. Especially on mobile connections where speeds can be slower, at least until 5G is in place everywhere. Yet, while technical teams see API issues and performance in their APM tools, most of these tools were not designed to measure and visualize the impact on experience and business metrics. Since there are always too many issues to fix, which ones should be prioritized?

That's where Experience Analytics comes in to extend the value from APMs. They visualize and quantify which of the many issues impacted experience and revenue. By connecting the dots between customer behavior and the underlying root cause of issues, Experience Analytics is like a Rosetta Stone that business and technical teams use to align around customer issues.

- Which of the many areas where performance can be improved is actually impacting user experience and conversion?
- What content elements and functionality are so engaging and persuasive to customers that they need to be kept? Which other content elements get ignored so that they can be removed to lighten the load and speed up performance?
- Going beyond errors and performance that the APM solution is surfacing, where are problematic areas where the site and app are performing exactly as designed but customers are still confused, frustrated, and exiting prematurely?
- When the APM solution surfaces errors, what are the steps leading up to the issues so that technical teams can recreate and resolve them faster?
- What should be resolved first based on business impact?

As an industry analyst once phrased it, "teams can quickly pinpoint the issues and recover revenue faster instead of chasing Unicorns."

No Pressure, Experience Analytics!

As we've seen in this tour of the existing digital intelligence ecosystem, Experience Analytics has the power to help nearly everywhere. But with great powers come great responsibilities. How can Experience Analytics solve all these challenges?

Let's find out in the next chapter by continuing our tour. We'll look at the Experience Analytics visuals and metrics that are required for pulling users out of the data quicksand and putting them onto solid ground for decision making.

Notes

1 Contentsquare, Digital Experience Benchmark Report, 2022, https://contentsquare.com/insights/digital-analytics-benchmarks/
2 Alien, 1979, www.imdb.com/title/tt0078748/
3 Always be Testing, The Complete Guide to Google Website Optimizer, 2008, by Bryan Eisenberg, John Quarto-vonTivadar with Lisa T. Davis.
4 Visual Website Optimizer, survey, updated 2021, https://vwo.com/blog/cro-industry-insights/

5 Gigaspaces, Amazon Found Every 100ms of Latency Cost them 1% in Sales, 2019, www.gigaspaces.com/blog/amazon-found-every-100ms-of-latency-cost-them-1-in-sales/ and WPO Stats https://wpostats.com/2015/11/04/walm art-revenue.html

6 CNN: Here's what your favorite websites looked like 20 years ago, May 2015, https://money.cnn.com/gallery/technology/2015/05/08/old-websites/6.html

Chapter 3

A Map of Digital Experience Analytics and Metrics

With so much talk about customer experience, it is ludicrous to think that the people tasked with delivering these experiences could do their job without a way to measure their success. We're finally ready to close that gap now.

This book focuses on behavioral metrics for understanding customers and their digital experience rather than data from surveys, feedback, or qualitative research. So, what is the data behind these behavioral experience metrics for websites and mobile apps? How is the data translated into metrics and visualizations? These will be the tools for enabling better decisions in the hands of digital professionals in virtually every role.

The Data Behind Digital Experience Analytics

If you think about it, an estimated 90%—or more—of user behavior on a website or app happens between clicks and taps. The tap or click is just the tip of the iceberg. It is the culminating result at the end of interacting with a page. The user first lands on the page, waits for the content to display, scrolls or doesn't, sees the content, engages with various content elements, and then makes up their mind on their next move. Will they tap somewhere or abandon? Fight or flight?

The data underlying behavioral experience metrics includes these granular interactions so that they can be quantified as metrics and visualized in insightful ways.

Experience and Behaviors Captured

Figure 3.1 shows the additional data captured by Experience Analytics tools beyond the traditional digital intelligence ecosystem. This is the data on which Experience Analytics for sites and apps are built:

DOI: 10.4324/b23273-5

Behavioral and contextual data typically captured ...	By traditional digital intelligence	By Experience Analytics
Traffic & User Data		
Number of pages viewed, sessions, users	✓	✓
Pages viewed by users from entry to exit	✓	✓
Site and page conversion rates and revenue driven	✓	✓
Marketing acquisition sources	✓	Add'tl. tagging
Marketing attribution comparison, e.g. first/last click	✓	X
Marketing ad costs	✓	X
Customer segment data	✓	✓
User retention data	✓	✓
User Experience		
Link clicks / touches	✓	✓
Events tagged on pages	✓	✓
Content element clicks within pages	Add'tl. tagging	✓
Scroll rate ... and attractiveness rate	X	✓
Active engagement time within pages	X	✓
Mouse hovers over content elements and correlation to conversions	X	✓
Time to click, hesitation, order of interactions	X	✓
Mobile behaviors such as rotation of the screen	Add'tl. tagging	✓
Click rage (frustration, non-responsive content, unclickable content)	X	✓
Form field interactions, struggle, refills, blank fields	X	✓
Accessibility	X	✓
Context		
Page background snapshots and content elements captured and stored	X	✓
Session Replay data ... combining of all of the above to recreate the actual experiences (excluding any personally identifiable information)	X	✓
Performance and Technical Experience Metrics		
Speed of pages	X	✓
Technical errors e.g. JavaScript and API errors	X	✓
Functional errors, e.g. form validation errors	Add'tl. tagging	✓
Merchandising and Content Metrics		
Content engagement, persuasion, and ROI	X	✓
Product interactions within pages vs. purchases	X	✓
Promotion interactions vs. purchases	X	✓
Pricing interactions vs. purchases	X	✓
Search filter interactions	X	✓
Video interactions	X	✓

Figure 3.1 Behavior and contextual data typically captured by traditional digital intelligence vs. Digital Customer Experience Analytics.

That's a lot of additional data. The only way to get value from this data is to

1. Translate it into consumable and relevant metrics via intuitive visualizations or by crunching it with data science algorithms;
2. Make it business-relevant;
3. Map the metrics to use cases.

We will discuss a more digestible map for experience insights shortly. But first, let's look at where this data is coming from and how it's collected without infringing on users' privacy.

How the Data Is Captured

The prevalent method of data collection for website Experience Analytics is via a JavaScript tag, that is, the same approach that has become standard for web analytics.

The web pages embed a standard JavaScript file provided by the analytics tool. This tag then captures the interactions and registers them to the data collection servers of the analytics provider.

For mobile applications, data is captured via embedded SDKs (Software Development Kits). That is also how web analytics tools are embedded in mobile applications. Analytics tools typically provide these for Apple iOS and Android mobile applications and some development frameworks for hybrid mobile applications such as ReactNative, Flutter, and so on.

Privacy by Design! No Personally Identifiable Information

With so many additional behaviors and contextual information captured, it's essential to very quickly address the frequently asked question about privacy and security. As consumers, we need to know that our data is private and secure. It is a critical part of our experience. It is also essential for trust in brands.

Experience Analytics metrics typically do not capture personally identifiable information (PII). Most Experience Analytics tools follow a "Privacy by Design" approach and ensure that their data is entirely anonymous.

- Any data entered by site users into form fields is blocked from being captured by default. Sensitive data does not leave the browser.
- Data displayed on pages that include personally identifiable information (e.g., on an order confirmation page) is also blocked from being recorded via automated anonymization or by selectively marking those areas of pages to be excluded from data collection.

Experience Analytics is not about spying on users but providing a better experience.

Experience Analytics tools have to provide the necessary means to comply with all required privacy regulations, for example, GDPR and CCPA. From a security perspective, many enterprise-level vendors have certified their software as a service solution based on recognized standards such as ISO27001, ISO 27701, SOC1, and SOC2.

Whenever we call a business by phone these days, we are very used to hearing a privacy-related disclosure—"This call may be recorded for training and quality assurance purposes"—before our actual call begins. It's the same idea with Experience Analytics and its online privacy policies. Businesses cannot manage what they don't measure. So, for providing the experiences that customers expect and deserve, there has to be a way to measure them. But without encroaching on customers' privacy.

A Map of Digital Experience Metrics and Visualizations

Here begins our tour of typical experience metrics and visualizations. The various Digital Customer Experience Analytics tool vendors provide different visualizations and metrics, so this tour focuses on the most common ones.

To not get lost in the weeds, Figure 3.2 provides a map of typical experience insights based on their most common applications. The features and report names may differ from one Experience Analytics tool to the next. However, many tools offer—or should offer—something that can be mapped to these categories.

Whole-funnel Insights Across all Stages of the Journey

At the center of the map in Figure 3.2 is a typical conversion journey represented by a funnel, that is, from Attract to Engage, Persuade, Checkout/Apply, and Conversion. Note that this journey funnel framework doesn't just apply before a purchase, that is, for prospective customers. Depending on the type of site or app, it can just as well be a post-purchase journey, for example,

- Self-service sites and apps: Attracting customers to complete their account management. Then helping them find the right options and complete their goal seamlessly.
- Media or informational sites and apps: Attracting customers to consume the information or media offered. Then helping them find what they are looking for and engaging them on the site to provide value.

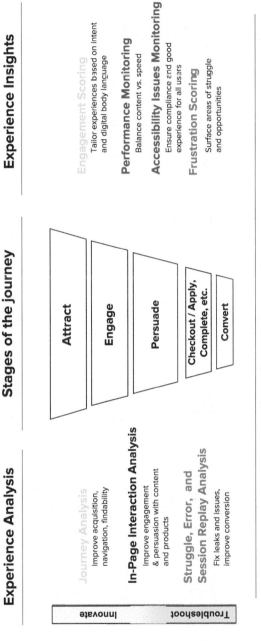

Experience Insights Framework

Automated Experience Insights

Engagement Scoring
Tailor experiences based on intent and digital body language

Performance Monitoring
Balance content vs. speed

Accessibility Issues Monitoring
Ensure compliance and good experience for all users

Frustration Scoring
Surface areas of struggle and opportunities

Stages of the journey

Attract

Engage

Persuade

Checkout / Apply, Complete, etc.

Convert

Impact Quantification, Customer Insight & Segmentation
Better understand customers. Prioritize action based on impact on experience and the business.

Experience Analysis

Journey Analysis
Improve acquisition, navigation, findability

In-Page Interaction Analysis
Improve engagement & persuasion with content and products

Struggle, Error, and Session Replay Analysis
Fix leaks and issues, improve conversion

Innovate

Troubleshoot

Figure 3.2 A framework for experience insights across the stages of a typical funnel.

The key for experience optimization is to understand and improve all journey stages, not just the checkout parts, for example. Yet, just as you use different tools in a toolbox for hanging a holiday wreath on the front door vs. fixing a clogged shower drain, Experience Analytics also provides different tools that are more likely to be useful in different parts of the funnel. Namely:

- In the green font on the map, you see the tools that are more likely needed at the top of the funnel, e.g., Journey Analysis and Engagement Scoring.
- In the red font, you see the tools that are more likely to be needed for troubleshooting issues toward the bottom of the funnel.
- In the black font, you see analysis tools that are almost always needed everywhere across the funnel.

Experience Analysis

On the left side of the map in Figure 3.2, we're seeing typical granular analysis tools and visualizations provided by many digital Experience Analytics products. These help users proactively investigate and answer questions about the experience, that is,

- *Journey Analysis*: helps improve journeys, e.g., acquisition, navigation, findability
- *In-Page Interaction Analysis*: helps improve engagement, persuasion, and conversion at each step in the journey
- *Struggle, Error, and Session Replay Analysis*: helps fix leaks and issues that negatively impact conversion

Automated Insights

On the right side of Figure 3.2, we're seeing more automated experience insights and visualizations. Some of these are provided by increasingly many digital Experience Analytics tools, that is, especially Frustration Scoring. These help surface issues automatically so that users don't have to analyze everything manually.

- *Engagement Scoring*: helps assess what's working well and how to tailor the site or app based on customers' intent and digital body language. Which users engage with what content and products?
- *Performance Monitoring*: helps monitor the responsiveness of the site or app so that investment in rich, immersive content experiences can be balanced against the need for speed that users expect.

- *Accessibility Issues Monitoring*: helps understand whether experiences are accessible to all users and how to make them compliant with accessibility regulations.
- *Frustration Scoring*: helps surface areas of struggle so that errors and other frustrations can be resolved and revenues recovered.

Impact Quantification, Customer Insights, and Segmentation

At the bottom of Figure 3.2, we mark the critical need to assess the above insights by their impact on business and experience. The issues and opportunities that matter most can then be prioritized.

The strategic value of Experience Analytics is better customer insights, that is, to help everyone on the team better understand and align around their customers. That also includes segmentation, that is, the ability to distinguish customer segments so you can discover their differing wants, needs, and behaviors.

Let's begin our tour of each of these insights, starting top-down.

A Day in the Life Using Experience Analytics

Let's use a typical experience optimization "day in the life" story as the common thread for our walkthrough of Experience Analytics visualizations. It will be like doing a test drive of Experience Analytics. This story is based on many real-life customer case studies.

Mary's Challenge at Marks and Spicy Inc.

In this story, we meet Mary, VP Digital at multichannel retailer Marks and Spicy Inc. On her first day at Marks and Spicy, Mary is presented with digital analytics and ecommerce data about the state and trends of Marks and Spicy's online business. Everything looks, well, "average" and "typical." Nothing sticks out from the ecommerce, web analytics, and IT reports as an obvious problem to investigate.

- The site conversion rate is trending steadily at 2–3%;
- There are no pages with unusual "bounce rates" where traffic is abandoning the site prematurely;
- No unusual error reports according to the IT team and no unusual customer complaints.

So, where should Mary begin to find low-hanging fruit for improving the digital business? Her first question will seem very intuitive for anyone coming from the world of brick-and-mortar businesses. Here, executives would just go to the store and take a look at how customers are shopping in the store, that is, what are they looking for and are they able to find it?

For a digital store, this question translates to seeing customers flow through the site and app. That question is answered by Journey Analysis. So, let's introduce Journey Analysis before switching back to Mary and seeing what she learns about MarksAndSpicy.com.

Experience Analysis

It's easiest to understand Experience Analytics by walking through the conventional visualizations first, that is, Journey Analysis, In-Page Analysis, Error, Struggle, and Session Replay Analysis. In the next chapter on automated experience insights we will see later how machines can do much of the legwork nowadays instead of users having to analyze everything manually and bottom-up.

Journey Analysis

Why did the chicken cross the road? It's hard to tell for any individual chicken, but if you see a whole flock of them moving to the other side of the road, then you can assume that there must be a common reason. You can investigate what that reason is. That is also the idea behind Journey Analysis, that is, to see customer flow through the site and app in aggregate so you can see where your most significant opportunities and issues are to investigate further.

We start from a bird's-eye view. This top-down approach enables the business to identify which journeys work well vs. which others do not. Then we can analyze these from an experience and customer perspective.

Journey Analysis is an innovation on top of traditional web analytics funnels and Sankey-diagram style path analysis. Unlike funnels, Journey Analysis reveals all journeys, including unexpected ones. Unlike predefined funnel views, no prior definition of ideal journeys needs to be configured. That is what enables them to uncover the unforeseen journeys so you can spot new opportunities and issues.

In Experience Analytics tools, Journey Analysis has come to mean a visualization of customer flow that is adept at reducing noise and surfacing unexpected journey patterns and their impact on the experience.

Sunburst Diagram for Journey Visualization

It's a tall order to visualize the entire customer flow through the whole site or app in a meaningful way. The first innovation that some Experience Analytics tools have brought to the table for Journey Analysis is the use of a sunburst diagram to accomplish this.

The Data Viz Project[1] defines a sunburst diagram as a "visualization of hierarchical data, depicted by concentric circles. The circle in the center represents the root node, with the hierarchy moving outward from the center."

For example, the Journey Analysis in Figure 3A.1 uses a sunburst diagram to depict the following:

- The innermost ring ranks the pages that are the most frequent starting points where users first land on a site or app. Each color is a different page or page type.
- Each additional ring is the next step in the interaction
- The black color shows the most common site and app exit points
- Traffic volume is expressed in the size of the slice or other relevant metrics

So, here you see at a glance the typical initial user behavior after landing on the site or starting in the mobile app. But wait a minute, where did

Figure 3A.1 Journey Analysis example in Experience Analytics.

all the hundreds of other pages and paths go? What happened to all the variations that clutter digital analytics path analysis reports and make them difficult to get value from?

That is where the next two innovations come in for Journey Analysis in Experience Analytics: First, a mapping of pages to page types, and second, a focus on the most prevalent journey patterns while suppressing outliers.

Noise Reduction by Mapping Pages to Page Types

Most commercial websites may have thousands or millions of URLs. Still, many can be grouped into typical page types or categories such as the following:

- Home page
- Campaign landing pages
- Product category or list pages (PLP)
- Product display pages (PDP)
- Cart page
- Login or registration pages
- Checkout (ecommerce) or account application (e.g. financial services) or lead forms (e.g. B2B)
- Search
- Customer service, account management, help, and support
- etc.

A bird's-eye view of customer flow in Journey Analysis typically begins at the level of page types rather than individual URLs to understand behavior at a high level.

But what if you are the product category manager responsible for TVs at an electronics retailer? You will not be served by Journey Analysis if TVs are lumped together with all other products on the site.

That is where the next innovation in Experience Analytics comes in, that is, making mappings flexible for each user. So, the category manager for TVs does not just see all TV PDPs as a single page category, but they can also map more granularly to distinguish, for example, Ultra HD TVs, 4k TVs, 8k TVs, and so on.

Where does this mapping data come from? Well-constructed websites and apps will already have this page category information in the data layer of each page. The page category information can be passed into Experience Analytics via its data collection tag. Otherwise, mapping or page categorization is left to be done manually within the Experience Analytics tool, which is much less fun but mission-critical.

Mary Spots a Journey Anomaly at MarksAndSpicy.com

Remember Mary, who is looking to learn how customers flow through her digital channel? Here is what her Journey Analysis is showing (see Figure 3A.2).

Can you see something that catches your eye? Yes, how about that interesting looping pattern between Search and Product Detail Pages (PDP), back and forth? But many of them don't ultimately go on to purchase anything.

As always in analytics, the answer to one question leads to multiple new ones:

- Is this normal behavior of customers browsing products in detail?
- Or are customers not finding what they are looking for?
- How are customers engaging with the PDP?
- What do they like, what puts them off?
- Why are they not adding anything to the cart, and how can we improve?

None of these questions are answered by web analytics, ecommerce, IT, or other data that Mary has available. We need to get insight into what's happening within the PDP page. That's what In-Page Analysis provides in Experience Analytics.

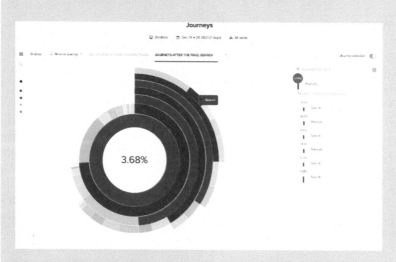

Figure 3A.2 Journey Analysis shows looping between Search (red) and Product (green) page types.

In-Page Interaction Analysis

Today, In-Page Analysis for sites and apps is mostly synonymous with heatmaps. However, as Experience Analytics expands to additional use cases and additional digital channels such as chatbots, In-Page Analysis can be generalized to any kind of interaction analysis that helps understand and improve the experience at each step of the journey.

Heatmaps

Heatmaps take advantage of the most granular behavior data collection in Experience Analytics, that is, not just clicks but all the behavior between clicks. They overlay these behaviors over the historical background of the page, thereby showing them in the correct context. Along with other Experience Analytics visualizations, this enables them to reveal why customers do or do not click (or tap) on the call to action that the business is hoping they will find attractive. That is vital information to understand customers and inform the enhancements most likely to increase the targeted journeys.

Traditional Heatmaps

The most common original heatmap types include the following

Scrolling Heatmaps

They color code how far users tend to scroll on a page (e.g. see Figure 3A.3). We can see what content most users see vs. the most frequently missed content. The color spectrum represents a metric called scroll ratio, that is, red indicates areas seen by more users while increasingly colder colors indicate areas seen by fewer users.

A fold line indicator shows where the page cuts off for the average visitor based on their devices used for browsing.

A variation to scrolling heatmaps is sometimes called an attention heatmap, where the color spectrum represents not scroll ratio but time spent in an area after scrolling. On attention heatmaps, an area is redder if users tend to stop and have that area exposed for longer times. This is useful for gauging interest in the content on that section of the page.

Mouse Move Heatmaps

For users browsing on desktop devices, mouse move heatmaps color code where they position their mouse cursors during interactions within the page (e.g. see Figure 3A.4). Experience Analytics tools capture and

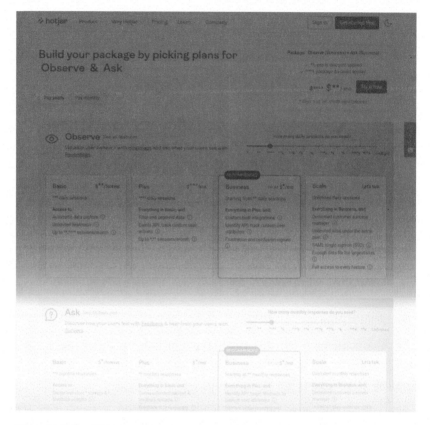

Figure 3A.3 Scroll Heatmap.
Source: Hotjar.

record the position of the mouse frequently enough to understand the mouse path, for example, every 15 milliseconds. Once again, the color spectrum represents the volume metric, for example, red are areas where most users positioned the mouse, whereas blue means fewer users moved their mouse on those locations. Mouse move is seen as correlated with where the user is paying attention within the page on average, but more to that point later.

Clickmaps

Clickmaps (also called Click heatmaps) color code where on the page users were most likely to click or tap (e.g. see Figure 3A.5). Analysts can typically see

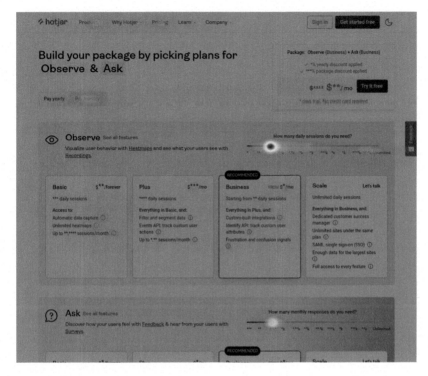

Figure 3A.4 Mouse Movement Heatmap.
Source: Hotjar.

- Where are users tapping anywhere on the page, even areas that are not hyperlinked? That is an indicator of potential user intent and frustration. It surfaces easy ideas for enhancing the page.
- In situations where multiple hyperlinks on a page lead to the same destination, which of these is clicked more often?

Heatmap Historical Page Backgrounds

Except for the most basic tools, heatmaps capture not just the behavior but also store a snapshot of the page background. That enables them to display behaviors over the correct historical version of the page even if the page changed over time. For example, if the analyst is running a heatmap for the previous month, the analytics tool has that historical version of the page background stored so that the heatmap will make sense.

Reproducing those historical page backgrounds accurately is already a significant technical challenge for Experience Analytics tools. However,

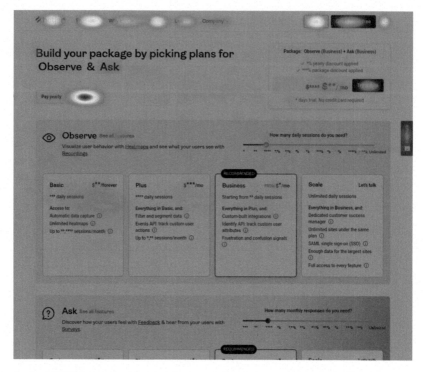

Figure 3A.5 Clickmap.
Source: Hotjar.

for most websites, capturing just one background per page is insufficient due to dynamic content such as the following.

Drop-down menus, sliders, carousels, etc.
Many sites and apps feature dynamic drop-down menus that expand over underlying content when users are interacting with the menu. If the heatmap didn't distinguish behavior with the menu open vs. closed, the information could be garbage-in, garbage-out. But when a page has multiple drop-down menus, carousels, or other dynamic content elements, reproducing the correct backgrounds is even more critical.

Personalized content
Websites and apps also increasingly show some amount of content that is different between user segments or even individual users. This content is meant to influence the individual's behavior, so to ignore it for analysis would be to oversimplify.

We will see shortly how Zone-based heatmaps overcome these challenges.

So Many Use Cases for Heatmaps

Heatmaps have been invaluable in the hands of analysts and product teams over the past decade. For example, some of their most popular use cases include the following.

1. Showcase your best-performing designs by seeing how users engage with the page;
2. Find call to actions (CTAs) on a page with the most (and least) clicks;
3. Measure how far users scroll to understand what content they are exposed to vs. not;
4. Spot problematic clicks such as clicks on non-hyperlinked content;
5. Optimize engagement on mobile and desktop by comparing the above behaviors for different device types.

Challenges for Traditional Heatmaps

Due to personalized and dynamic content, pages can have hundreds of permutations within their content elements so addressing this by retaining all of those backgrounds as separate pages does not scale anymore. A different approach is needed that goes beyond treating the page as one big block and instead understands the content zones and elements within those pages.

Additionally, traditional heatmaps are insightful in the hands of product teams and analysts that can take the time to analyze them and who have an analytically oriented mind. They can interpret the colors, compare and contrast behaviors of different groups of users, for example those that completed a journey vs. didn't. Heatmaps are rarely used by business users, however.

But when experience metrics are mission-critical for business users for decision making, it does not scale to have everyone standing in line for analysts to interpret the data and make recommendations. Business users need clear metrics that everyone can understand and act on, in the moment when they need to make decisions.

Zone-based Heatmaps

Zone-based heatmaps were designed as an innovation on traditional heatmaps. Unlike conventional heatmaps, they treat the page not as one undistinguished content block, but see the page as a collection of individual content elements and zones (e.g. see Figure 3A.6). Experience Analytics tools that offer Zone-based heatmaps do this by reading the document object model (DOM) in the page source code and identifying the various content elements on the page.

Figure 3A.6 Example of a Zone-based heatmap.

The DOM has a nested structure, much like nested boxes of content. These boxes came to be called "Zones" by the vendor that pioneered the approach, that is, Contentsquare.

When behavior data such as mouse hovers, clicks, and taps are captured, they are mapped to the correct content elements within the page. This is done for the correct state of the page, for example see Figure 3A.7 where a drop-down menu is open.

Thanks to this approach, behavior is associated with the correct content elements. That's what opens the path for understanding:

1. Reliable data for dynamic pages;
2. Experience metrics relating to the content elements and zones that business users are responsible for;
3. More contextual metrics. For example, repeated clicks on a slider button typically mean positive engagement whereas repeated clicks on a call-to-action button signify struggle.

Zone-based Experience Metrics

Now that we see how Zone-based heatmaps work, we are ready to talk about behavioral experience metrics at the level of zones. These metrics show from a bird's-eye perspective how most users see a page and engage with it, what content elements attract them vs. put them off, and ultimately what enhancements or redesigns of the page are most likely to improve the experience and business outcomes.

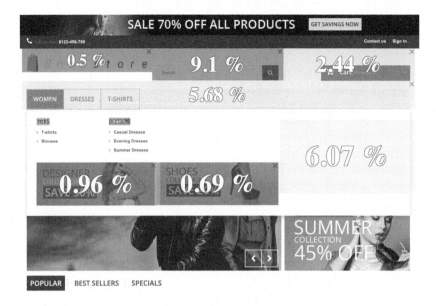

Figure 3A.7 Zone-based heatmap for a page state with a drop-down menu open.

Have a glance at the high-level summary of these metrics below. It will be much more interesting to define and understand these metrics in the next part of this book, where we will put them to use for typical use cases.

Engagement Metrics

- *Exposure rate*: What percent of users on a page scroll far enough to see content elements?
- *Engagement rate*: What percent of users on desktop devices engage with the content element by hovering over them with their mouse cursor?
- etc.

Interaction Metrics

- *Click or tap rate*: What percent of users click or tap on the content elements?
- *Attractiveness rate*: Normalizing exposure versus clicks and taps, what percent of users scroll far enough to see a content element and then find it attractive enough to tap on it? This is a key indicator for

engagement. It is a mission-critical metric for Experience Analytics on mobile device interactions where there is no mouse cursor to hint to users' attention.

- etc.

Conversion and ROI Metrics

- *Conversion rate*: What percent of users that hover or click on a content element go on to complete a given journey goal, e.g., a transaction or account registration;
- *Revenue attribution in total*: How much revenue resulted from users who engaged or interacted with a content element, i.e., the combined value of their conversions?
- etc.

Merchandising Metrics

- *Promotion metrics*: How effective is a promotional content element for driving purchases of the targeted products? What other products are viewed or purchased alongside the targeted ones? Or, instead of them?
- *Placement metrics*: When different users see personalized content within the same content zones, which placements are most effective?
- *Product metrics*: What are products with opportunities worth getting more real estate on a page?
- Etc.

Struggle and Error Metrics

- *Recurrent or "rage" clicks*: What content elements draw a fast succession of clicks or taps indicating struggle and frustration due to malfunction?
- *Errors*: What content elements trigger JavaScript or API errors when users interact with them?
- *Unresponsive clicks*: What content elements don't lead users to their intended next step after they try to tap or click on them, e.g., content elements that are not hyperlinked or that aren't responsive?
- etc.

These metrics and Zone-based visualizations have revolutionized the adoption of experience insights by business users.

Mary Spots an Opportunity

Let's switch back to Mary who is investigating why her customers are looping back and forth between Search and PDPs. What is their experience on the PDPs? What should she invest in for turning more traffic to the PDPs into "add-to-carts"? Here is what Mary's Zone-based heatmaps show for exposure rate and conversion rate metrics (see Figure 3A.8).

No surprise on exposure rates (see on the left of Figure 3A.8). Not everyone is scrolling very far on the PDP to see lower content elements on the page. So what? We cannot possibly put everything above the fold. Some things have to be more down on pages. By itself, this isn't an actionable insight.

But is there something lower on the page that is engaging and per-suasive to customers if they scroll far enough to see it? That question is answered by various experience metrics. In this case, Mary looks at "conversion rate" for add-to-carts, that is, if customers viewed and interacted with content elements, did that lead to add-to-carts?

Figure 3A.8 Zone-based heatmaps with exposure rate metric (left) and conver-sion rate metric (right).

Anything that jumps out to you on the right side of Figure 3A.8 for conversion rate? Yes, the product recommendations at the bottom are highly correlated with add-to-carts. But we know from the exposure rate metric that very few customers scroll far enough to spot these.

Mary sees an opportunity now. What if we help more shoppers find these recommended products? The data suggest that this will increase sales. So, Mary calls in her Product Manager for the PDP, UX Designer, and A/B Testing Team. They develop an A/B test that moves product recommendations higher up on the page so more customers will see them.

Will the A/B test work? Or will it introduce new points of confusion or even accidental errors?

Struggle, Error, and Session Replay Analysis

When you work in a physical store and see customers struggling in front of you, of course, you drop everything to rush to their help. You also resolve recurring problems quickly. If the store has a broken door or a slow cash register, of course, you will have it fixed quickly. But how do you do the same things on digital channels where "nobody can hear customers scream"?

It would be easy to spot if the website was totally broken. You could check and confirm that fact immediately. Then, all hands would be brought on deck to resolve the issue swiftly.

The problem that drives everyone crazy, that is, customers, business, and technical users alike, is that in most cases, the site and app are working just fine for the majority of customers, while at the same time, significant pockets of customers are struggling or running into errors.

Their problems remain difficult to recreate, pinpoint, and fix even if they leave complaints on customer feedback tools. Many tickets and problem reports remain unresolved. Sometimes weeks or months go by before the issue is identified. Meanwhile, millions in revenue go down the drain. There are thousands of case studies of companies that tell a tale about this.

As we discussed under APM tools in the previous chapter, IT systems are very good at capturing all errors and slow performances. Still, they are usually not designed to track the impact on the business and experience. Since there are too many potential issues to fix, which ones should be prioritized?

And above all, so often customer confusion and struggles happen even where the sites and apps are working as designed and free of errors. These points of friction fly under the radar of APM and IT systems. Typically, the IT team is not tasked with resolving usability issues. That's where Struggle Analysis, Error Analysis, and Session Replay come in within Experience Analytics.

Session Replay

When you hear about an error or problem, the first thought usually is: "I wonder what happened? I wish I could have been there to see it." And thanks to Session Replay (e.g. see Figure 3A.9), you can go back in time and recreate the issues in question by replaying the (completely anonymized) sessions.

When the digital team sees the customer's struggle in a replay, it creates that same feeling of empathy that staff have in physical stores, which prompts them to jump up to help. For example, it is one thing to hear that there is a point of friction in the checkout that is causing some users to abandon. It's another to watch a user try 15 times to check out and still fail in the end. Seeing that with their own eyes makes the team want to drop their lunch sandwich and fix the issues first.

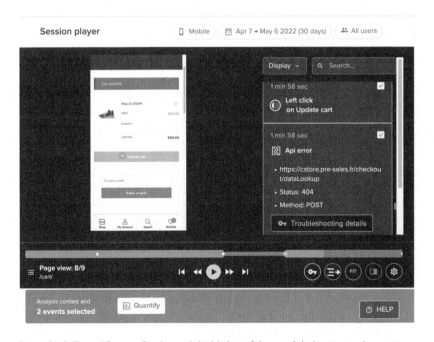

Figure 3A.9 Typical Session Replay with highlights of the user's behaviors and experience.

Session Replay Meets "the Matrix"

In the movie "The Matrix," characters can see their virtual world as it appears, but they can also see the underlying firehose of data creating the virtual experiences. Wouldn't it be helpful if Session Replay offered the same granular perspective onto the "backstage" when users have a question as to why something is happening "on stage"?

That is where the event stream comes in and goes alongside the replay of sessions. The event stream shows underlying events and behaviors as they unfold. For example, it shows taps, key user events, and errors. It helps pinpoint why nothing happens when a user is frantically tapping a call-to-action button multiple times. It's the ultimate "smoking gun" that enables business and operational teams to open better support tickets for technical teams and developers to dig deeper into the root causes of an issue. When those teams combine this view with their APM tools and IT logs, they get to the bottom of the problem more quickly and stop the revenue leak.

Examples of events that Session Replay can highlight in an event stream include the following:

• Clicks and taps on content elements;
• JavaScript and API errors that occur;
• User struggle behaviors such as rage clicks, multiple form field interactions, multiple button clicks;
• Capture event data, e.g. what selection was made from a drop-down menu;
• etc.

From "Movie Nights" to a Scalable Way to Get Insights from Session Replays

With thousands and millions of customers, however, there wouldn't be enough hours in the day to watch everything. Many businesses that invested in Session Replay initially found that business users rarely use them. They were typically only adopted by analysts and technical teams tasked full time with understanding and improving issues on the site.

They would find some insightful sessions to watch and sometimes invite the rest of the team to review them as part of a "movie night," popcorn included. But, how do we reap the benefits of Session Replay for busy business users more systematically and at scale?

Session Replay only becomes scalable as a source of insight when combined with macro-level insights such as Journey Analysis, In-Page Analysis, and Struggle and Error Analysis. There are not enough hours in the day to watch Session Replay randomly. Macro and micro-level insights need to work together as one.

Shortcuts to Session Replay

Experience Analytics tools facilitate this connection by enabling drill-down to Session Replay from macro-level visuals such as Journey Analysis and Zone-based heatmaps. You spot potential issues from a bird's-eye view and can then zoom down to Session Replay to investigate why metrics indicate certain common behaviors and struggles.

Shortcuts from Session Replay to Impact Quantification

Just as well as drilling down, some Experience Analytics tools enable drilling up from individual Session Replay to quantify how many look-alike sessions struggled with the same issues or behaviors. This enables users to quantify the business problems and prioritize where to invest (e.g. see Figure 3A.10).

In the next part of the book, we will see this in action, where we put these insight tools to work for typical use cases.

Error Analysis

The case for Error Analysis is a no-brainer. Of course, we want to eliminate errors that stand in the way of business and experience. Since sites and apps build on layers of code and technologies behind the scenes that all need to work correctly, errors can originate from anywhere in that stack. We can group the types of errors captured by Error Analysis as follows.

Figure 3A.10 Impact Quantification from Session Replay.

JavaScript Errors

Much of the dynamic functionality within website pages is facilitated via JavaScript program code. This client-side code runs within the browser and depends on compatibility with each browser. That also explains why the site can be working fine for many users while it is broken for others.

Most websites have many—if not hundreds—of JavaScript errors that occur for different browsers or in different situations. Most of these never become noticeable to site users, though. But,sometimes JavaScript errors can have a significant impact on the business and experience.

Case Study: Kusmi Tea

At Kusmi Tea, the digital team ran an A/B test to improve shopping experiences for their assortment of fine teas. The A/B testing solution indicated that the test candidate was not performing well upon launching the experiment. Its conversion rate was ten times lower than the control. This would have amounted to an annualized revenue impact of 160,000 Euros.

But how could that be? The team spotted a JavaScript error associated with the A/B test variant with a glance at Error Analysis. Customers exposed to the error had a much lower conversion rate. The team fixed the error quickly and turned their experiment into a resounding success (e.g. see Figure 3A.11).

(A) 0.05% (90) of all sessions match the conditions		(B) 7,68% (14,587) of all sessions match the conditions	
Conversion		**Revenue**	
No. of conversions	Conversion rate	Revenue	Median cart
(A) 2	2,22%	88,0€	44,0€
(B) 3,487	23,9%	215,795€	53,0€
VS. 3,610 for All users	1,90% for All users	223,279€ for All users	54,0€ for All users

Figure 3A.11 Error impact analysis at Kusmi Tea.

API Errors

APIs are critical for modern websites and apps, as discussed in the previous chapter. API Error Analysis ranks the malfunctioning API calls by their impact on conversion so that the most critical issues can be resolved first (e.g. see Figure 3A.12). The analysis workflow involves reviewing the error codes and the specific API requests that lead up to the errors and the server's response.

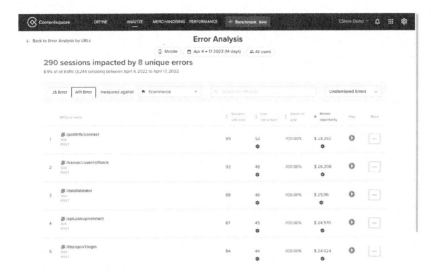

Figure 3A.12 Error Analysis ranked by the missed opportunity.

Business and Functional Error Messages

Even when the site and app are working as designed, they will still often raise issues to the user's attention. For example, when the user is trying to submit a form but has not completed a required field.

These issues block the user from proceeding. Frustrations with these error messages can run just as high as in the case of technical errors, so improving these experiences is equally important. But IT systems do not typically report on these messages because they are by design.

Typical examples include

- *Form validation errors*: An entry is missing or needs to be corrected before submitting the form.

> Case study: At one luxury goods brand, a form validation error in the checkout was challenging to see for shoppers on mobile devices. They were frantically trying to resubmit their purchase multiple times and finally giving up. This represented an over $5 million annual revenue leak for the brand.

- *Product out of stock messages*: A product is presented to shoppers but cannot actually be purchased. But instead of proceeding to select other products, this can be a "buzzkill" to shoppers and prompt them to abandon the site, perhaps to find the same item at other retailers.

Case study: It is widespread on fashion websites that a product is out of stock for the most popular sizes and only available for very large or small sizes. At a well-known British retailer, this was causing a revenue leak of multiple hundred thousand pounds on an annual run rate. Simply taking these products down from inventory fixed the leak and increased revenue.

- *Content or products not found errors*: A search leads to no results. This brings users to a "dead-end" in their journey. They may try a few times to keep searching but eventually give up and try their luck on another site.
- etc.

Mary's Team Traps an Error

Remember Mary's A/B test on her PDP to move product recommendations higher up on the page? A/B tests often need to run a few weeks before obtaining statistically relevant results. But instead of just sitting back and waiting, it is always a good idea for the A/B test team to see whether the test variation is working as expected.

When the A/B test team at Mary's company runs the Error Analysis, they immediately spot an error on their test. It's impacting conversion rates of the test variant.

Replaying sessions with the error, it jumps out the error is happening on the add-to-cart button. Unfortunately, as often occurs when innovating new experiences, the test variation introduced a bug.

The team files a ticket to resolve the issue and then restarts the A/B test without losing precious time. The A/B test becomes a resounding success increasing add-to-carts by 13% vs. control.

But, purchase conversions did not go up at the same rate. Why not? What's happening to these shoppers after adding the product to the cart?

Struggle Analysis

It often doesn't need a site or app error to trip up customers on their journey. Frustrations quickly turn from anger to rage when sites and apps are confusing or seemingly malfunctioning. Even though the experience is working as designed, it fails customers and the business. The damage is extensive; it may not only lose the transaction but may lose the customer for good. So, Struggle Analysis is a critical aspect of experience optimization.

We will cover automated tools for surfacing many different kinds of frustrations top-down in the next section. Here, let's introduce the tools used by digital teams every day to closely understand what's frustrating their users and derive better designs or A/B tests for remedying the issues.

Click Frustration

Often referred to as rage click in the industry, click frustration refers to users trying multiple times to get a response from the site or app without any luck. This can happen for various reasons.

Deactivated Buttons

A button looks like it should be clickable, but it is grayed out because the user hasn't completed all of the required steps before the button is activated.

Case study: A well-known British shoe retailer's site enables shoppers to choose shoes by selecting the size and the width of the shoe, e.g., standard vs. wide fit. However, Experience Analytics uncovered that some shoppers missed the need to pick a shoe width. As a result, they were confused why the add-to-cart button remained grayed out. Many abandoned the site in frustration.

After seeing this behavior, the digital team decided to pre-select widths when only one width-fit is available anyway. This helped remove customer frustration. The retailer drove $1.1m annual revenue from this one experience improvement alone.

Non-hyperlinked Content

Users think an image or text should be clickable when it isn't hyperlinked.

> **Case study:** On a well-known site for travel books, users viewed a travel destination attraction and clicked the city name under the name of that travel attraction. It appears they were looking for other attractions nearby, but the city name wasn't hyperlinked. Of course, some users worked around this by using the site's navigation menus. But the more effort something requires, the more users run out of time and patience, and abandon before completing their goal. The page was updated by hyperlinking the city name. This reduced bounces on the page by 15%.

Other Confusions

All of the above can exacerbate the already laborious effort of completing online forms on the way to a conversion. For example, in the Figure 3A.13, a popular metric is click recurrence, another name for rage click behavior. It immediately jumps out that one form field, the city field, is causing a struggle, and users are trying to tap it repeatedly without success. The proverbial smoking gun indicates a usability problem and draws users' attention to dig deeper into the situation via Session Replay. Improving form completions is such a critical use case that it is supported by dedicated Form Analysis which we will introduce next.

Form Analysis

Nobody likes completing forms, but almost all conversions and customer service transactions ultimately require completing a form. Online forms are no less frustrating than their paper-based cousins. How often does it happen that you start to fill out a paper-based form only to find that you wrote something in the wrong field, need to scratch out your entry, and start again? (It happens to me almost every time.)

So, how do we find the fields that most commonly trip up users? That's what Form Analysis enables, a standard part of Experience Analytics today. Typical Form Analysis reports and metrics include the following.

Form Funnel

At a glance, how many users don't even start the form and give up before they try? How many others begin but abandon along the way? And how many are making futile attempts to submit the form? Form completion funnels answer these questions. They direct the analyst's attention on where to dig deeper to find the cause of the problem. In Part II, Chapter 9 of the book we will see this in action with a visual example.

Drop Rate

How often is a field the straw that breaks the camel's back, that is, the last field users interact with before deciding to turn their back on the whole thing and abandon?

Blank Rate

How often are fields left blank in an attempt to save effort or due to unwillingness to provide the information?

Refill Rate

How often do users need to try before they get a field right? This shows areas of laborious effort, which is usually the precursor to abandonment/

The above is combined with other Experience Analytics insights such as Error Analysis, click frustration metrics, and Session Replay to provide a complete capability for helping alleviate trouble with form completions.

Mary Spots and Resolves Friction During Checkout

Back to Mary. Her team's A/B test on moving product recommendations higher up on the PDP successfully raised add-to-carts by 13%. But the purchase conversion rate did not go up at the same rate. Why?

There is nothing in Mary's web analytics or IT data to suggest why customers with products go to the checkout but abandon the journey before completing it. However, Mary does see in Journey Analysis that a lot of the abandonment is happening on the new shipping form page in the checkout.

So Mary runs a Form Analysis looking at the Drop Rate metric, i.e., what is the last form field before customers give up and abandon (see Figure 3A.13)?

What jumps out? The city field is a sore point for customers. Refill Rate and Click Recurrence Rate metrics confirm that customers have to try multiple times. But why?

Session Replay shows customers skipping the postal code field and going straight to the City Field. But the form was designed to auto-populate the city field with a choice of selections after customers enter their postal code. That was meant to be for customers' convenience but turned out to be a bad idea for UX. The City Field is

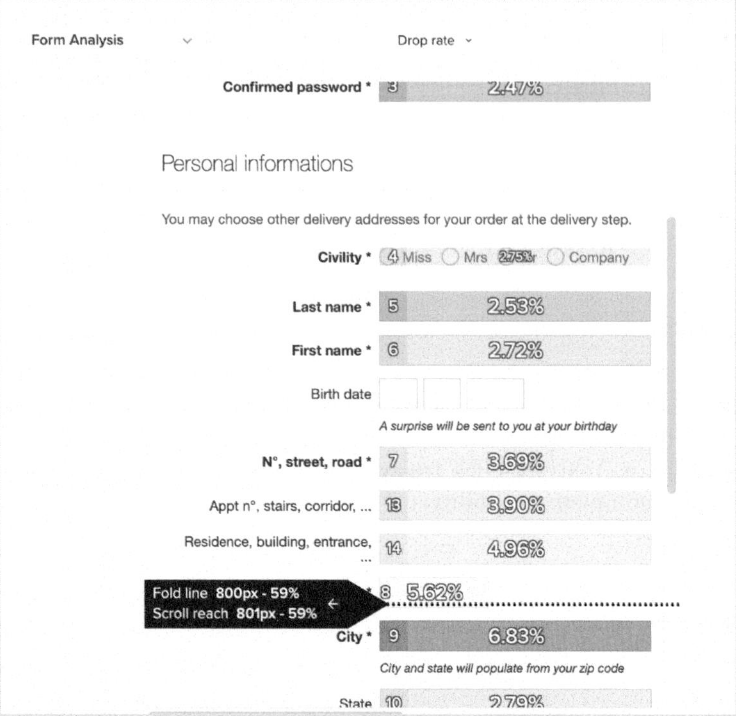

Figure 3A.13 Form Analysis example with Drop Rate metric.

not accepting entries that don't match the missing postal code. Even though the site is working as designed and no errors are present, customers are frustrated and give up.

Mary's team decouples the Postal Code and City fields and resolves the revenue leak within the same day. Following her big win earlier on the PDP raising add-to-carts by 13%, now her conversion rate and revenue also increased by 13%.

Customer Feedback and Complaint Forensics

One of the most valuable uses of Experience Analytics is to contextualize the issues leading up to customer feedback via Voice of Customer tools. However, we will cover these use cases in the next chapter, that is, under connection points with the ecosystem.

Likewise, Triage teams often need to investigate customer support issues and complaints at the call center. We will cover that in the use cases section of the book.

Automated Experience Insights

Now that we've seen the kind of data and insights that Experience Analytics provides, the question becomes how we can make their use practical. The answer is that automation needs to do some of the legwork on behalf of users. Let's see how that works.

Frustration Scoring

Given how big most sites are and how diverse users' devices and behaviors are, it doesn't scale to look for friction and frustrations manually. And there are never enough hours in the day to analyze every frustration and every customer segment. So, how can digital teams surface issues top-down and rank them by their impact? How can machine intelligence assist the digital team with prioritizing where to focus their time and effort for troubleshooting?

That's where automated Frustration Scoring is required. The issues that surfaced represent opportunities for improving the experience and recovering leaks of revenue and conversion proactively before customers complain.

How Frustration Scoring Works

Depending on the Experience Analytics tool, different scores and algorithms are provided. But at a high level, many have the following approach in common.

Automated algorithms crunch the Experience Analytics data, including all the granular micro behaviors such as clicks, taps, scrolls, and more. They scan for patterns that are associated with frustration and count how often they occur in a session or within a page or journey. Examples of those patterns include the following.

Click frustration
Rage clicks, i.e., multiple consecutive attempts at clicking or tapping a content element, e .g. a form field or button.

Errors
Errors associated with clicking or tapping an element.

Repeated attempts during a pageview
Whether it is multiple attempts at completing a form field or multiple attempts at completing a call to action (even if not consecutively), these are signs that a user has to work much too hard.

Navigation frustrations
Navigation patterns such as "fastbacks" where a user arrives at a page but quickly makes a U-turn and reverts back to the previous page because they clearly didn't see what they were expecting. Similarly, multiple revisits of the home page can indicate that a user is not finding their way and having to restart their journey at the top to get back on track.

Performance frustrations
How is slow load performance of pages correlated with abandonment?

Surface the Worst Issues Top-down and Explain Why It Is Happening

All the scores across all the pages and sessions are aggregated up to provide a bird's-eye view of where the biggest issues and revenue leaks are (e.g. see Figure 3B.1). See at a glance where to focus.

Tally up frustrations by issue, page, or journey
Show the locations most prone to issues.

Rank frustrations by the impact on the experience and business
Bubble up the issues that are leading to the highest amount of frustrations vs. the biggest loss of conversions and missed opportunity for revenue. Identify the issues that should be addressed first.

Explain the issues
A common challenge with AI-based or automated insights is that they can sometimes feel like a "black box." A score goes up or down but users are unclear why and how to validate the underlying concern.

That is why the notion of "Explainable AI" has become very attractive. Here, automated Frustration Scoring lays open the specific types of frustrations that occurred and caused the score to spike up. The user can pinpoint which issues are correlated with abandonment.

To see the steps leading up to the issues, it is very typical for Experience Analytics tools to provide a drill-down to Session Replay. Recreating sample sessions that experienced the frustrations enables teams to see exactly when and where the frustrations were detected.

Figure 3B.1 An example of automatically scored opportunities.

Examples of frustration events that Session Replay can highlight in an event stream include for instance:

- Rage clicks, i.e., repeated quick clicking or tapping;
- Multiple form field interactions;
- Multiple button clicks;
- Fast backs, i.e., quick return to the previous page after arriving on a page;
- Multiple home page visits, i.e., indicating that a user isn't finding what they are looking for;
- etc.

Bottom-up Analysis

A frustration score is calculated for each individual session or pageview, indicating which ones to examine more closely (e.g. see Figure 3B.2).

Replay the sessions worth watching
Whenever you have an experience issue to examine, instead of choosing sessions to watch randomly, wouldn't it be great to identify the most likely ones to showcase the frustrations? That's exactly

	4min 15sec	Jan 4, 2020 at 23:08	FR ❚❚	Chrome 97	😞 97	14 URLs ⌄
	Engaged 2min 15sec					
		🖵 1920 x 1080	Visitor ID: 12345			

Frustration score

! High frustration

The user has encountered many frictions during his browsing and may have had a bad experience

Frictions total:	Frictions type:
8	6

Figure 3B.2 Session Replays ranked by user Frustration Scoring.

where Frustration Scoring helps in the bottom-up use case. Each session is associated with a frustration index so that the analyst can start with the ones where there was the biggest amount of "smoke."

Compare behaviors by frustration score
In Journey and In-Page Analysis, segment by high vs. low frustration to contrast the behaviors that are behind these experiences. See common issues at a glance instead of individual session replays which can sometimes be misleading.

Find "look-alike" sessions and quantify the impact
Since we started from a single anecdotal session, we still need to quantify whether a point of frustration is an outlier or a common issue that is impacting many users. We will cover Impact Quantification later in this chapter.

Mary Uncovers a Pocket of Frustrated Customers

Let's tune back to Mary and Marks and Spicy Inc. Monitoring Frustration Scoring she sees that a number of customers exhibit click frustration during the checkout just before submitting their transaction. Instead, many of them abandon. Neither IT reports, nor Error Analysis had detected any issues. What's going on?

A replay of the sessions reveals exactly when the frustration is happening. Customers see a free shipping offer for purchases above $20. For some customers, the combination of their purchase and shipping costs is just over $20. Yet, the offer is unavailable to them. That is because the offer is only for purchases that exceed $20 before shipping costs.

Many customers did not catch this nuance however and are confused. They are repeatedly clicking on the offer in the hopes of unlocking it. Many abandon the checkout in frustration. The site is working exactly as designed but the experience of these customers is terrible anyways. Mary works with her product design team to update the page and clarify the offer. Scanning frustration scores after the update she sees that the issue has been resolved.

Engagement Scoring

Many years ago, I remember a discussion among leading web analytics professionals about how to measure engagement.

- If a user is viewing many pages and clicking frequently during their session, does that mean they are very engaged? Or does it mean they are very frustrated because they are scrambling to find what they are looking for?
- When a user stays on a page for a long time before opening a new page, does it mean they are very engaged? Or does it mean they left the page open and went to go get a coffee or browse on another tab?
- When a user lands on a site and bounces without seeing a second page, does that mean they hated what they saw? Or did they actually really engage with the content and were able to answer their question without needing to view a second page for now?

The truth is, web analytics are lacking the data to be able to measure engagement in any useful way. That is where digital Experience Analytics closes the gap with the benefit of much more granular behavioral insights.

What Is Engagement and Can It Be Measured at Scale?

Positive engagement is the opposite of frustration. Yet, making users happy on the digital channel requires a number of things beyond just avoiding frustration. Namely, it requires enabling customers to achieve their goals by providing good experiences. What's a good experience? We discussed the criteria in the first chapter:

Inspiring
Is the content engaging and inspiring to customers? Is it attractive and even exciting? Are the products the right ones, and for the right prices?

Rewarding
How easy is it for customers to accomplish their goals, e.g. find and acquire the products they are looking for? Or accomplish their customer service goals? Do they get the information that they came for? How accessible is the site and app for all customers?

Seamless
Are customers having a smooth experience free of technical issues, frustrations, and perceived performance problems?

Automated Frustration Scoring helps digital teams with the last one, that is, bringing seamless experiences to market faster. Automated Engagement Scoring needs to help with the first ones, that is, making sure experiences are inspiring and rewarding.

Digital Experience Analytics provides data to be able to score these criteria and calculate an engagement score. For example, by exporting data from the Experience Analytics and scoring sessions on the criteria suggested below. This kind of scoring is the closest thing to being able to measure positive engagement at scale, short of having a microchip embedded in everybody's mind.

Inspiring: Are users engaged with and excited about the content? Are customers attracted to the site or app and returning frequently?

- *Active engagement time*: How long do users engage actively, moving the mouse, scrolling on a page vs. merely having the page open in a tab?
- *Scroll and exposure rates*: To what level do users scroll ... because they can't get enough of the content?
- *Hover time*: During desktop interactions, how long are users hovering over content elements with their mouse cursor?
- *Attractiveness rate*: On mobile and desktop interactions, how likely are users to click on content if they are exposed to it after scrolling?
- *Engagement time with inspirational content*: To what degree are users noticing and engaging with content designed to inspire them, e.g. videos on the page started vs. completed?
- *Dynamic content interactions*: How much do users interact with dynamic content elements on a page, e.g. sliders, accordions, menu, etc.
- *Journey completion rates*: To what degree do all of the above interactions then make it more likely for users to complete journeys, e.g. transactions, registrations, applications, etc.?
- *Return rates and frequencies*: How often do users return in total?
- *Stickiness*: After becoming a first-time visitor to the site or first-time user of the app, how often do users come back in repeat sessions and transactions?

Rewarding: How easy is it for customers to accomplish their goals?

- *Navigation*: How easy is it for users to understand the menus, e.g. what is the ratio of drop-down menu opens vs. clicks?
- *Effort*: How hard are users having to work on search and category pages to filter the list of offerings down until they find the options they are looking for, e.g. think about travel booking sites?
- *Product page reach*: How does the use of those filters translate into finding products and reaching product display pages?
- *Misleading clicks*: How good is the site or app at avoiding clicks that are followed by a fast click on the browser's back button?
- *Hesitation*: How good is the site or app at avoiding long hesitation on content elements such as call to actions on cart and checkout pages, application, or registration forms? How long does it take them to go from exposure and hovering to clicking?
- *Confusion*: How often are users clicking on unclickable content?
- *Journey completion rates*: What is the ratio of users beginning vs. completing journeys, e.g. looking for information on products, searching for products to purchase, starting a lead registration or account application, self-service task, account management task, etc.?

Meanwhile, we've already covered the scoring of seamless experiences earlier with Frustration Scoring.

Mary Detects an Opportunity

Mary looks at her customers that are most engaged during their sessions and achieve their goals. In Mary's case that is indicated by users reaching product pages and adding products to the cart. She notices a commonality (see Figure 3B.3).

Sessions engaging with search filters on the product category and search pages are more likely to have a higher score on achieving their goals. Looking at the specific search filters that are most helpful to customers, the filters for product availability and price range jump out. Users that scroll far enough to see and click on these filters have much higher conversion rates of 10.1% and 9.64%, respectively. However, the filters are under the fold, that is, many users don't scroll far enough to be exposed to them.

This gives Mary a hypothesis for an A/B test to run. What if Marks and Spicy moves these filters up on the page by eliminating some of the least used filters instead? More users will see the filters and this has a good chance of increasing the ratio of rewarding sessions and sales.

Figure 3B.3 Zone-based heatmap on the search category page, displaying a conversion rate metric.

Mary gets buy-in for the test. The adjusted test version of the search page is developed easily. Mary's launch checklist includes a few more mission-critical items to check off before launching the test.

Web Performance Monitoring

Web Performance, also called Site Speed Optimization, is the usability domain that focuses on users' perceptions of the speed at which the browser responds to their interactions. As we saw in an earlier chapter, site speed plays a major role in the success of any online venture. High-performing sites and apps engage, convert, and retain users better than low-performing ones. Better site speed typically also means better search engine presence and rankings, as Google announced their use of the "Core Web Vitals" metrics to influence search listing rankings.

Case study: Readers in the US may remember when the Affordable Care Act first became available providing the ability for anyone in the USA to sign up for healthcare. The option was so popular that the websites that were initially created for enabling citizens to sign up had crushingly low speed in 2013. This didn't just hurt the perception of the sites and their developers but hurt the perception of the program in total at the time. It's a warning for any brand.

Web Performance focuses on users' perceptions of the speed at which the browser responds to their interactions. The slower an experience is perceived, the more users abandon before we've even got a chance to engage them with our content.

APM tools are great at measuring web performance and alerting to slow speeds. Their insights are even more valuable when combined with Experience Analytics to show the impact of those slow speeds on how customers perceive the experiences.

Balancing Speed vs. Engaging Content

Web Performance Monitoring is here to proactively analyze the speed of our pages and help balance the need for speed against the need for content-rich pages with attractive content. Of course, a barebones site without any images and videos would be faster. But it would also be less attractive. So the trick is to find the right balance between engaging content and satisfactory speed.

Synthetic (Lab) vs. Real-User Monitoring

There are two ways that site speed is measured, namely synthetic measurement, similar to lab testing, and Real-User Monitoring (RUM), a type of field measurement.

My colleague Boris Schapira uses the following analogy to explain the value of both synthetic and Real-User Monitoring.

Analogy: Testing a waterproof jacket

If my company wanted to manufacture a waterproof jacket, we would certainly use a lab to test that the jacket we produced is indeed waterproof. But at some point, we would also need to put the jackets on testers for trial runs.

> Only by observing them in the field would we discover, for example, that people need to sometimes go jogging with their jackets. So, the experience of actual customers guides us that our jacket should also be breathable in order to provide the best customer experience.
>
> Research is a constant back and forth between reproducible and controlled lab analyses and market observation.

Lab Data: Synthetic Monitoring

Also called active monitoring, here we run automated tests that emulate users within steady and precise browsing contexts (various locations across the globe, bandwidth, browser, etc.). See for example Figure 3B.4.

Field data: Real-User Monitoring (RUM)

Also called passive monitoring, here we gather individual session performance data in real-user sessions, while they are browsing the website.

Each approach has its advantages and disadvantages, so neither can replace the other. Most companies use both together for different use cases.

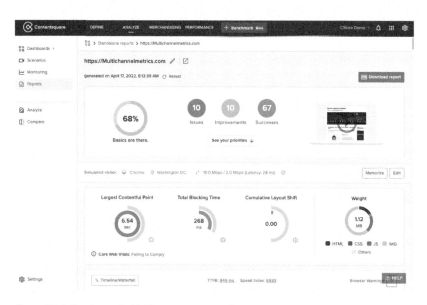

Figure 3B.4 Synthetic (Lab) Monitoring example.

Synthetic Monitoring Advantages

- Enables testing newly developed experiences before rolling them out to avoid potential blunders;
- Provides specific insights for improving the speed of pages;
- Measures site speed within test conditions and contexts that are totally under control and steady between tests over time so they can be trended and compared (i.e., test by browsing from the same location, same browser, etc.);
- Can measure the speed of any competing websites as a benchmark for comparing to your own site's performance;
- Provides metrics that are not swayed by changes in user population, e.g. if a new, faster device and browser comes on the market this does not artificially change the test metrics you are running and make it seem as if the website became faster.

Real-User Monitoring Advantages

- Let's you calculate the business impact of slow speeds;
- Enables troubleshooting how site speed impacts specific sessions and experiences by directly correlating performance at the session level;
- Reveals the complexity related to the diversity of actual users and their actual browsing conditions (users' locations, devices, Internet connection speeds, …);
- Can provide some additional metrics that depend on user interactions, e.g. the first input delay (definition follows shortly);
- Metrics do reflect perceived changes due to changing user population, e.g. if a new, faster device and browser comes on the market and improves perceived site speed for users, your RUM performance indicators automatically improve.

Site Speed Metrics

We cannot characterize the loading of a page in a single measure. A page load is a user experience with an action, a feedback, and a confidence threshold that leads to the next user action. To accurately capture the finesse of this, there are a lot of metrics to measure page speed, both from a field and lab perspective. Their measurement and computation are well-defined for performance professionals. Here is an overview in the context of how they map to users' perceived experiences.

Checkout typical site speed metrics in this book's online supplemental materials

https://ExperienceAnalytics.Live/SiteSpeedMetrics

Google Core Web Vitals

Google is famous for providing relevant search results to its users. Google's approach demonstrates that they consider a good experience to be part of what makes a search result more relevant. Following the Smartphone revolution, that included ranking sites better that provide a mobile-friendly experience. In 2020 Google announced that page experience, that is, specifically performance, will also influence rankings going forward. As a result, it has become a new consideration for search engine optimization (SEO).

In their initial approach to this, Google crystalized three metrics for assessing page experience, calling them the Core Web Vitals. Namely, these are the following three metrics.

- *LCP (largest contentful paint)*: The amount of time to render the largest content element visible in the viewport, from when the user requests the URL. The largest element is typically an image or video, or perhaps a large block-level text element. This is important because it tells the reader that the URL is actually loading.
- *FID (first input delay)*: The time from when a user first interacts with your page (when they clicked a link, tapped on a button, and so on) to the time when the browser responds to that interaction. This is important on pages where the user needs to do something because this is when the page has become interactive.
- *CLS (Cumulative Layout Shift)*: CLS measures the sum total of all individual layout shift scores for every unexpected layout shift that occurs during the entire lifespan of the page. This is important because having page elements shift while a user is trying to interact with it is a bad user experience. (Source: Google's Search Console Help[2])

How does Google get data for these metrics? It uses real-user data via its Chrome User Experience Report.[3]

Impact of Site Speed on Experience and Content Engagement

Speed—like beauty—is "in the eye of the beholder," that is, it is the user's perception of adequate speed. With that perspective, measuring speed by itself is an incomplete assessment of performance. Only when speed and experience metrics are combined do we get a view that enables balancing the benefits of greater speed with the benefits of attractive, engaging, and persuasive content.

- In Journey and In-Page Analysis, compare the experiences of users that saw quick vs. slower page loading times.

- Replay their sessions to see what they experienced.
- Quantify the impact of slower speeds on their journey completions, conversions, and revenue.

Insights for Improving Site Speed

Metrics and alerts for site speed are great—but tips for how to increase the speed of inadequate experiences are even better. Web Performance Monitoring tools can provide automated insights for what is impacting the speed of given pages and how to improve it (e.g. see Figure 3B.5). That is what turns Performance Monitoring from an alerting capability into actionable insights.

There are many more practical opportunities for improving performance beyond just limiting heavy images, videos, and choosing speedy Content Delivery Networks. For example, these tips include items that are under the control of the page developer:

- Deferring JavaScript code so that it executes asynchronously instead of blocking page load progress;
- Limiting the number of fonts and third-party resources that are loaded but never used;
- Image compression and sizing;
- etc.

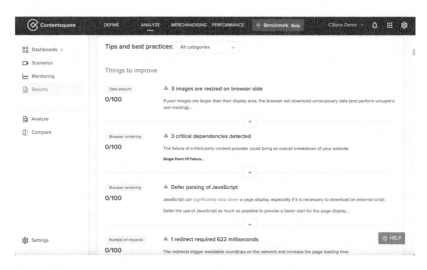

Figure 3B.5 An example of automated tips for improving speed.

Mary Gets Her New Search Experience Ready to Test

Before launching the test that she requested for the product search experience, Mary scans the test page with synthetic Web Performance Monitoring. This uncovered that the loading of the page is being slowed down mostly due to scripts, images, and numerous DOM elements—many unused or used inefficiently.

It's an easy fix for her developers to make the page faster without losing any content. A fix that is well worth it given that even sub-second slowdown of pages has been shown to impact conversion.

Accessibility Issues Monitoring

With over one billion people in the world having an impairment that affects their ability to use the web, experience optimization would be incomplete without including accessibility for all. Yet, sadly accessibility has remained a blind spot for most digital businesses and even within analytics efforts. As my colleagues write in the Contentsquare Digital Accessibility Handbook, today, it is estimated that over 70% of digital content is not accessible, including 80% of news sites and two-thirds of ecommerce sites.

Thankfully, governments around the world are implementing web accessibility standards that come with fines for businesses that are not compliant. Accessibility has become a hot topic across public and private websites. These regulations put power behind the accessibility goals that any digital business should have in place anyways, not just because of moral obligation but also in order to reach their full potential audience.

Accessibility issues reporting is designed to scan sites for content that isn't accessible and doesn't comply with regulations. This includes the following examples, as outlined in the Digital Accessibility Handbook linked below.

Visual Impairments

Visual impairments include not just loss of sight entirely but also color blindness (affecting a surprising 1 in 12 males), glaucoma, cataracts, and various kinds of conditions leading to low vision. Some of the accessibility criteria toward a better experience for these customers include

- Clear and concise site navigation that is compatible for customers using screen readers;
- Sufficient font sizes and contrast ratios of font vs. background colors;
- Alternative text supplied for images;

- Responsive page design so that the page displays correctly even when zoomed in by 500%;
- etc.

Auditory Impairments

For customers with impairments affecting their hearing, it is important that ...

- Videos include subtitles, captions, or sign language;
- Any notification that relies on sound also provides a visual queue;
- etc.

Physical Impairments

For customers with paralysis or lack of motor control, we need to ensure that

- Site navigation is hierarchical, logical, and concise so that it is usable also while tabbing through links rather than using a mouse;
- Form fields are labeled correctly so that browser autofill can put the right content into the right fields;
- Page structural elements (header, footer, etc.) and skip-links acting as shortcuts are well labeled and designed to allow users to navigate more easily using a keyboard;
- etc.

Cognitive Impairments

Customers impacted by cognitive impairments include many different situations, including Dyslexia, Autism, ADHD, and memory loss (up to 20% of adults over 65). For these customers, it helps to ...

- Keep experiences simple and concise;
- Don't overload experiences with information that can easily overwhelm customers;
- Add images and pictograms to illustrate textual content and lighten the amount of text;
- Avoiding difficult-to-read fonts and font styles, e.g. italics;
- etc.

Learn more about these experience optimization opportunities by requesting the Digital Accessibility Handbook from the Contentsquare Foundation, a non-profit organization aiming to promote digital accessibility.

https://foundation.contentsquare.com/

Accessibility Auditing

Some of the above optimization opportunities can be surfaced by accessibility issues reporting tools such as Microsoft Accessibility Insight, Chrome's Lighthouse, WAVE, and many others.

WAVE (Web Accessibility Evaluation Tool), is developed and made available as a free community service by WebAIM, a non-profit organization based at the Center for Persons with Disabilities at Utah State University. Originally launched in 2001, WAVE has been used to evaluate the accessibility of millions of web pages.

Supplemental Online Materials: Example of a Wave Report

For an example of a Wave report see this book's supplemental online materials at the following URL

https://ExperienceAnalytics.Live/Figures

See the Wave report example in Chapter 3B

Accessibility Experience Monitoring

Catching the issues where the site is not compliant is only step one. The second and even more crucial step is to then understand and quantify with Experience Analytics, which of these issues impact customers' ability to have a good experience and achieve their goals. That enables the digital team to prioritize what they improve first.

Mary Launches Her New Search Experience

After scanning her new search experience for accessibility issues and addressing opportunities to make the experience better for all, Mary is ready to launch the new experience as an A/B test.

Expectations are high after all the data and effort that went into getting this launch right. It's Friday afternoon, champagne bottles and flutes are ready for the celebration.

And yet ... the A/B test results are negative, the new search is performing poorly. Why? What went wrong?

To find out, we need to connect the dots between digital Experience Analytics and the other analytics tools used in Mary's arsenal. How to triage issues across the digital experience ecosystem is the topic of the next chapter.

But first, Mary needs to assess how bad the issue is. That is where Impact Quantification helps.

Impact Quantification, Customer Insights, and Segmentation

Impact Quantification, customer insights, and segmentation make the data that we've already reviewed actionable. For example, by quantifying how often a behavior or issue is happening for a given group of customers, and how that is impacting their experience and conversion.

Impact Quantification

In one sense, Impact Quantification is the most critical of all Experience Analytics because it helps distinguish outlier behaviors from the opportunities and issues that matter because they affect many customers and impact the business.

That is why Impact Quantification is used everywhere together with the other insights we've seen.

Quantifying Opportunities Top-down

For example, are you seeing a looping behavior in Journey Analysis? Before going further, first, quantify how often the issue is happening and how the customers in question fared in comparison to others for their ability to achieve their goals on the site and app (e.g. see Figure 3C.1).

Quantifying Look-alike Sessions Bottom-up

Did you watch the replay of a user that struggled and abandoned their session? Find out how many others also struggled with the same content elements or encountered the same error events. For example, your Experience Analytics tool may allow you to click from a Session Replay to quantify how many historical sessions had the same behaviors and error messages (e.g. see Figure 3C.2).

Figure 3C.1 Example of quantifying impact top-down, e.g. starting from an unexpected journey.

How Impact Quantification Is Supported by Experience Analytics Tools

Quantifying the impact of behaviors and issues sounds like a no-brainer. However, it is a technical challenge for Experience Analytics tools. First, we need to describe the customer segment in question, based on their behavior including in-page interactions. Then, the analytics tool needs to be able to identify and quantify the historic sessions that included the same behaviors or errors. This requires retroactive analysis capabilities on data that has already been collected, without needing to preplan event flags or tags. Ask your Experience Analytics provider how the tools facilitate Impact Quantification.

Segmentation

As a German saying goes, "stupid questions get stupid answers." The way to ask good questions is to use segmentation. Analytics without segmentation is useless. Since different customers come to a site or app to accomplish different things, it makes no sense to analyze everybody's behaviors as if they were trying to accomplish the same goals.

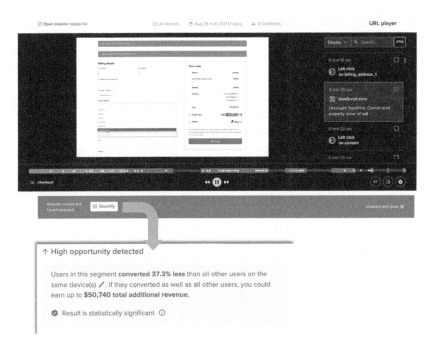

Figure 3C.2 Example of quantifying impact bottom-up, e.g. starting from one user's session that struggled due to an error.

The more flexible and granular the segmentation capabilities in an Experience Analytics tool, the better the questions that users can ask.

Most answers delivered by Experience Analytics lead to many new questions that also need to be answered before arriving at an actionable insight. Those increasingly specific new questions are answered by narrowing the analysis context to the specific behaviors in question. All of that is accomplished by using segmentation capabilities in analytics.

Experience Analytics Segmentation

Segments can be created at different levels. Here are key levels to think about.

Customer/User-level Segmentation

- *Customer profile*: for example, are they a registered customer? Are they a new vs. tenured customer? What CRM segments do they belong to, if available?

- *User and technical profile*: E.g. browser, operating system, etc.
- *Interaction history*: Session frequency, recency, purchase history.
- etc.

Session and Journey-level Segmentation

- *Session context*: For example, the marketing source of the sessions. What is the location from where they are browsing? What type of device and browser are they using?
- *Goals achieved*: Depending on the analysis, a goal can be a purchase transaction, lead registration, or simply the engagement with targeted content such as a video.
- *Sequential behaviors*: Focus on users that took a specific path through the site or app. For example, how many users directly reloaded the cart page multiple times in a row, as a telltale of struggle?

Pageview-level Segmentation

- *Exposure rate*: For example, focus on users that were vs. weren't exposed to a given area under the fold of the page.
- *Activity rate*: For example, focus on users that deeply engaged with the page vs. users that merely had it open but didn't engage.
- *Errors encountered*: For example, users that experienced an error on a specific page in their journey, not just somewhere within their session.

Content-element-level Segmentation

- *Hovers*: For example, focus on users with mouse-overs on specific content elements to understand the influence of those elements.
- *Clicks/taps/swipes*: For example, understand what leads up to interactions with specific content elements and how that influences the rest of the customers' journeys.
- *Sequential behaviors*: For example, focus on users that did vs. didn't engage with content elements in the expected order, or users that skipped part of the page by clicking an anchor link.
- *Time and effort*: For example, focus on users that engaged with content elements for a long time, or struggled on a given form field for a long time, or repeatedly.

Merchandising-level Segmentation

- *Products, promotions, pricing*: For example, focus on users with certain merchandising interactions vs. completed purchases.

Event-level Segmentation

- *Errors*: For example, focus on users that experienced specific errors, what led up to these errors, and what happened next.
- *UX frustrations*: e.g. same as above but for struggle behaviors such as clicks on unclickable elements, repeated attempts, and rage clicks
- *Custom events*: e.g. on a car manufacturer site, focus on users that selected a high-end engine option in the car configurator vs. price-sensitive.

When we discuss connection points between Experience Analytics and the ecosystem in the next chapter the above segmentation list can be extended further by many more practical segments such as …

- A/B test variations;
- Personalizations;
- Customers that provided positive vs. negative feedback;
- Customers from specific marketing campaigns or in specific customer segments;
- Segments already defined in the Digital Analytics tool;
- etc.

Check with your analytics provider's documentation on how these types of segmentation are achieved in your Experience Analytics tool.

Supplemental online materials: Segment definition example

For examples of a segment definition see this book's supplemental online materials at the following URL

https://ExperienceAnalytics.Live/Figures

See the Segment examples in Chapter 3C

Mary Measures the Impact of Her New Search Experience

Comparing the customer segments that were vs. weren't exposed to the new search experience, Mary validates that the new experience negatively impacted revenue on a run rate of a million in revenue per month if it were to be made live for all users.

A fast answer is needed to the question of why the A/B test failed. In the next chapter, we will review how Experience Analytics connects the dots with Mary's ecosystem of analytics tools to extend segmentation and get Mary the answer that she needs.

Customer Insights

When you listen to business leaders describing the value of Experience Analytics, what you hear them talking about the most is the strategic opportunity of better understanding customers. Yes, conversion and experience improvements are urgent and mission-critical. But as business people, they know that it's even more strategic for their teams to be close to customers and understand how they make decisions, what influences them, what excites them vs. puts them off.

Often coming from the world of offline commerce, these executives are used to being able to connect with their customers and seeing their faces to build empathy. But in digital, customers are invisible. With Experience Analytics we have the opportunity to close the gap.

Digital Body Language

When we see someone browsing in our physical store we can intuitively read their body language and facial expression to understand their experience, for example happy and engaged vs. confused or frustrated. We can also see what their mindset seems to be, for example quick shopping behavior vs. casually browsing and looking for options and inspiration. Digital Body Language is a term that goes back to Dr. Liraz Margalit. working at Experience Analytics vendor Clicktale back in 2016. It highlights that digital customers' behavior also gives clues to their experience and mindset.

A user may complete their journey and convert during the session which would mean that their experience is rated as a success in traditional digital analytics data. Yet, any frustrations they had to overcome along the way and their digital body language might suggest that the experience actually failed the user and that they might never return because of that.

Frustration Scoring at the session level provides one part of the data that makes up a user's digital body language. Engagement Scoring provides the other part, that is, how inspiring and rewarding the user's sessions have been.

Opportunities for using digital body language come at macro and micro levels.

Macro-level
If for example, the digital body language for too many users flips from happy to frustrated when they reach a certain page in their journey, that page and journey need some work to improve.

Individual customer level
Digital body language presents an opportunity to understand the intent of individual users and calculate propensity and risk scores.

These can then trigger helpful customer services or tailored offers to better meet the customer's needs. These actions can be extended during their session or via retargeting after their session.

We will review more opportunities from digital body language and customer insights in the last part of this book.

A New Approach to Measuring Net Promoter Scoring

Many brands go a long way to measure customer satisfaction and the overall customer experience via metrics such as the Net Promoter Score (NPS). NPS depends on customers that respond to a survey which is inherently a subset of customers and one that can potentially be skewed by customers that are particularly engaged or frustrated with the brand.

Automated frustration and Engagement Scoring round out measures such as NPS by assessing the digital experience of customers at scale. They are great indicators to display and trend alongside NPS and other customer satisfaction metrics.

The exhaustive data collection with Experience Analytics means that scoring can be segmented easily, to compare and contrast specific experiences that customers were exposed to, for example:

- Areas of the site and app
- Content, products, and page features they interacted with
- Customer segments, e.g. new vs. tenured
- Customer profiles, e.g. geographic region.

The teams tasked with measuring and improving NPS typically provide scorecards to the business within the company's standard dashboarding tools. Frustration and Engagement scores can be incorporated into those dashboards by exporting the data from the Experience Analytics tool. Many Experience Analytics tools provide APIs or exports to facilitate this.

In this chapter we've seen how rich the world of insights from digital Experience Analytics is. Before we continue into the heart of this book with practical use cases, we have one more foundational aspect to understand. Namely, how Experience Analytics typically integrates with the existing digital intelligence ecosystem to connect the dots.

Notes

1 DataViz project: datavizproject.com and ferdio.com.
2 Google Search Console help: https://support.google.com/webmasters/answer/9205520?hl=en
3 Google Chrome User Experience Report (CrUX): https://developers.google.com/web/tools/chrome-user-experience-report

Chapter 4

Connect the Dots Between Experience and the Digital Intelligence Ecosystem

When an artist gets ready to throw a great painting on a canvas, they have all their paints prepared to use and mix on the palette. Imagine what would happen if their colors were incompatible with each other, for example, red was in oil paint, blue was pastel chalk, and green was a watercolor? How would they mix the colors and create that coherent painting?

Similarly, when a digital team lead gets ready to develop and improve experiences, their digital intelligence ecosystem of tools needs to work together just as well as the colors of a paint palette. For example, suppose Web Analytics shows that your best customers are abandoning the site on the loyalty program page. In that case, it should be easy to find that exact issue and customer segment in your Experience Analytics.

As Tom Davenport says in the foreword to this book, "to really make sense of any business domain—and the most important one, your customers—requires using all the data available." Given how broad the marketing and digital intelligence ecosystem is today, there are dozens of integration opportunities with Experience Analytics. So here, we will focus on just a few of the most common ones.

Integration with Traditional Digital Analytics

The most mission-critical integration is, of course, the one with Web Analytics, that is, known by their more modern name of Digital Analytics today. Traditional Digital Analytics tools such as Google and Adobe Analytics are widely considered the heart of web tracking at nearly every digital business today, Digital Customer Experience Analytics needs to work in lockstep with them.

Look for your analytics tools to integrate in two different ways so you can connect the dots between web and Experience Analytics.

DOI: 10.4324/b23273-6

Session Replay Integration

Supported by many popular Experience Analytics tools, session replay integration enables a user looking at a session-level report in Google and Adobe Analytics to link from each session to the corresponding session replay in the Experience Analytics tool.

This is a popular and helpful way to get a first idea of what's going on with specific sessions that an analyst examines in their Web Analytics tool.

For example, in our story for a day-in-the-life of Mary at Marks and Spicy, she can create a Web Analytics report of all the sessions with her new on-site search experience where users didn't continue to view a Product Display Page. She can then drill to replay some of those sessions to get a first idea of any potential struggle with searching for products.

This approach is instrumental for analysts to shed some light but is still rather laborious. It requires watching many session replays to glean the best enhancements for reducing abandonment. That is because we are jumping straight from aggregate level reports all the way down to session-by-session, replays. There has got to be something more methodic that provides faster speed to insights. In fact, there is, namely, segment-level integration with Digital Analytics.

Segment Import Integration

Ask your analytics provider about importing customer segments you have already created in your Digital Analytics tool to use the same segments in your Experience Analytics. This integration is available in several Experience Analytics tools.

Many Google and Adobe Analytics users have created dozens or hundreds of segments in their Web Analytics. Since segmentation is vital for asking the most important analytical questions and answering them in an actionable manner, this integration leverages that investment. It enables users to ask those same great questions across their web and Experience Analytics. Importing these segments ensures consistency, so everyone is working with the same customer segment definitions.

When you import Web Analytics segments into your Experience Analytics tool, you can typically apply them to all the reports that you are looking at. This helps understand and improve the experience of the customers in question.

For example, at Marks and Spicy, Mary can pull up a Zone-based heatmap of the new search experience and apply the customer segment from Web Analytics that narrows the audience to those that experienced the new A/B test variation and didn't continue to view a Product Display Page (e.g. see Figure 4.1).

Instead of needing to start from individual session replays which at this stage of the analysis would be impractical and time-consuming, she can leverage Zone-based metrics to reveal what is happening when the experience is awry. For example, recurring clicks are common for this group on the search by the size filter element in the image. On average, shoppers are clicking 3.15 times in this section. What's going on? They can't possibly change their minds whether they are looking for a small, medium, or large?

So, Mary can create a segment of users' replays that included multiple interactions with this element and watch only the moment of friction with this filter. The session replay event stream reveals an error every time these specific users click this filter.

By quantifying the business impact, she can then contrast how much business is lost due to this issue. And she can narrow the

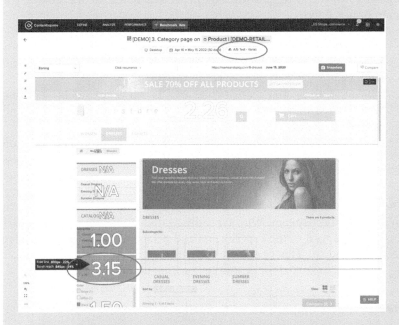

Figure 4.1 Zone-based heatmap filtered by a Digital Analytics imported segment.

issues down to various technical profiles, for example, in this case, the problem is happening with Firefox users much more than others. So, now we have all the dots connected that will help Mary's team fix the problem and restart their A/B test.

Integrations with A/B Testing and Personalization

You might be forgiven to think that A/B testing is just a tactic. Far from it, the teams specializing in experimentation see it as a mantra and a key driver for business innovation. All ideas for improving experiences are welcome, but let's test them out and let the numbers decide. Instead of debating, let's just run a test.

Likewise, personalization is strategic too. How can we make our site and app smarter by way of personalization, more like a living and breathing brick-and-mortar store clerk?

However, as previously discussed, both A/B testing and personalization are more challenging in practice than most businesses expect. After all the effort, results of many experiments can be flat or sometimes even negative. So, the synergy with Experience Analytics we are looking for again is as follows:

- *Before testing and personalizing*: What are the most likely experiments to generate uplift and why? Which groups of users should we target and what exactly should we be personalizing for them?
- *During testing and personalization*: Is my experiment working as intended or is there something I should be fixing quickly and restarting the experiment before weeks are lost?
- *After testing and personalization*: Why was a given variation successful (or a failure) and, what were the most significant success factors to create even better experiments?

These use cases are much more efficient and effective to address with an integrated ecosystem. With typically available integrations, each user session is mapped to the experiments and personalization that they have been exposed to. This opens up the path to compare how experiences A vs. B vs. C impacted users' journeys within and across pages.

Side-by-side Comparison of Experiences

Many Experience Analytics tools enable users to view variants of experiences side by side to compare behaviors from a bird's-eye view.

Let's look at an A/B test example here inspired by a real-life case study from a Beauty and Cosmetics brand.

Challenge

Google Analytics shows lots of customers reaching the Product List Page (PLP) but not proceeding to view any of the products. Why?

The "Aha" with Experience Analytics

Many users land on this page, view the beautiful big marketing banner up top but do not scroll enough to view the Product Carousel under the fold line (see Figure 4.2). Only 47.9% scroll down to see the products. There is nothing to suggest scrolling for the rest of the shoppers, so they completely miss the good stuff on the page.

The Attractiveness Rate on the same page shows that users that do scroll enough to see the Product Carousel are much more likely to click through to a product page, that is, 36.5% of these users click on a product once the products are in view on the PLP screen.

You do not need to be a genius to figure out that an A/B test that improves exposure to the Product Carousel should improve sales conversions driven from this page.

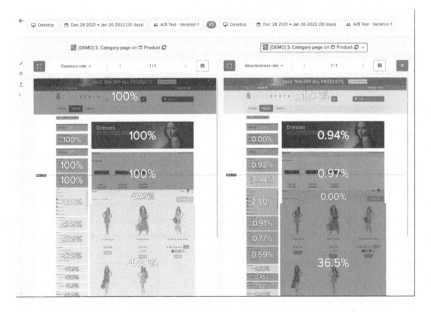

Figure 4.2 Side-by-side comparison of Exposure Rate vs. Attractiveness Rate.

The Action

With the visuals and data in hand, the team gets buy-in for running a test that could be viewed as controversial, namely reducing the size of the Marketing banner. The purpose is to lift some of the underlying content just sufficiently above the fold to hint that there is more content to scroll to.

The Result

The well-informed test shows a 44% increased scroll rate, and a 35% improved conversion rate from the PLP page, that is, from one of the most highly trafficked packages on the site. A side-by-side comparison proves the biggest success factors, that is, with improved scrolling, improved revenue was driven by the Product Carousel.

Success Factors Learned

Some of the success factors learned for future experiments include the following:

• Identify the fold line for most users and make sure they have an indication that there is further content to scroll to;
• A beautiful and immersive marketing banner doesn't have to be full page in order to be effective.

Integrations with Customer Feedback Management

"On the web nobody can hear you scream," as we were quoting Eric Peterson earlier in this book. Occasionally a scream does break through the silence, namely via customer feedback. Usually, it is either a scream of joy from your biggest fans because they found something they loved on your site or app. More often, it is a scream from the most disgruntled users that run into confusion, frustration, or plain errors.

The only thing that can be even more frustrating than these disgruntled feedbacks is the challenge that the digital team is facing in making them actionable. They worked so hard to create the best experience they could, and they really want to learn from the feedback and improve experiences for all. Customer feedback is a goldmine of information about customer wants and needs. All too often however it is not clear from the feedback by itself ...

• What steps led up to the frustrations?
• Was the problem due to errors or confusion?
• Was it an outlier or how many others are also experiencing the same frustrations?

- What journeys lead up to the worst frustrations and should be addressed first?
- How much business is lost due to these issues so resources can be prioritized for resolving them?

That's exactly where the integrations between customer feedback management tools and Experience Analytics help. As before, integrations are available at multiple levels, ask your analytics tool provider which ones your solution supports.

Session Replay Integration

When users read their customer feedback in their Voice of Customer tool, they can click to replay the exact sessions where feedback was given. Users can see the steps and experiences that lead up to providing feedback.

Impact Quantification Integration

But how do we discover if this complaint and frustration is an outlier or a common issue that is impacting many? That is where the Impact Quantification that we discussed earlier in the book is mission-critical. It enables users to go from one session replay to quantify how many look-alike sessions there are, and then compare their success rates vs. the rest of the population.

Rating Integration

The rating that users provide on pages via feedback (e.g. 1–5 stars) is provided to the Experience Analytics tool. In side-by-side heatmaps, the digital team can compare a bird's-eye view of the differences between users that came away happy vs. dissatisfied (e.g. see Figure 4.3). In the example below, for instance, users that had to try multiple times to complete the City field in the analysis form were correlated with negative feedback on the page.

Supplemental Online Materials: Voice of Customer Integration Examples

For additional visual examples of Voice of Customer integrations see this book's supplemental online materials at the following URL

https://ExperienceAnalytics.Live/Figures

See the Voice of Customer examples for Chapter 4

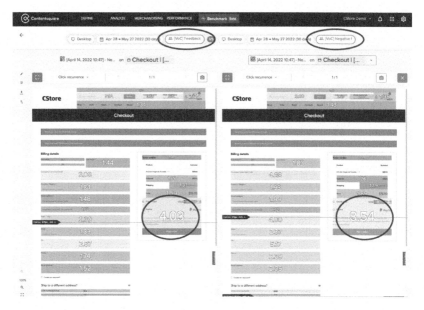

Figure 4.3 Ratings integration comparing positive vs. negative feedback side by side.

Journey Integration

Digital teams often plan proactively where they are going to invest the next set of improvements on the site. A great input into the prioritization can be to identify which journeys are most frequently associated with positive vs. negative feedback. This can be facilitated by running a reverse journey analysis of all the paths that lead to each feedback and segmenting on 1 vs. 5-star ratings. Help more customers find the golden paths and invest in improvements to the paths that are frequently causing friction.

Experience Scorecard Integration

The complete picture of experience usually comes together from combining multiple sources into a common balanced scorecard. For example, a scorecard can combine online feedback with the company's customer satisfaction metrics such as the Net Promoter Score. Scorecards can also include data beyond those customers that provided feedback, for example combine the rate of negative feedback vs. how many users complete their goals successfully on that page.

Together, these integrations open up the goldmine that is to be found in customer feedback by making it actionable.

Integrations with Business Intelligence, Data Science, and Multichannel Marketing

The power vested in Experience Analytics data is the power of your customers. Experience data is about their behavior, their intent, and their perception of the experiences that you are providing.

It holds clues as to how customers want to be browsing your site and app. They are guiding you to better design decisions by way of their behavior data. They are also telling you about their wants and needs along the way.

Since the customer is king and experience data is about customers, this data holds a lot more value than just improving sites and apps. It is a valuable contribution to your understanding of customers, that is, customer analytics and customer satisfaction.

That is why attentive users of Experience Analytics are keen to extract the data and metrics and surface them alongside other customer data and dashboards for a more balanced and broad understanding of customers. The way to achieve that is by tapping into the export functions and Application Programming Interfaces (APIs) provided by many Experience Analytics tools.

We will cover opportunities and use cases in the third part of the book.

Back at Marks and Spicy, Mary and the team have popped the champagne bubbles and toasted to their second round of the on-site search experience A/B test. Now that the errors were fixed, the test has been a resounding success.

To top off their success, the team now has a dashboard running on a big monitor on the office floor. It shows the trend of interactions with various search filters which lets the team see what's trending currently, e.g. in terms of product categories, price ranges, brands, colors, and more.

Now that we have laid out all of our Experience Analytics "tools" we are ready to leave Mary and Marks and Spicy behind and step into your shoes, and the shoes of your colleagues. Let's apply the insights for everyday challenges that will hopefully (or unfortunately) be all too familiar to you.

Solve Everyday Business Challenges Faster with Experience Analytics

Part II of the book is here to provide you with practical examples for the everyday use of Experience Analytics on digital channels. Let's step into the shoes of champions in every role within digital teams and see how they let their customers guide them how to design a better site and app.

We will orient the use cases by the stages of a typical customer lifecycle from the top to the bottom of the funnel. For most sites and digital businesses, the mapping of use cases looks as follows.

Chapter 5: Solve Common Challenges at the Top of the Funnel
5A For Marketing Acquisition teams
5B For Brand Marketing and Content teams

Chapter 6: Solve Common Challenges at the Middle of the Funnel
6A For Ecommerce and Ebusiness Teams
6B For Visual Merchandising

Chapter 7: Solve Common Challenges at the Bottom of the Funnel
7A For Customer Feedback Management Teams
7B For Operations, Triage, and Technical Roles

Chapter 8: Solve Common Challenges at the Flip Side of the Funnel, that is, customer relationship
8A For Customer Experience, Support, and Service Goals
8B For Customer Marketing Teams

Chapter 9: Solve Challenges Across the Entire Customer Journey
9A For Product Management and UX/CX
9B For Conversion Rate Optimization and Analytics Teams

The funnel concept is a simplified way to look at the customer lifecycle to help us with our walkthrough of teams and use cases. Think of the lifecycle as a literal cycle. Customers are always in the acquisition phase for certain products, consideration and purchase phase for others, and customer service phase for yet others.

DOI: 10.4324/b23273-7

Chapter 5

Solve Common Challenges at the Top of the Funnel

When you are walking down your favored shopping street in your town, sometimes a new store catches your eye. Within seconds you decide whether you are interested in going inside. Does anything capture your attention and persuade you to engage? Sometimes, it's the brand or the name of the store. Sometimes, it's the shopping window display or the products and prices that attract you.

It is no different at the top of the funnel on websites. Once the customer lands on the site, what do they see that attracts them, persuades them to the brand, and gets them to engage with the content and products? What are some of the golden paths you can discover and learn from to reduce bounces for all customers?

Let's visit each team focused on the top of the funnel with the mission-critical goal of fueling the site with qualified traffic. Without them, everything else is useless.

Chapter 5A: Solve Marketing Acquisition Challenges

- Business pressures on the Acquisition Team
- Challenge 1: Paid traffic: Are we paying for the right audiences?
- Challenge 2: Most A/B tests fail to reduce bounce rates
- Challenge 3: Different acquired audiences expect different experiences
- Challenge 4: Page experience impacts SEO rankings
- Challenge 5: Improving landing page form completions

Chapter 5B: Solve Brand Marketing and Content Challenges

- Business Pressures on the Brand Marketing and Content Teams
- Challenge 1: Is the content strategy working for engaging and persuading customers?
- Challenge 2: How to fit engaging experiences onto small screens?

DOI: 10.4324/b23273-8

The C-SUITE Method: Cheat Sheets for Solving Challenges

For each challenge, we will walk through real-life case studies. It's the most practical way to step into the shoes of your peers that are experts at using Experience Analytics. At the end of each challenge, we'll have a cheat sheet to help you extract the lessons to be learned.

Our cheat sheets have a fun and fitting name, that is, the C-SUITE method. Figure 5.1 shows what each letter stands for.

Challenge	What's the challenge we are looking to solve?
Surface	What are some clues that Experience Analytics can surface based on our customers' behavior and context? What are the golden paths? Where is there "smoke" that suggests potential trouble?
Understand	Why are those behaviors happening? What is the underlying intent of our customers? What new ideas for revenue jump out? Where are points of hesitation, confusion, and friction? What is the root cause?
Impact	There are always too many issues that could be fixed and too many potential opportunities to invest in. So, how can we prioritize based on impact on experience and the business?
Test	What enhancements, new experiences, or fixes are most likely to address the challenge?
Evaluate	Why did certain tests or new experiences win or lose? What were the biggest success factors that we can extract toward even better tests?

Figure 5.1 Cheat sheet: C-SUITE analysis blueprint explained.

Solve Marketing Acquisition Challenges

It's a constant hustle and bustle on the marketing floor at most companies. It is a never-ending production of campaigns to acquire the right audiences to your site, persuade them to your brand, and drive them into the funnel.

Toward that mission, advertising and other marketing campaigns are where the biggest portion of the digital budget goes at most companies. It is a competitive sport, with marketing teams racing each other to reach their target customers and persuade them to their brand. Did you just succeed in running a great Black Friday campaign? Congrats! Now go back and start all over again for the Christmas holiday campaign.

All that would be an easy job if the marketing budget was infinite. It is always finite, of course. What's not finite are the goals for acquisition, it seems, that is, they only go up and up every year. So do prices for advertising. How can marketers improve ROAS (Return on ad spend)? Marketing Acquisition is an extreme endurance sport.

Doing all this without Experience Analytics would be like flying a plane with insufficient instruments to tell you how you are doing. Let's step into the shoes of acquisition marketers using experience metrics added to their analytics ecosystem.

Here is a typical mindmap of what's going on in many Marketing Acquisition managers' minds and where Experience Analytics help them (see Figure 5A.1).

Business Pressures on the Acquisition Team

Acquisition efforts involve many different channels and types of marketing. Each of these come with their unique challenges.

Paid Traffic Costs a Lot, Yet Bounce Rates Remain High

Despite decades of using marketing analytics and optimization tools, bounce rates for paid traffic remain high. The Marketing Education

MINDMAP Marketing Acquisition		
Proactively innovate & troubleshoot top-down		
CHALLENGES		
Acquisition goals are going up, but ad budgets are limited. How can we do more with less?	If we miss our acquisition goals, business will fall short	Ad spend is our biggest spend. How can we improve ROAS?
QUESTIONS TO ANSWER		
Why is traffic bouncing on the landing page? How can we reduce?	What's the intent of acquired users? How can we better engage them?	How can we improve SEO by improving Google Core Web Vitals?
What's the business impact and priority of potential actions?		
SUCCESS CRITERIA		
Increase traffic reduce bounces, improve journeys	Hit acquisition goals	Improve ROI on advertising & campaigns

Figure 5A.1 Typical Marketing Acquisition Team mind map.

blog CXL by Peep Laya,[1] lists typical traffic bounce rates by acquisition channel, ranging from 35–85% depending on the channel of traffic acquisition.

> See the CXL marketing education destination blog on benchmark bounce rates statistics by channel. CXL shows bounce rates ranging between 35–85% depending on the channel.[2]
>
> https://cxl.com/guides/bounce-rate/benchmarks/

For example, for display ad traffic, out of 100 users you are paying to bring to the site, 56 are leaving without giving you another thought. As advertising costs are high and going up, it would be impossible to win this game in the long run by throwing more money at advertising.

If you could persuade an extra five users to take an interest in your offering and go into the store or site funnel, in the example above, it would mean a reduction of bounces from 56 to 51. That would be an 11% improvement on your ROAS.

How can customer behavior on your landing pages guide you on what it is that they are looking for, what puts them off, and what would be the most effective way to persuade them to enter the store?

Organic Traffic Is Free, But SEO Is Tricky and Competitive

Is your search listing not showing up on the first page of search results for relevant keywords for finding your business? Forget it; you might as well not exist at all for those searches.

Content relevancy and references from elsewhere on the Internet are not the only criteria that factor into SEO. As we reviewed in earlier chapters, customer experience plays a role too. Specifically, Google (with a share of over 90% of searches) now considers site speed as part of its ranking algorithms, specifically based on the Core Web Vitals metrics, reviewed earlier.

Social Media and Other Acquisition Marketing Channels

Besides the above, many different marketing channels share the same challenges. For example, social media marketing doesn't come easy. So, when traffic referred by influencers lands on your site, you want to make the most out of the opportunity by minimizing bounces.

Acquisition Optimization Challenges and Use Cases

Let's step into a typical day in the life of a Marketing Acquisition team now working on improving their success rates. Let's see how they are using Experience Analytics to overcome challenges.

- Challenge 1: Paid traffic: Are we paying for the right audiences?
- Challenge 2: Most A/B tests fail to reduce bounce rates
- Challenge 3: Different acquired audiences expect different experiences
- Challenge 4: Page experience impacts SEO rankings
- Challenge 5: Improving landing page form completions

Challenge 1: Paid Traffic: Are We Paying for the Right Audiences?

With limited control over who sees your ads, the first question to ask is whether your advertising budget is even going toward attracting the right audience. Is the traffic you are paying for qualified? To which degree are you wasting your ad budget?

Where Traditional Metrics and Experience Metrics Come Together

Traditional marketing and Digital Analytics provide key performance indicators for your campaigns, including revenue, conversion rates, and bounce rates for ad-driven traffic. When bounce rates are higher than desired, your immediate next question becomes what you can do about it. Is the culprit that your content on the landing page is inadequate? Or, did the ad message somehow attract the wrong target audience?

Supplemental online materials: Example of Acquisition channel KPIs in Web Analytics

For examples of Acquisition channel KPIs in Google Analytics™ see this book's supplemental online materials at the following URL

https://ExperienceAnalytics.Live/Figures

See the Web Analytics example for chapter 5a

That's a perfect use case for Experience Analytics to come to the help of traditional analytics by illuminating the intent of paid visitors coming to your site.

Case Study 1: Financial Services and B2B Companies Qualify What Acquired Traffic Users Are Looking for When They Click Their Ad

Where users navigate on the site after landing indicates what they came for. Using Journey Analysis (as introduced in Chapter 3), we can see whether that intent aligns with the purpose of our advertising campaign.

The Challenge

Our first case study tells the story of multiple Financial Services and B2B companies that all experienced this same blind spot with their pay-per-click advertising on search engines. Namely, conversion rates were lower than desired. Yet, the cost of clicks adds up quickly. What can they do to improve the ROI on their pay-per-click advertising?

Step 1: What Do Users' Journeys Say About Their Intent?

If traffic is qualified, we expect visitors to engage with the journeys that we designed to inform and persuade them to become customers. Yet, here is how several Financial Services and B2B companies looked at the traffic they acquired and what they found. They used the Journey Analysis reports in their Experience Analytics but filtered these reports to focus on traffic received via given advertising channels.

How to Filter Experience Analytics by Acquisition Source

Creating a segment to filter reports by Marketing Acquisition source is typically done in one of two ways. If your Experience Analytics tool enables it, you can import your ad traffic segments that you will have already configured in your web analytics. This approach saves time and effort. It also ensures that your metrics will be consistent between your web analytics and Experience Analytics tools.

If the Experience Analytics tool does not provide this option, you can work around it by customizing the tags of your Experience Analytics tool. Here, you write JavaScript code to capture your advertising URL tracking parameters on the ad landing page and pass them into the tag of your Experience Analytics tool. For more information on how to do this, refer to your tool provider's

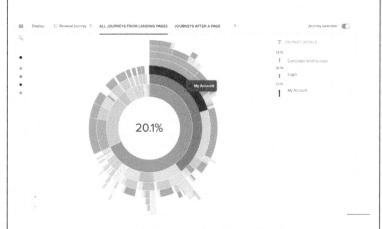

Figure 5A.2 Journey Analysis example showing 20.1% log in to their account from the ad landing page, and nearly twice that many try to log in.

documentation, or see any book on Digital Analytics, including my book on Multichannel Marketing.

What did these Financial Services and B2B companies find in Journey Analysis in our case study?

Instead of going into the acquisition funnel, a large portion of users that clicked through from pay-per-click advertising embarked on the existing customer section of the site. Journey Analysis shows them logging into their account right away (see Figure 5A.2).

This reveals that many acquired users were not prospective customers but existing customers who just clicked the ad link for convenience. Some of this was expected, of course, but the extent to which it happened surprised them, with 40% of the ad budget potentially going to waste.

So far, everything in this case study could have also been accomplished using any traditional web analytics tool. But before jumping to conclusions, the marketing team needed to confirm whether these existing customers still engaged with the advertising messages on the landing page so that they could consider it a benefit toward cross-selling to additional accounts and products. That would still qualify as a benefit for the campaign. That's where we need to look at the in-page behavior of the acquired traffic to answer the question. It is where Experience Analytics is mandatory.

Step 2: What Does Their In-Page Journey Say About Their Intent?

If the traffic from existing customers is qualified, we expect to see engagement with the content on the landing page. Before users continue on their journey into the existing customer section of the website, do they spend time with the content on the page?

That's a question we can answer with Zone-based heatmaps by filtering on the users in question, that is, existing customers re-acquired to the site by the ads.

How to Filter on Existing Customers

There are various ways to create a segment for existing customers; however, the simplest of these methods suffices for the current case study. Namely, we just need to create a segment of users that started on the ad landing page and *directly then* continued to the login for the existing customer area.

In some Experience Analytics tools, you can create this segment instantly from the Journey Analysis. It requires an ability to specify a navigation path type filter, i.e., we don't want to look at users that viewed other pages between the landing page and the login into the customer area.

For visual examples of creating a segment in this way, see this book's supplemental online materials at the following URL

https://ExperienceAnalytics.Live/Figures

See the Segmentation examples for chapter 5a

When the Financial Services and B2B companies in our case study applied this analysis, they found the following insights by looking at various experience metrics:

- *Scrolling or Exposure heatmaps*: These existing customers did not scroll on the ad landing page to get exposed to much of the content.

Definition: Exposure Rate

This metric identifies how far down the page the average visitor is scrolling (see Figure 5A.3).

Calculation

$$\frac{\text{Number of pageviews that displayed a given content zone or area of the page}}{\text{Total number of pageviews}}$$

Figure 5A.3 Exposure Rate calculation.

Exposure rate is calculated as the number of pageviews that displayed a given content zone or area of the page, divided by the total number of pageviews.

- *Hover heatmaps*: The customers in question did not engage with any content elements aside from the login button.

Definition: Hover Rate

The percentage of pageviews using a desktop device in which visitors hovered over a given content zone with their mouse cursor at least once (see Figure 5A.4). This metric determines which zones are consumed the most. Using this metric, you can rank zones and see if users engage with them.

Calculation

$$\frac{\text{Number of pageviews with at least one hover over the content zone}}{\text{Total number of pageviews}}$$

Figure 5A.4 Hover Rate calculation.

- *Time before first clicking on the login button*: The speed at which these customers clicked the log-in button (within seconds of landing) was the final nail in the coffin for this segment of the ad campaign. This insight confirmed that users did not even visually engage with the content above the fold.

Definition: Time Before First Click

This metric identifies which elements users interact with first. It helps rank zones according to the time spent before users engage with the zone.

It is calculated as the average time from when the page loads and the data collection tag executes to the first click on the content element for a pageview with at least one click on the content element.

The bottom-line is that users weren't interested or did not see enough incentive to scroll within the content of the page. They just wanted to log in to see their accounts (see Figure 5A.5).

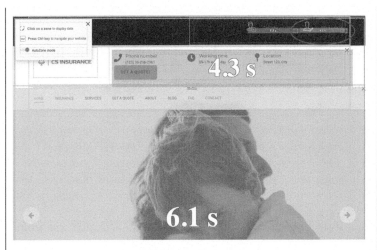

Figure 5A.5 Zone-based heatmap example shows a short time before the first click on login (top right).

The Value: Clarity on Customer Intent Drives Better Decisions and Saves Time

So, now the companies in our case study knew that a lot of their ad budget invested here was going to waste. It was not driving new customer acquisition, and it was not engaging existing customers for cross-sell purposes. But what should they do about it?

In competitive markets, it is often necessary to make sure that your PPC ads appear even on keywords that are used by existing customers. Sometimes, marketers even advertise on their company's brand name because competitors also advertise to appear alongside. So, the companies in our case study did not stop advertising on these keywords. But marketing attributed ROI to customer retention benefits instead of customer acquisition benefits. And instead of embarking on costly and futile experiments to improve their ad landing pages, they understood that content had nothing to do with the low conversion rates. That is time and money saved.

C-SUITE Cheat Sheet for Solving the Challenge

In summary, here is a visual overview of how Marketing Acquisition teams qualify the audiences acquired by various campaigns to shift ad placements where necessary and attract the right audiences (Figure 5A.6).

Challenge 2: Most A/B Tests Fail to Reduce Advertising Bounce Rates

Once we have validated that we are attracting the right audiences, how can we engage these audiences to increase conversion rates? We can stumble upon great improvements by A/B testing various versions of our landing pages. Yet, it is the experience of most marketers that too many A/B tests finish flat, that is, they don't move the needle in a significant way.

What if the best ideas for improving your bounce rate came from your customers? So, here is where our marketers will use Experience Analytics to understand why some users are bouncing while others are continuing their journey. That will inform the best A/B testing candidates that are most likely to improve conversion rates.

Challenge	Acquired traffic: Are we paying for the right (qualified) audience?	
Surface	Review performance of campaigns to focus first on the ones with relatively lower success rates.	
Understand	Is there a mismatch of the audience's qualification and expectation vs. the marketing team's goals?	
	What do users' journeys reveal about their intent, i.e. why did they click the ad and what are they looking to do on the site?	Are users engaging with in-page content in a way that suggests their interests are aligned with the campaign's purpose?
Impact	Quantify volumes for potential value of changing ad placements	
Test	Change ad placements or creative in order to clarify the purpose of the campaign and attract the right audience.	
Evaluate	Why did the changes help/hurt? What were the biggest success factors we can learn for future campaigns?	

Figure 5A.6 Cheat sheet: Qualify acquired traffic.

Case Study: Software Company Improves Landing Page Effectiveness by Informing the Best A/B Test to Run

For our case study, we will step into the shoes of marketers at a well-known software company. They ran a large-scale B2B advertising campaign targeted at executive audiences for one of their enterprise software offerings.

The Challenge

They were asking themselves the same questions that any marketer would do:

- With so much content to engage audiences on our ad landing pages, what content is attractive and persuasive? What content is ignored and should be dropped?
- We can't put everything above the fold. So, where should we place the content that works the best on our landing pages?

What metrics you use to answer these questions depends on how you have constructed the experience. In this case study, the lead registration call-to-action was not on the ad landing page itself but required a deeper foray into the site. That would be the case on any ecommerce website as well. In these situations, the first question becomes which content elements are persuasive enough to get users to click deeper into the site.

Step 1: What Can We Learn from Click Rates to Inform the Next A/B Test? (Not Much)

A simple Click Rate metric tells us how many users click on any content element. That is a good start, but the Click Rate will be lower for content elements under the fold because fewer users are scrolling even to see them. A Click Rate analysis would often misleadingly suggest that the content elements above the fold are the most valuable ones. Yet, the most clicked element will often be the menu or search bar on any page on any site. While it is an intuitive metric, we often learn nothing actionable about the content by looking at Click Rates.

Definition: Click Rate

This metric tells you how many visitors clicked at least once on a zone per pageview (see Figure 5A.7).

Calculation

$$\frac{\text{Number of pageviews where the zone}}{\text{Total number of pageviews.}}$$

Figure 5A.7 Click Rate calculation.

Step 2: What Can We Learn from Attractiveness Rates to Find Hidden Gems?

Attractiveness Rate enables us to normalize Click Rates based on how users scrolled and viewed content elements. It answers the question, if users scrolled and were exposed to a content element, were they attracted to it and clicked on it?

Definition: Attractiveness Rate

This metric translates the attractiveness of an element. It calculates the percentage of visitors who clicked on a zone after being exposed to it (see Figure 5A.8).

Calculation

$$\frac{\text{Number of views with zone displayed and at least one click}}{\text{Number of views with zone displayed}}$$

Figure 5A.8 Attractiveness Rate calculation.

Why is Attractiveness Rate a huge deal? It's because we also learn about the relevancy of content to our customers.

We see what content meets their interests. For example, if I had an Attractiveness Rate metric on the paragraphs in this book, I would learn from my readers which sections they would like to learn more about vs. which others I might want to eliminate.

Attractiveness Rate Examples

For visual examples for Attractiveness Rate, see this book's supplemental online materials at the following URL

https://ExperienceAnalytics.Live/Figures

See the Attractiveness Rate examples for chapter 5

At the software company in our case study, it became clear that content toward the bottom of the ad landing page was very attractive for clicks but only for the small subset of visitors that scrolled far enough to reach this content.

With this information in hand, our software company sought to help more visitors to find these valuable content elements. In their case, they did this without changing the location of this content. Instead, they added an anchor link in the middle of the page. Clicking that link enabled users to skip ahead to the bottom of the page. A/B testing this approach resulted in a 12% increase in clicks deeper into the site from their ad campaign (see Figure 5A.10).

Attractiveness Rate is a metric that works equally well for mobile and desktop traffic because it does not depend on a mouse cursor. That makes the metric particularly valuable for analyzing mobile traffic because you have a more limited choice of metrics available here. If users scroll down, what content makes them stop and tap and continue their journey?

Step 3: What Can We Learn from Conversion Rates About What Changes Will Improve Business Outcomes?

"But ultimately, you probably don't care about clicks; you care about conversions," as the founder of Contentsquare, Jonathan Cherki, often says.

In our case study, when ad traffic visitors clicked the anchor link to skip forward to the bottom of the page, they were more likely to click and continue their journey without bouncing. But were they also more likely to convert into a lead? Or, did they skip and miss content that would have been critical for persuading them?

Our marketers need to measure beyond just click behaviors to answer that question. They need to look at conversion rates.

Definition: Conversion Rate per Click

This metric shows you if clicking or tapping on a zone impacts the behavior toward downstream conversion goals (see Figure 5A.9).

With Conversion Rate per Click, we can also learn something important about our customers (see Figure 5A.10). It reveals the customers' decision-making journey in their minds: the journey to narrow down and find what they are looking for, and the journey to answering questions that they have along the way before making up their minds.

Calculation

$$\frac{\text{Number of users that clicked on the zone and accomplished the goal behavior}}{\text{Total number of users that clicked on the zone}}$$

Figure 5A.9 Conversion Rate per Click calculation..

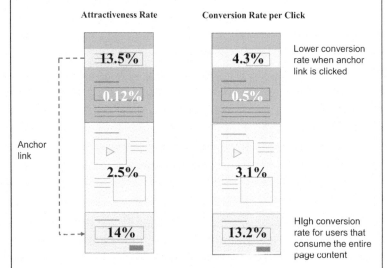

Figure 5A.10 Illustration of the difference between Attractiveness and Conversion for users that click on the Anchor link to skip to the bottom of the page.

Conversion Rate per Click

In our case study, marketers found that the anchor link for skipping content drives clicks and journeys deeper into the site. But the conversion rate of that traffic is indeed lower because they have missed messages and videos designed to persuade them. We can see this from the relatively lower lead conversion rate of clicks on the anchor link.

Conversion Rate per Hover

Great, so which of the many content elements that users missed are critical for persuasion and lead conversion? That is the million-dollar question that all visual content marketers face for improving their content strategy. When users engage with a page, they are influenced by many content elements, but they only click or tap one of them in the end. How can we understand which content elements helped with persuasion to convert?

That is where the *conversion rate per hover* helps. It shows where users stopped and lingered with their mouse cursor, then later completed the conversion goal that you are targeting

---

Definition: Conversion Rate per Hover

This metric shows you if hovering on a zone with a desktop mouse cursor impacts a conversion goal (see Figure 5A.11).

Calculation

$$\frac{\text{Number of users that hovered on the zone and accomplished the goal behavior}}{\text{Total number of users that hovered on the zone}}$$

Figure 5A.11 Conversion Rate per Hover calculation.

Most importantly, with Conversion Rate per Hover, we learn how our customers make decisions toward conversion. What influences their perception? Aggregated over sufficient traffic, this shows us what content is persuasive.

The "Aha": Informing the Next Best A/B Tests for Increasing Engagement

At our software company in the case study, conversion rate per hover showed the content elements that were commonly associated with conversions if desktop users hovered over them with their mouse cursor (see Figure 5A.12). This informed the next set of A/B tests to improve the landing page. Namely, by placing these persuasive content elements higher up on the page—before users click on the anchor to skip forward—we have an A/B test that is very likely to move the needle in a significant way.

Et-voilà, data-driven decisions in action!

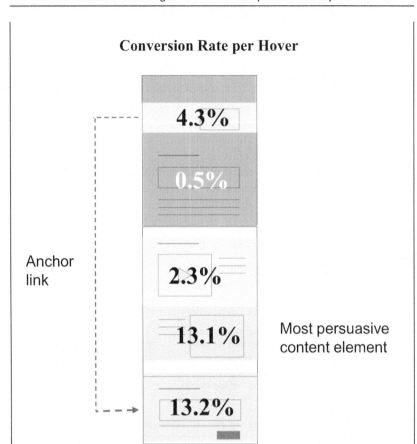

Conversion Rate per Hover

4.3%

0.5%

Anchor link

2.3%

13.1%   Most persuasive content element

13.2%

Figure 5A.12 The software company in the case study identified the persuasive content elements impacting conversion when users hovered over them.

C-SUITE Cheat Sheet for Solving the Challenge

In summary, here is a visual overview of some of the most typical ways in which Marketing Acquisition teams inform their A/B tests with the best chance for reducing bounce rates and increasing ROAS (Figure 5A.13).

Challenge 3: Different Acquired Audiences Expect Different Experiences

It's intuitive for flesh and blood marketers to address our audiences differently depending on the context. We adapt our pitch based on our

Challenge	Reducing bounce rates on marketing landing pages	
Surface	Compare behaviors on the landing page side by side for sessions that bounce vs. those that continue into the site.	
Understand	What content helps engage and persuade audiences vs. puts them off? How can we help more users find the ideal path?	
	Are users scrolling + exposed to our pitch? If users scroll, are there gems under the fold that engage them and get them to click? (Attractiveness)	Which content elements are best at persuading, i.e. correlated with conversion?
Impact	Quantify the potential impact of promoting the most attractive content elements with the biggest persuasion power.	
Test	Test changing content placements and eliminate irrelevant content.	
Evaluate	Why did the changes help/hurt? What were the biggest success factors we can learn for future campaigns?	

Figure 5A.13 Cheat sheet: Lower bounce rates to increase ROAS.

intuitive understanding of what is most likely to resonate. For example, if I am selling vegetables at the farmers market and people are walking by fast, I might yell out my great prices. But if shoppers are walking slowly and carefully scanning my stand with their eyes, I might instead point out how fresh and organic my vegetables are.

Does that translate to acquisition marketers online? It does in fact, as case studies show.

Supplemental Case Studies on the Book's Accompanying Website

Check out the following case study on this book's accompanying website.

Case Study: Flash Sales Site Increases Ad Conversion Rates 22% by Tailoring Their Landing Pages to Each Advertising Channel

https://ExperienceAnalytics.live/CaseStudies

Select the Flash sales site case study for chapter 5

Challenge 4: Page Experience Impacts SEO Rankings

As discussed earlier, Google is now providing better SEO rankings for sites that offer better Page Experiences, per Google's definition, that is, based on Core Web Vitals metrics.[3] So, it is already a best practice to keep an eye on Core Web Vitals metrics and improve them. The investment will benefit marketers to the power of two:

1. Conversion rates are likely to go up with better performance.
2. Better SEO rankings will drive more traffic.

Case Study: M6

Check out the supplemental materials online for this book for a recommended approach and a case study from M6, also known as Métropole Television, that is, the third most-watched television network in the French-speaking world.

https://ExperienceAnalytics.live/CaseStudies

Select the M6 case study for chapter 5

Challenge 5: Improve Landing Page Form Completions

If, like many B2B websites, you also have your conversion form directly on the landing page, you've essentially got a single page that is both the top of the funnel and the bottom of the funnel. Of course, it pays to study what is causing frustration with the forms and how to eliminate friction.

We will cover metrics and use cases for Form Analysis in the chapter on *bottom*-of-funnel use cases. Please refer to that chapter for tips and tricks.

Solve Brand Marketing and Content Challenges

"A brand is the set of expectations, memories, stories and relationships that, taken together, account for a consumer's decision to choose one product or service over another," as Seth Godin defines it in his blog.[12] So, the customer experience with content and products is a massive contributor to brands, if not the most important. On digital, that experience includes every content element designed to persuade customers to the brand and make them feel they have arrived at their brand of choice.

Customers have a choice of what products they purchase and where. So, aside from the products, the brand experience needs to create differentiation and value. That value helps avoid the race to the bottom on pricing and drives greater loyalty and word-of-mouth.

A quote from Ian Rogers, as CDO at LVMH Moët Hennessy Louis Vuitton, encapsulates this challenge beautifully for the digital channel:[4] "Our job is not to bring luxury online; our job is to make online shopping luxurious. We need to focus on the customer experience in a world where customers move seamlessly between our stores and their mobile phones."

The same can be said for many other industries.

- In travel and hospitality, how can we make travelers feel that their vacation has already begun when they are on the site or in the app?
- In beauty and fashion, how can we make customers feel a bit of that happiness that they get when using the brand's products?
- In financial services, physical branches increasingly look like cafes, and there is even a bank clerk at the door greeting customers as they enter. So, how can we make clients feel that same level of trust and welcome as they arrive on the site or in the app?
- In B2B, how can we increase the performance of our content for improving perception and lead generation?

MINDMAP Content / Brand Marketing		
Proactively innovate & troubleshoot top-down		
CHALLENGES		
Need to tell our brand story effectively to engage customers and win them to the brand	Need to understand and engage different customers differently	Content creation is expensive, how can we increase ROI?
QUESTIONS TO ANSWER		
Is the content strategy working for engaging and persuading customers?	What content & placements work best for which segments?	I know 50% of my content spend is wasted, but which 50%?
What's the business impact and priority of potential actions?		
SUCCESS CRITERIA		
Improve engagement, persuasion, and brand equity	Avoid the race to the bottom on pricing	Increase ROI on content spend

Figure 5B.1 Typical Brand Marketing & Content Team mind map.

All of that is the job of the brand marketing and content teams for the digital channel. Here is a typical mindmap of what's going on in many Brand Marketing and Content Team managers' minds (see Figure 5B.1).

Business Pressures on the Brand Marketing and Content Teams

Brands invest heavily in digital content and need to see returns on that investment. But, of course, that's easier said than done, as many brands have found out when designing their digital experiences.

Content Can Cost a Lot, Yet Most of It Is Never Even Seen

According to sources familiar with the brand, the annual photography and content production investment added up to $30 million at one world-famous jewelry brand. Yet, the 2021 benchmark report from Contentsquare[5] based on customer interaction across thousands of websites showed that 45% of content on sites is typically never seen by customers, for example, because they don't browse or scroll far enough.

Just like the adage for marketing advertising goes, how can Brand Marketing and Content Teams know—and prove—which half of their investments is making a difference vs. which half is wasted?

The New Wealthy Are Digital-Natives, but Many Marketing Executives Are Not

Brand experiences are essential for luxury-oriented brands. So, their perspective on challenges with getting content strategies right is very informative for our purposes. Many luxury brands got a late start on digital as they relied on store experiences longer than other industries. After all, customers want to touch and feel the luxurious products hands-on. But their primary target audience of well-to-do individuals are now the new generation of wealthy who grew up with a Smartphone in their hands. Their expectations on digital experiences are set by the brands that do it best, such as Apple, Amazon, and Google. That's the level to which they hold any brand.

As a result, even the luxury industry has woken up to the fact that growth will come from digital: "LVMH and Kering's new battlefield is online," as Vogue Business wrote in June 2020.[6] This was exacerbated by the Pandemic and temporary store closures. Yet, the Pandemic only accelerated a trend that the luxury industry already recognized in the years just before. "Our physical stores provide among the best experiences in the market," says Kering's CEO Grégory Boutté in the same article. "Our ambition is to do the same thing online."

Traffic Is Shifting to Marketplaces, But "Direct to Consumer" Remains a Key Channel for Building the Brand

Marketplaces such as Amazon, Alibaba, and others already have an overwhelming share of ecommerce transactions, and that share is only growing. If Alibaba's Tmall Luxury Pavillion is a telltale, this market share will also extend to luxury-oriented goods, not just commodity products.

But "We can't shut down and go through Amazon," as GoPro's Kathy Ando, head of ecommerce, said in a DigiDay article in September 2018.[7] "A sale on Amazon is just a sale for us, but a sale through gopro.com is a relationship."

Since manufacturers don't typically compete on price with their retail networks, they need to compete on better brand and content experiences. That puts pressure on Marketing and Content teams to identify and deliver the right experiences. Of course, that's easier said than done!

Content Optimization Challenges and Use Cases

The pressure is on. What if your customers would tell you which brand stories resonate with them? When and where in their journey do these brand experiences make a difference for them?

Let's now step into a typical day in the life of Brand Marketing and Content teams. Let's see how they understand their customers better and solve challenges with the help of Experience Analytics.

- Challenge 1: Is the content strategy working for engaging and persuading customers?
- Challenge 2: How to fit engaging experiences onto small screens?

Challenge 1: Is the Content Strategy Working for Engaging and Persuading Customers?

The only way to know whether our content strategy is working is via Experience Analytics because conventional analytics cannot measure engagement in a meaningful way. With experience metrics, we can see whether the brand and content elements designed to engage customers are being seen and consumed, and then the impact on conversion.

This gets us to my two favored case studies in Experience Analytics. They show that what works well for one brand's customers may not be the right approach for another brand's customers. The only way to know is to let your customers show you what gets them excited about interacting with your brand.

Case Study 1: L'Occitane En Provence Increases Mobile Sales by 25%

When people walk into a L'Occitane store, the company aims to provide an experience that connects the customer to the brand and promotes engagement. At L'Occitane's flagship stores in New York, London, and Melbourne, for example, they offer hand massages, product customization, gift engraving, and the chance to enjoy a special Provençal treat.[8]

L'Occitane operates more than 50 websites in 30 countries, generating $1 billion in annual revenue.[9] "It's critical to provide the same high level of experience for our online customers as we do in our bricks and mortar stores."

Typical for the beauty industry, L'Occitane sees more than 60% of the traffic coming from mobile devices. So, not only do they have to adopt a mobile-first approach, but they have to balance providing an aesthetically pleasing and highly visual brand experience versus providing quicker access to products. So, at the time, L'Occitane had designed their mobile site focusing on aesthetic imagery first.

The Challenge : Increasing Flow to Product Display Pages

L'Occitane's content team identified in their Google Analytics that on the then-current mobile site, the rate of visitors clicking from the mobile home page to reach their product pages was not as high as it could be. But there was no information to show how this could be improved.[9]

Step 1: What Does In-Page Behavior Say About the Attractiveness of Each Content Element?

To get to the bottom of the question, L'Occitane analyzed the attractiveness of content elements on their homepage to understand what mobile users were interested in seeing on the homepage.

For this purpose, they looked at the metric "click distribution" for each "block" of content. This metric shows which content zones receive the highest and lowest shares of clicks on the page.

Definition: Click Distribution

This metric identifies the content zones with the most clicks (the total sum equals 100% distributed across all the zones on the page) (see Figure 5B.2).

Calculation

$$\frac{\text{Number of clicks on the zone}}{\text{Sum of clicks on all zones}}$$

Figure 5B.2 Click Distribution calculation.

They combined this with assessing the "scroll-depth," that is, Exposure Rate, to see on average what percentage of the mobile page was viewed.

L'Occitane's team found that a specific block of content near the bottom of the page drove a lot of clicks, but customers did not always scroll enough to see it. This content element focused on L'Occitane's attractive products.

Step 2: Which Content and UX Elements Are Driving Revenue?

Driving engagement and clicks is good, but only if it results in the outcomes that customers and the business are looking for. That's why it's essential to go beyond exposure, engagement, and clicks in assessing your content strategy. There must be a way to attribute conversions and revenue to the content elements that best engage and persuade customers. And there is.

Definition: Revenue Attribution to Content Elements

The total revenue generated by visitors who clicked on a zone.

This metric ranks elements based on their contribution to revenue, calculated as the total purchase amount of all sessions where visitors clicked on the content element.

For examples of Zone-based heatmaps with the revenue attribution metric see this book's supplemental online materials at the following URL

https://ExperienceAnalytics.Live/Figures

See the Revenue attribution examples for chapter 5

With this metric in hand, the L'Occitane team confirmed that the content block promoting its iconic products lower on the mobile homepage was driving clicks and correlated with higher purchase rates. And that was the critical piece of data needed for justifying a significant new investment for redesigning the mobile site.

Step 3: Redesign Mobile in the Way That Our Customers Prefer to Engage

Based on this data, L'Occitane hypothesized that their fans wanted faster and more direct exposure to the products they love. So, L'Occitane redesigned the mobile experience to surface their products right from the top of the home page. They replaced some of the previous content elements designed primarily to engage customers with visual content (see Figure 5B.3).

Along with this change, they also reordered elements in the hamburger menu based on similar analysis, that is, which menu selections customers use most frequently in successful visits.

The Result and Value

The hypothesis for L'Occitane's customers was proven right. Taken together, the impact of the site redesign was a 25% increase in

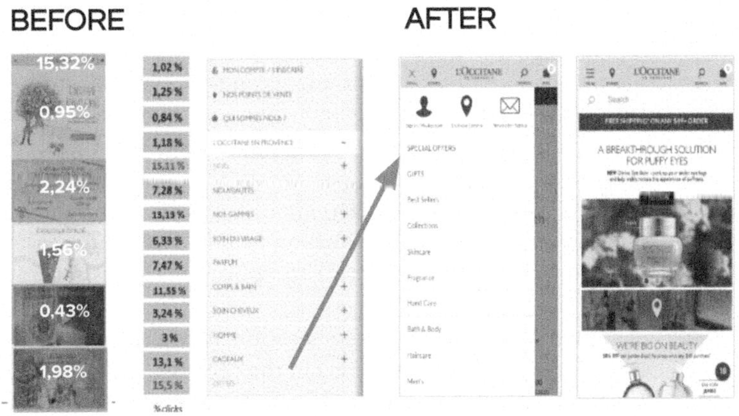

BEFORE   AFTER

Figure 5B.3 L'Occitane mobile website before and after optimization.

mobile sales. Considering that more than half of traffic to the site is on mobile devices, this is an extraordinary success for the brand and provides the rewarding experiences that customers are looking for.

Case Study 2: GoPro Increases Mobile Sales from the Product Page by 80%

A lifestyle-dedicated supplier of action cameras since 2002, GoPro isn't just providing a camera—it's providing the ability to create lasting visual memories of life's adventures. Their website is much more than just a showcase of the product; it communicates the possibilities of the brand.

The Challenge

The challenge in 2019 was:[10] "How to go bold with the content while keeping the customer journey friction-free. How to know what content was encouraging engagement and conversions? And more to the point, how much content is too much content?"

This is essentially the same question that L'Occitane En Provence faced on their mobile site, as discussed in the previous case study. Would the same answer prove true for GoPro? Would promoting quick access to products over aesthetically pleasing content also be how GoPro customers prefer to engage online?

Step 1: Understand the Correlation of Content to Engagement and Conversion

To achieve the broad objective of increasing direct-to-customer sales, the GoPro team began by focusing on its most heavily trafficked page (and primary revenue stream) at the time: the Hero camera product detail page.

GoPro looked at the in-page behavior of users on this product page using Zone-based heatmaps. The brand studied individual page elements to determine what gave rise to conversions, hesitations, and bounces.

Looking at metrics such as Engagement Rate, Attractiveness Rate, and Click Rate (refer to the definitions in the previous chapter), the team understood how fans consumed the content, which elements triggered interactions, and which were UX dead-ends.

The overall "aha" was that for GoPro fans, more content consumption did lead to higher Click Rates deeper into the site. Namely, the further users scrolled on the Hero page, and the longer they stopped to engage with product images, the more likely they were to click and view additional pages on the site; and this also correlated with increased conversion rates.

Step 2: Redesign the Way That Users Want to Engage

Based on this data, GoPro confidently redesigned the product page by bulking it up with more content. Since videos received a lot of clicks and views, there was clearly a hunger for this kind of content, and the client decided to design for that.

The Result and Value

This resulted in a whopping 80% increase in conversions from the product page. The mission of upping direct-to-customer sales was decidedly accomplished.

GoPro's Visual Website Design

For examples of GoPro's highly visual website design, simply visit GoPro.com and scroll down on any of the product pages.

The Moral of the Stories

Both L'Occitane and GoPro were highly successful with their site redesigns. They achieved their success by following the exact opposite design directions from each other because that's what was the right thing to do for their fans.

The moral of the story from these two case studies is that customer wants and needs are not all the same. Unless we measure experience and let our customers show how they prefer to interact with our specific brand, we cannot know what the right content strategy will be for our site and app.

What's right for one brand may not be right for another. Therefore "best practice" UX design tips and tricks are not enough for success. The ultimate experience design skill that will differentiate winners from losers is to understand customers first by measuring their experience and learning from their behavior.

In other words, we're back to : "The Customer is king (queen)."

C-SUITE Cheat Sheet for Evaluating Content Strategies

Here is a visual cheat sheet for solving the seemingly impossible, that is, making the impact of the content strategy something that is measurable and therefore manageable (see Figure 5B.4).

Challenge	Is the content strategy working for engaging and persuading customers?		
Surface	Does engagement with brand content improve persuasion, conversion and sales for our target audience?		
Understand	At what rates does engagement with brand content engage and persuade our audience vs. being ignored or putting customers off?		
	Are users scrolling to see more of the content?	If users scroll, does it increase their engagement with content?	Are users engaging with the content more likely to convert at higher rates and average order values?
Impact	Quantify volume of these behaviors and assess the impact of the content strategy on the goals of the site and app.		
Test	If necessary, adjust the brand content strategy of the site to change the balance between immersive brand storytelling vs. product displays.		
Evaluate	Why did the changes improve the success of the content strategy? What were the biggest success factors we can learn for future efforts?		

Figure 5B.4 Cheat sheet: Assess the success of the content strategy.

Challenge 2: How to Fit Engaging Experiences onto Small Screens?

We want to convey so much to our customers on the site and app, but all that content cannot possibly be seen and consumed. And it sure won't all fit above the fold line. So what do we keep vs. eliminate, and where do we place it on each page?

We looked at content strategy at a high level in the previous challenge. Now we want to look at the more tactical day-to-day use case of choosing the best placements and alternative content selections within pages.

Case Study 1: Credit Card Company Increases New Account Applications by Eliminating Content

Depending on your business type, you probably have Product Marketers or Merchandisers that get paid to know what buyers want and bring that knowledge into the company. As folks in that role, our job is to help everyone better address our customers by knowing what it is that the market is looking for.

This was also the case at the credit card company in our case study. Specifically, they provided a set of product detail pages (PDP) for students as the target customers for certain credit card products. When creating an experience, we start from what we think our customers are interested in. So, in this case, the credit card page included a big content block to assure students that they can service their accounts from their mobile phones and that their data is safe and private. After all, anybody would agree that this will be especially important to the new generation of customers.

The Challenge : It's Great, and How Could it Work Even Better?

Once launched, the performance of the new experience seemed in line with expectations. But, of course, the question at any company is always, could the experience work even better? What A/B test is most likely to improve outcomes?

Step 1: What Are the Golden Paths of Content Interactions that Lead to Success?

To understand this, the credit card company looked at the in-page behavior of prospective customers to understand what is most engaging and persuasive to students (see Figure 5B.5).

For this purpose, they used metrics such as

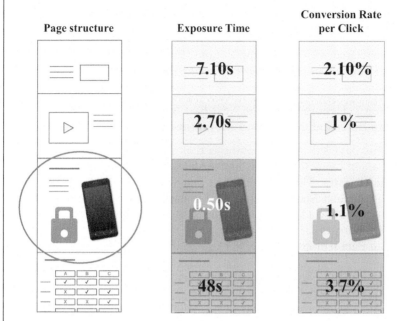

Page structure	Exposure Time	Conversion Rate per Click
	7.10s	2.10%
	2.70s	1%
	0.50s	1.1%
	48s	3.7%

Figure 5B.5 Time spent with content and conversions rates per click.

- Exposure Time, i.e., how much time did students spend looking at content elements after scrolling to expose them?

Definition : Exposure Time

This metric allows you to identify areas of the page and zones viewed the longest during a pageview while scrolling. It is calculated as the time that the area is visible in the viewport when displayed.

- Attractiveness and Conversion Rates, i.e., if they saw a content element, did they click and ultimately convert? (Defined earlier in the previous chapter.)

What jumped out on that occasion was that the content block on mobile access and security was not seeing engagement at all. Instead, students were scrolling right past it and were clearly looking for something else. They only stopped to consume content at the bottom of the page if they reached it. They would find the detailed comparison table of multiple credit card options there.

Engagement with the comparison table content was highly correlated with deeper applications. But most students didn't scroll far enough and gave up before seeing this information.

Step 2: Hypothesis for the Next Best A/B Test to Help More Students Find the Golden Path Journey

This data led to the hypothesis that shrinking or eliminating the content block for security and mobile access should increase application rates. That is an A/B test that would never get buy-in from the Product Marketers in charge if it weren't for the data in hand. You would get laughed out of the room if you suggested eliminating the content that is deemed to be most important to the target buyer. But data trumps opinion.

The A/B Test Result and Value

The credit card company did run this test and found that shrinking the content increased conversion rates somewhat, but eliminating the content was even better. Applications increased by 2%, which is a big deal for such a small and inexpensive change to the site (Figure 5B.6).

The Moral of the Story

It turns out that students, already at the time of this case study in 2016, took mobile access and security for granted. But, come to think of it, behaviors change from generation to generation. For example, it may have well been true that Gen X students would have been wowed by visual content on phone access and security. But this generation of Millennial students was much more interested in facts and substantive information, as conveyed through the credit card options table at the bottom of the page.

So, the moral is that we need to measure how our customers want to engage with our brand and content. We need to do this for each of our target customer segments. We also need to do this continuously as buyers' wants and needs change over time.

"Without data, it's just another opinion," as my colleagues like to say.

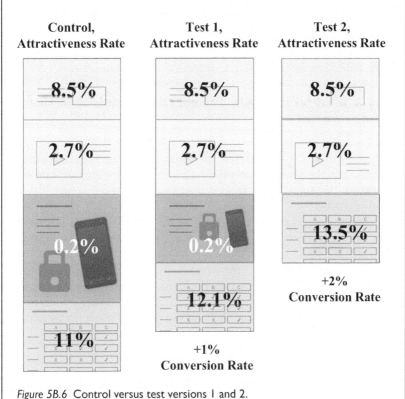

Control, Attractiveness Rate	Test 1, Attractiveness Rate	Test 2, Attractiveness Rate

Figure 5B.6 Control versus test versions 1 and 2.

Case Study 2: Avon Increases Customer Engagement and Sales from the PLP by 6% with One A/B Test

The content optimization use case that we just saw is common across industries. So, for example, here is a use case from Avon that is very similar.

New Avon is a beauty brand with an enviable reputation built in part by a vast community of representatives. In addition, the company has invested heavily in digital transformation to bring a seamless customer experience to its hyper-connected audience.

Being in the business of beauty, New Avon's website includes highly appealing content elements designed to engage its fans. One such element is a banner at the top of New Avon's Product List Pages designed to draw attention to some of their customers' favorite products and promotions.

The Challenge : It's Great, and How Could it Work Even Better?

As with most companies and situations, there isn't a huge drop or problem that is the starting point. But while performance is going fine, could we do something to improve on the status quo?

Step 1: What Are the Golden Paths of Content Interactions That Lead to Success?

As Lorraine Ryshin wrote in a blog published on this case study,[11] when Avon's team analyzed the makeup category page, they found that the product carousel had a low 60% exposure rate on desktop—meaning, 40% of customers were not even seeing it (see Figure 5B.7).

Visitors viewed the banner image at the top of the page but were not scrolling down to the product carousel, which was located beneath the fold.

At the same time, the Attractiveness Rate of the area was high, with those visitors exposed to the carousel likely to click on it. Even better news, the conversion per click showed that a high percentage of visitors who did click on the carousel went on to make a purchase.

Figure 5B.7 Zone-based heatmap with Exposure rate metric.

Step 2: What Can We Change to Help More Users Find the Golden Paths?

Armed with this new customer knowledge, the team decided to test the impact of a banner redesign to see if a permanent design change was the way forward.

The test subject on this occasion was primarily the banner, which the Avon team decided to shrink to determine if doing so would lift the exposure rate. The benefit of the test was moving the carousel higher up on the page to be in better view of the visitors.

The area of concern for Avon with cutting down the banner was that it might devalue this area of the site—the team was concerned that with the product carousel more prominent, consumers might disregard the banner. Therefore, running the test was a crucial step to take before executing any changes—even the newly data-backed ones.

The A/B Test Result and Value

The page with the shorter banner saw positive outcomes across the board (see Figure 5B.8). It led to a 44% increase in exposure, which climbed from 57% on the control page to 82% on the variant page. In addition, the Click Rate on the product carousel increased by 24%, and the bounce and exit rates dwindled.

These uplifts resulted in a 35% increase in overall revenue in the carousel zone. The revenue on the variant page was 6% higher than that of the control page.

Figure 5B.8 The New Avon category page control vs. new test version.

The Moral of the Story

A/B testing can often be a political question. That's because a change that increases flow to one product or content can often reduce the flow to other products and content, sometimes owned by different teams within the company.

However, this case study showed that this isn't always the case. It's not necessarily a zero-sum game. Namely, the test resolved Avon's original concerns of reducing the banner in that it did not negatively affect its performance—quite the opposite! Revenue generated by the banner increased by 2% during the test, strengthening the argument to change the standard size of the category page banner.

Supplemental Case Studies on the Book's Accompanying Website

The credit card company and New Avon case studies that we reviewed were ultimately both about identifying what content is most persuasive to customers and lifting that content further.

There are of course many different content optimization use cases. For example, check out the following case study on this book's accompanying website.

Case Study: A Beauty Brand Reduces Bounce Rates by 20% with an Unexpected Approach to Content Placement

https://ExperienceAnalytics.live/CaseStudies

Select the Beauty brand case study for chapter 5

C-SUITE Cheat Sheet for Solving the Challenge

Here is a visual cheat sheet for fine-tuning content choices, placements, and layout to increase the impact of content on conversion and sales (see Figure 5B.9). It is very similar to the cheat sheet we saw earlier for acquisition marketers on reducing bounce rates on landing pages.

Challenge	How to fit engaging experiences onto small screens by adjusting placement and layout of content?		
Surface	Does exposure to and engagement with specific content elements improve persuasion, conversion, and sales?		
Understand	Which content elements and placements help engage, persuade, and convert each audience vs. being ignored or putting customers off?		
	Are users scrolling + exposed to content?	If users scroll, are there gems under the fold that engage and attract them?	Which content elements are best at persuading, i.e. correlated with conversion?
Impact	Quantify the volume of these behaviors and assess the impact of potential changes to help more users find the content elements that work best.		
Test	Test adjusting content choices, placements, layout, and eliminating irrelevant content.		
Evaluate	Why did the changes improve engagement and conversion? What were the biggest success factors we can learn for future efforts?		

Figure 5B.9 Cheat sheet: Fine-tune content placement.

Notes

1   CXL, marketing education destination, https://cxl.com
2   CXL, marketing education destination, Bounce Rate Benchmarks: What's a Good Bounce Rate, Anyway? https://cxl.com/guides/bounce-rate/benchmarks/
3   Web Vitals, web.dev, https://web.dev/vitals/
4   *New York Times*, Luxury Retail Technology, 2018, www.nytimes.com/2018/11/19/fashion/luxury-retail-technology.html
5   2021 Contentsquare, Digital Experience Benchmark Report, https://contentsquare.com/insights/digital-experience-benchmark/
6   Vogue, LVMH and Kering's new battlefield is online, 2020, www.voguebusiness.com/companies/lvmh-and-kerings-new-battlefield-is-online-covid-19
7   DigiDay, " 'We can't shut down and go through Amazon': How GoPro is making DTC part of its growth strategy," 2018, https://digiday.com/retail/cant-shut-go-amazon-gopro-making-dtc-part-growth-strategy/
8   Retail Innovation Hub, 2018, https://retailtechinnovationhub.com/home/2019/1/17/loccitane-en-provence-opts-for-contentsquare-ai-alerts

9   Retail TouchPoints, UX Analytics Drive L'Occitane Mobile Sales Boost, 2017, https://retailtouchpoints.com/features/retail-success-stories/ux-analytics-drive-l-occitane-mobile-sales-boost

10   Contentsquare blog: Community, Content and eCommerce Conversions: How GoPro's Bold Brand Experience Strategy Paid Off, 2019.

11   Contentsquare blog: Beauty giant Avon sees sharp increase in engagement and revenue, Lorraine Ryshin, https://contentsquare.com/blog/beauty-giant-avon-sees-sharp-increase-in-engagements-and-revenue/

12   Seth Godin, Seth's Blog, Define Brand, https://seths.blog/2009/12/define-brand/, 2009

Chapter 6

Solve Common Challenges at the Middle of the Funnel

In a physical store or branch, you've got a whole team present to engage, persuade, sell, and service customers. They see the customer's body language, listen, ask questions, and offer help. They gain a good read of customer wants and needs along the way.

With that understanding, they can sometimes almost read a customer's question from their face before the customer even needs to say anything. Then, if there are recurrent areas of confusion or opportunity in the store, they will make changes to improve the situation once and for all.

On digital, the site and app team have to accomplish all of the above without seeing their customers. It's like having a blindfold. That's a big handicap.

Many teams are tasked with configuring and improving digital stores and branches. Let's visit each of these teams that are focused at the middle of the funnel. They have the mission-critical goal of enabling everyone to find what they are looking for and accomplish their goals quickly, for a win-win with the business.

Chapter 6A: Solve Ecommerce and Ebusiness Sales Challenges

- Business Pressures
- Challenge 1: Inform the redesigns, A/B tests, and new experiences that are most likely to move the needle in a lasting way
- Challenge 2: Create more uplift from the campaigns, A/B tests, and new launches that you are working on
- Challenge 3: Identify what puts customers off and fix it faster

Chapter 6B: Solve Visual Merchandising Challenges

- Business Pressures
- Challenge 1: Are Promotions effective for sales of the targeted products?
- Challenge 2: How can Placements of Products be improved based on performance?
- Challenge 3: How can Prices be fine-tuned relative to the market?

DOI: 10.4324/b23273-9

Solve Ecommerce and Ebusiness Sales Challenges

The digital channel's sales and business goals are only going in one direction, namely up and up every year. Not only because every company wants to grow but also because the shift to digital channels is ongoing. Every company needs to run faster on their digital channel just to stay in the same place in the overall market.

Where does the buck stop for achieving the higher targets? Yup, the Ecommerce team or the Ebusiness team is held accountable depending on the type of site and app. They sign up to achieve the revenue number. That's why (or when) they get paid the big bucks. But that's also what makes their job challenging.

Here is a typical mindmap of what's going on in many Ecommerce and Ebusiness managers' minds (see Figure 6A.1). First, we see it from the perspective of proactive innovation and enhancements. Then from the perspective of reacting faster to issues.

Business Pressures

The job of the Ecommerce and Ebusiness team would be easy if they could just throw more money at the problem, that is, request their Acquisition Marketing colleagues to send more traffic. But that's not how it works. Budgets and markets are limited. So, the pressure is on the Ecommerce or Ebusiness team to make more out of the same traffic volume.

But how? Magic? Well, actually, the magic is in better understanding customers and their experiences.

Proactively Drive Strategy and Investment by Finding the Best New Ideas for Revenue

There are always too many ideas for new campaigns, experiences, improvements, but which will actually move the needle in a lasting way? Or are there "lower hanging fruit" ideas we haven't discovered yet?

Rather than letting the highest-paid individual decide based on their best guess, how can we let our customers show us what to prioritize?

MINDMAP
Ecommerce / Ebusiness Team
Proactively innovate & troubleshoot top-down

CHALLENGES		
We've got higher sales goals, but not higher traffic.	So, we need to improve our conversion rate and cross-/up-sell.	Most A/B tests and new launches fail to move the needle.

QUESTIONS TO ANSWER		
What journeys are working well and we should help more shoppers find them?	What frictions put customers off when they are ready to buy?	What is the intent of different customer segments?
What's the business impact and priority of potential actions?		

SUCCESS CRITERIA		
Innovate best new experiences (build new peaks)	Resolve revenue leaks faster (fix potholes)	Better target customers

MINDMAP
Ecommerce / Ebusiness Team
Prioritize & resolve the biggest issues, working from bottom-up

CHALLENGES
We've got so many reported issues and complaints. Which of them impact sales so we can have them resolved faster?

QUESTIONS TO ANSWER	
How can the team recreate each issue and identify the root cause?	How can we quantify the impact of each issue to prioritize what to address?

SUCCESS CRITERIA	
Prioritize and fix the issues that matter before it's too late.	Free up time to innovate more.

Figure 6A.1 Typical Ecommerce/Ebusiness Team mind map.

Understand and Close the Gap Between Customer Expectations and the Actual Experience

A website and app interaction is like a conversation. The customer is arriving with set goals. Often, their expectations are set by an ad that they clicked on. What are those expectations? Is the site or app able to meet them? Where are the gaps? The pressure is on to understand customers really well so that the team can engage them with a clear offering and UX.

As leaders at businesses from Ecommerce to Financial Services have all pointed out, in 80% of cases, customers behave differently, and most new initiatives or A/B tests don't pan out the way as planned. So we need to get data quickly.

"One of the first things we discovered was that our customers rarely behave in the way we all thought they did. In fact, 80% of the changes we introduced provoked a customer response that was totally different to what we were expecting," as the Head of Digital put it at a retail bank.[1]

Eliminate Struggle and Errors Faster to Recover Revenue and Free Up Time for Innovation

While it's not the Ecommerce business manager's job to fix UX or technical points of friction, their success is dependent on ensuring that all blockers and hurdles are identified and removed quickly. Relying on their Operations and Support teams for this responsibility is great but even better than that is a way for business users to validate that no more points of friction are hurting their success.

Course Correct/Improve a Campaign or Test While it Is Still In Progress

It's been typical for business teams to get post mortem campaign reports. But campaigns are too important for the business to wait until campaigns are over. If a campaign is underperforming, the team needs to course correct it while it is still in flight. We need a way to understand whether a campaign or new experience is working as intended, starting right on day one.

Ecommerce Optimization Challenges and Use Cases

Let's now step into a typical day in the life of Ecommerce and Ebusiness teams working on improving their sales. Let's see how they are using Experience Analytics to know their customer as well as their counterparts in the offline stores do. With that customer knowledge, they can then overcome the everyday challenges.

- Challenge 1: Inform the redesigns, A/B tests, and new experiences that are most likely to move the needle in a lasting way
- Challenge 2: Create more uplift from the campaigns, A/B tests, and new launches that they are working on
- Challenge 3: Identify what puts customers off and fix it faster

Challenge 1: Inform the Redesigns, A/B Tests, and New Experiences That Are Most Likely to Move the Needle in a Lasting Way

What to do? There isn't usually a lack of ideas. There are too many! But without experience data and customer insights, it's just another opinion. So how can we change the culture from having the loudest person or the highest paid professional (HIPPO) trumpeting a roadmap to letting customers show us the way to create better experiences?

Case Study 1: How Moss Bros Identified a Winning A/B Test Idea That Increased Mobile Sales by 13%

Let's start with the most common use case, that is, identifying A/B tests that are most likely to improve results.

This case study is from Moss Bros, one of the UK's top menswear shops specializing in dress wear for formal occasions. Moss Bros has over 150 shops throughout the United Kingdom.

The Challenge

The digital team at Moss Bros noticed visitors were dropping off between product pages and the checkout. In fact 90% of sessions on the product pages were not continuing to the checkout. But as always, with Web Analytics alone, it's not clear why the drop-off is what it is and what A/B test is most likely to improve results.

Step 1: Use Zone-based Heatmaps to Understand Engagement and Golden Paths

Looking at the Exposure Rate metric in Zone-based heatmaps, Moss Bros saw the scroll rate on their product pages wasn't as high as other pages on the site.

Using the Attractiveness Rate and Conversion Rate metrics, they found some content elements under the fold line that were highly correlated with a completed purchase. When users scrolled

Figure 6A.2 Zone-based heatmap shows a higher Conversion Rate if customers find and interact with the product reviews further down on the former PDP page at Moss Bros.

far enough to see product reviews down the page, they were more likely to stay on the site, click, and convert (see Figure 6A.2).

This revealed a golden path. If we can help more shoppers see the product reviews, it is likely to make a difference for them. So, an A/B test with a better placement for product reviews would be a promising test for improving results.

Step 2: Run an A/B Test Providing Better Exposure to Product Reviews

Through Dynamic Yield, Moss Bros' testing platform, they built a tabbed approach, ensuring that customers could see the product description, reviews, and recommended products just below the fold (see Figure 6A.3).

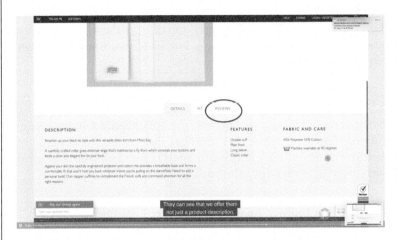

Figure 6A.3 A/B test variant with Reviews in a tabbed approach.

The Result and Value

This A/B test led to a +14% increase in progression from product page to basket, a +13% increase in conversion, and a +13% increase in revenue. A huge success!

The Moral of the Story

The best optimizations come from understanding what is happening but also the why. Through their behaviors, customers didn't just show what makes their experiences successful, but they gave us an insight into how they make decisions and what they value the most. We can best understand what makes customers tick by listening to their wants and needs. From there, it's easy to identify the best A/B tests to invest in for a win-win.

Case Study 2: How Leeds Building Society Identified a Redesign That Led to 40% Higher Conversions from Their Product Pages

Now, let's look at a story about identifying a promising redesign to improve Ebusiness results. This case study is from the Leeds Building Society (LBS), a financial institute based in England. LBS serves over 700,000 customers across the United Kingdom and is the fifth largest building society in the UK.

The digital channel is the top branch for most financial services these days (besides the call center). Often, it is the top avenue for new customer acquisition as well. For LBS, too, online customer acquisition is a key objective.

The Challenge

When reviewing site performance, the LBS Digital Channel team noticed that their conversion rate was low compared to some of their competitors. They decided to analyze user behavior and see if users were following the sales path as it was designed.

Step 1: Using Journey Analysis to Uncover User Intent

Using Journey Analysis, they discovered customers were not following the ideal sales path. Instead, they moved from product pages to the product homepage and back again—looping between the two before exiting the website (see Figure 6A.4).

Figure 6A.4 Journey Analysis shows looping between full savings range and product pages (left hand side). Site exits are shown in black, with over a 50% bounce rate for visitors landing on a product page.

The team hypothesized that this behavior was caused by users trying to compare products. However, they found that some of these users left the website eventually after viewing a product page.

Step 2: Using In-page Analytics, Confirm Users' Intent and Assess Points of Friction

Using the Exposure Time metric in Zone-based heatmaps, they identified which areas of the product page were being interacted with the most, and which were causing frustration. For example, they noticed that users were spending a long time reading product pages, which were typically long and text-heavy (see Figure 6A.5).

Definition: Exposure Time

As defined earlier, this metric enables users to identify zones that customers viewed the longest during a pageview. It is calculated as the time in seconds that the content zone is visible when displayed.

Figure 6A.5 Zone-based heatmap shows high amount of Exposure Time on the LBS Cash ISAs page.

The team knew they needed to remove distractions in the acquisitions journey and provide a better approach to legal requirements versus visitor experience to improve overall conversion.

Step 3: Translate the Insights into the Right Redesign and Get Buy-in

Typically, changes to the content on the site are dependent on first getting legal approval in financial services. The legal team is ensuring that the site meets required disclosures.

The digital team presented their analysis back to the legal department, who were hesitant about simplifying the legal information on the product pages. However, by clearly showing the lack of user engagement on the page, the digital team convinced them that the product pages needed restructuring.

As a result, the LBS team redesigned their product home pages (see Figure 6A.6).

The team also introduced a comparison tool by understanding their customers' intent on the site.

The Results and Value

The changes led the average conversion rate of product pages to increase by 40%. And for some product pages, that conversion rate increased by 80%.

Pre-October page   October   Phase 1 – redesign (Nov)

Figure 6A.6 Evolution of product page design at LBS.

The Moral of the Story

Whoever comes with the best data-driven documentation has the best chance at winning the battle for legal approvals.

Journey and In-Page Analysis enable us to compare customers' natural behaviors against the expected ones. Brands design their website and app pages to serve a specific objective. But does that meet customers' goals and expectations? Experience Analytics gives us a clear picture when we've got any gaps and opportunities.

Supplemental Case Studies on the Book's Accompanying Website

We've seen how customers can better guide A/B testing and redesign. Can customers also guide decisions on the best new experiences to design? You betcha. Check out the following case study on this book's accompanying website.

Case Study : How a Jewelry Brand Identified a New Experience That Increased Conversions By 27%

https://ExperienceAnalytics.live/CaseStudies

Select the Jewelry brand case study for chapter 6

C-SUITE Cheat Sheet for Solving the Challenge

In summary, here is a visual overview of how Ecommerce and Ebusiness teams often inform the redesigns, A/B tests, and new experiences that are most likely to move the needle in a lasting way (see Figure 6A.7).

Challenge 2: Create More Uplift from the Campaigns, A/B Tests, and New Launches That You Are Working On

In Challenge 1, we saw how Ecommerce teams strategize on the best new launches, redesigns, and A/B tests to invest in. However, while a quote from Sun Tzu says that "Tactics without strategy is the noise before defeat," the quote starts by saying "Strategy without tactics is the slowest route to victory."

The same is true for Ecommerce and Ebusiness teams. A/B testing that is not informed by data is the noise before defeat. But A/B testing without tactics for making the tests successful is a very long route to victory.

Challenge	Nothing seems wrong, but how can we improve further?			
Surface	Compare successful vs. abandoned journeys. Are there any journey opportunities and issues?			
	Do journeys show signs of opportunities, e.g. high engagement?		Do journeys show signs of friction, e.g. high effort, looping, or premature exits at certain pages?	
Understand	Look for common patterns within those pages			
	Do in-page behaviors reveal a previously undiscovered intent?	In-page, look for deviations from the purpose and "ideal path" you designed content for	Which content elements/ behaviors are associated with success vs. not?	Compare successful vs. unsuccessful engagement with the content elements
	What new experience would better serve this intent?	What changes would help more users find the ideal path and move the needle?		
Impact	Quantify the business impact i.e. potential value of investing in these improvements.			
Test	Develop & test the new design.			
Evaluate	Why did the test win/lose? What were the biggest success factors we can learn for future tests?			

Figure 6A.7 Cheat sheet: Proactively improve Ecommerce/Ebusiness sales.

So that's why Experience Analytics is essential for verifying whether the initiatives are working as hoped and otherwise driving quick course corrections. Let's see a few examples of what that has looked like in practice for some well-known brands.

Case Study 1: How Pizza Hut Improved Their "Deals Page" to Drive a $7.8 Million Annualized Uplift in Revenue

Pizza Hut needs no introduction. Many pizza lovers know that ordering a pizza online often involves many deals that diners can take advantage of. For the Ecommerce team, these deals help drive sales and cross-sell. Yet, our case study shows that it's easier said than done to extend these deals in a way that is as intuitive as possible for guests.

The Challenge

The Pizza Hut Digital Ventures team noticed in their Web Analytics that guests on their highly-visited "Our Deals" page weren't clicking on the deal cards to go to the deal builder experience they had invested in. But they couldn't understand why.

Step 1: Use Zone-based Heatmaps to Answer "the Why"

Using the zoning analysis tool with the "time-to-first-click" metric, the Pizza Hut team identified that customers were much quicker to click the "View Basket" CTA than the deal cards (see Figure 6A.8).

Step 2: Formulate a Hypothesis for an Improvement to the Campaign

Why aren't hungry pizza customers tapping on the deals banner? The team hypothesized that the lack of a CTA on the deal cards themselves might be making them look unclickable to customers when they are in a rush to get to their pizza. So they decided to run a test to find out. We already saw an image of this A/B test in Figure 2.3 in Chapter 2.

Control: No CTA visible on the deal card
Variant: "Select" CTA visible on the deal card

When a customer clicked on the deal card CTA in the variant, it opened up the deal builder experience where they could select their pizza, toppings, and drinks and then add that to their basket.
They ran the test for two weeks.

The Results and Value Driven

The variant (with the deal card CTA) was the clear winner. Extrapolating on the results, Pizza Hut anticipates an annualized uplift of $7.8 million in revenue.

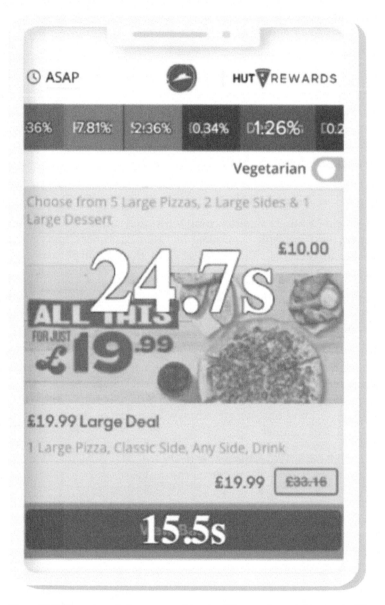

Figure 6A.8 Zone-based heatmap with the Time-to-first-click metric. The average time to click the call-to-action at the bottom is much faster than the average time to interact with the deal displayed on the screen (green).

The Moral of the Story

There is nothing like stepping into the shoes of a hungry pizza buyer to see the site from their perspective. Things that we might miss when feeling well-fed and sitting at our office desks will suddenly become crystal clear. When we improve the experience, it doesn't just increase sales, but it also means more rewarding experiences for guests. But the devil is in the detail. Tiny modifications can bring a massive uplift in revenue and user experience if they are the right ones.

Case Study 2: How Lovehoney Improved Their Black Friday Landing Pages to Drive Driving +30% Conversion

The pressure to optimize campaigns quickly is never more prominent than during the year's biggest holidays and sales seasons. We will switch from hunger for pizzas to hunger of a different kind for this case study. Lovehoney is a British business that sells sex toys, lingerie, and erotic gifts on the Internet. In this case study, let's see how the Ecommerce team at Lovehoney improved their search filters to achieve a big win.

The Challenge

Lovehoney pushed their landing pages live roughly a week before Black Friday. The team then used Journey Analysis to carry out an early performance assessment.

They discovered that 12% of users saw four list pages, and less than 24% got straight to the PDP: 12.5% were exiting the site directly (see Figure 6A.9).

This showed that their campaign should have room for further improvement. But what would move the needle?

Users were heading straight to view Black Friday deals but evidently couldn't find what they wanted, that is, viewing multiple list pages before exiting the site.

Step 1: Use In-page Analytics to Understand the Golden Journeys vs. What Leads to Abandonment

When Ecommerce teams need to understand why a journey behavior is happening, in-page analytics come to the rescue. So the team at

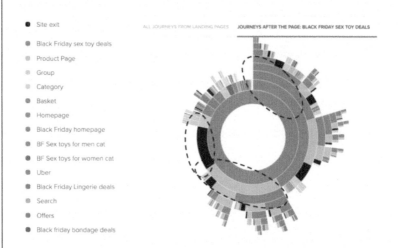

Figure 6A.9 Journey Analysis showed many users seeing multiple list pages and exiting straight away.

Lovehoney used Zone-based heatmaps to review the Product List Pages (PLP) to understand why customers aren't finding what they are looking for (see Figure 6A.10).

What jumped out is that the Conversion Rate per Click was 13.5% on the sort and filters buttons but just 11.8% on the pagination buttons—indicating users that filtered results were more likely to convert. But Click Rate on the sort and filter buttons was low, highlighting a missed opportunity.

Step 2: Data-driven Hypothesize for the Enhancement That Is Most Likely to Improve Campaign Outcomes

Since customers using the sort and filter buttons are more successful on average, the hypothesis for improving the sales campaign was obvious. We need to help more users spot the sort and filter buttons and take advantage of them.

Step 3: A/B Test the Improved Campaign Experience

On the Tuesday before Black Friday, Lovehoney acted (as seen in Figure 6A.11). They pulled the three main categories out of the filters dropdown and onto the page itself so that users could click right away, that is:

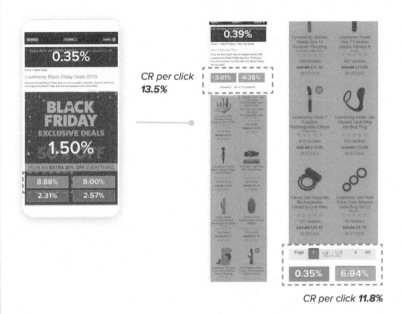

CR per click **11.8%**

Figure 6A.10 Zone-based heatmaps with the deals PLP on the right.

- Toys for couples
- Toys for her
- Toys for him

The Results and Value

Would this test succeed, though? After all, expanding the filter section means that more products get pushed under the fold to make room. We've seen so many case studies where moving products above the fold was the key to success.

Not only did they see a massive uptick in the number of users interacting with the filters, but they also saw a 30% increase in on-page conversions, a 20% reduction in exit rate, and a 17% reduction in bounce rate.

The Moral of the Story

When time is of the essence during a running campaign, it is even more apparent why Experience Analytics is key to success. You

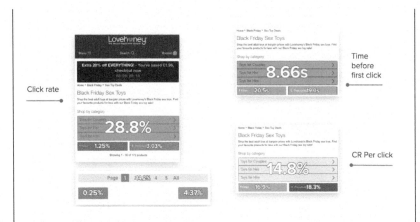

Figure 6A.11 Zone-based heatmaps with the improved metrics for Click Rate, Time before first click, and Conversion Rate per Click.

don't have time to randomly test different versions of the campaign experience based on who-knows-whose opinions and guesses. Yet, every design has potential pros and cons. So, data rules.

C-SUITE Cheat Sheet for Solving the Challenge

These were just two stories about course-correcting the path of an experience. In both cases, the improvements that increased sales had nothing to do with fixing bugs or friction. Yet, they were highly effective for increasing campaign results. There are countless more stories like these across industries.

Common to all of the stories is that our sites and apps include quite a few content elements, offers, and call-to-actions because most things that companies sell are complex. Few businesses are straightforward. So, there is always room for improvement.

As we saw in the stories, even minor improvements can go a long way if they are the right ones. And every time that our pages and customer behaviors evolve, Analytics keeps informing us about new opportunities and issues so we can keep iterating. It's a virtuous cycle.

In summary, here is a visual cheat sheet for troubleshooting campaigns and new launches while they are in flight (see Figure 6A.12).

Challenge	Create more uplift from the campaigns, A/B tests, and new launches that we are working on		
Surface	Review whether engagement inside related pages and impact on conversion is as planned and hoped.	Review journeys across the new experiences to look for signs of friction.	Score new experiences for signs of frustration.
Understand	Look for common patterns:		
	What behaviors and content engagements commonly lead to engagement with the campaign offer or new experience vs. not?		Replay examples, understand points of friction.
	What enhancements will help more users find the ideal path?		What would resolve the struggle & issues?
Impact	Quantify the business impact i.e. potential value of investing in these improvements.		
Test	Re-develop & test new designs.		Fix any bugs or issues.
Evaluate	Why did the improvements win/lose? What were the biggest success factors we can learn for future tests?		

Figure 6A.12 Cheat sheet: Improve campaigns and new experiences that you've launched.

Challenge 3: Identify What Puts Customers Off and Fix It Faster

Now that we've informed strategy and quickly course-corrected our campaigns and experiences, it's time to talk about the obvious need: Identifying friction points so that the Ecommerce team can have them fixed quickly. It's not always due to errors that customers struggle. Sometimes, the site works exactly as designed, but the design is confusing and can still lead to frustrations.

There are teams tasked full time with identifying, quantifying, and eradicating these hurdles and blockers based on business impact. We will cover their use cases in a later chapter. But when the Ecommerce team is launching a new experience, they need to be able to quickly see for themselves whether any points of friction hamper their success.

Case Study 1: How Hobbycraft Identified and Resolved a Surprise UX Issue Relating to Free Shipping

Hobbycraft is an arts and crafts superstore retail chain in the United Kingdom. Their Ecommerce sales have grown by double digits year after year after year. As Jennifer North, Head of Digital Experience, said, she is always looking for "what else can we do?" Understanding the areas of the site driving performance and having actions in place that drive them further is giving Hobbycraft the 20% growth year each year. Here is an example.

The Challenge

As with many retailers, Hobbycraft has a popular offer for free shipping on their site. To qualify, customers need a minimum spend of £20 GBP.

As always, when rolling out experiences, it would be easy to see if there was a big problem that was blocking everybody. But the many minor points of friction experienced by pockets of users are much harder to spot and quantify.

Step 1: Friction Surfaced via Frustration Scoring

When Hobbycraft scanned their site with the frustration scoring algorithms in their Experience Analytics, pockets of friction surfaced on the checkout page. Some customers are trying multiple times to interact with the "Free standard delivery" option element but ultimately abandoned the site, resulting in significant revenue loss.

Step 2: Replay the Sessions That Experienced the Biggest Frustration

What's going on? Replaying the related sessions revealed why the site and free shipping offer worked just as designed, but some customers experienced confusion and frustration nonetheless.

Namely, from the point of view of these customers, their spending seemed above 20 GBP, so they assumed they qualified for the "Free standard delivery" option. Yet, this option was grayed out for them, leading them to tap multiple times to activate it (see Figure 6A.14).

The reason for the field staying grayed out was easy to identify for the Ecommerce team. Namely, the customers' actual purchase amount was under 20 GBP, with discounts applied. Yet, this was

Before	After

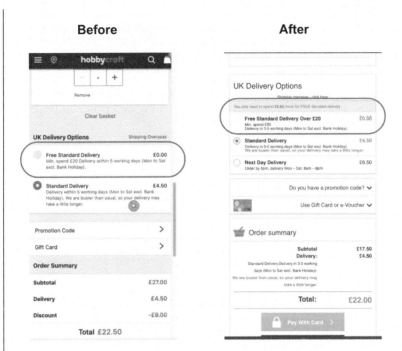

Figure 6A.13 Hobbycraft's checkout page before the case study and after improving it by clarifying the free delivery option.

confusing for shoppers. The team easily identified over a thousand sessions that ran into this confusion.

Action and Value

The team quickly rolled out a redesign with a clarifying message to shoppers, encouraging them to add the missing amount of spend to their cart to qualify for free shipment (see Figure 6A.13). This enhancement immediately eliminated the confusion. It enabled Hobbycraft customers to complete their purchases while taking advantage of the free shipment offer. A win-win!

The Moral of the Story

Points of friction don't always come from errors. If they did, the technical colleagues would probably always be the first to catch and report them. But as we saw here, the business side of the house needs a way to detect and remedy all the unexpected frustrations even when everything is working just as designed.

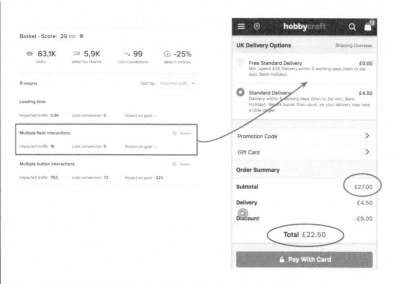

Figure 6A.14 Points for friction during checkout surfaced..

Supplemental Case Studies on the Book's Accompanying Website

Sometimes, the reason for frustrations are not just UX issues but hard core bugs and issues. Ebusiness leaders are equally interested in capturing those blockers and frictions as quickly as possible. Check out the following case study on this book's accompanying website.

Case Study : How a Top 20 US Retailer Eliminated an Issue That Would Have Impacted $1.7 Million During Black Friday

https://ExperienceAnalytics.live/CaseStudies

Select the Black Friday case study for chapter 6

Challenge	Proactively identify what puts customers off, regardless of whether it is due to errors, UX, performance, etc.	
Surface	Score experiences automatically for signs of struggle.	Review Error Analysis for leaks from the funnel due to errors.
Understand	Compare successful vs. abandoned journeys. Do differences jump out?	
	Replay examples, understand causes of friction & errors.	
	What behaviors inside related pages are commonly associated with friction and lead to exits?	
Impact	Quantify impact i.e. potential value of improving.	
Test	Develop & test new designs.	Fix the issues.
Evaluate	Why did the investments win/lose? What were the biggest success factors we can learn for future tests?	

Figure 6A.15 Cheat sheet: Proactively identify friction and frustrations.

C-SUITE Cheat Sheet for Solving the Challenge

In summary, here is a visual overview of how Ecommerce and Ebusiness teams go about identifying what is putting customers off, so they have it fixed faster (see Figure 6A.15).

Solve Visual Merchandising Challenges

When you enter a physical store and see those beautifully assorted products laid out in front of you, don't they just tempt you to want to touch them and bring one home? That's Merchandising in action. The masters in the profession often have a real passion for their products and what customers love about them.

Online too, Visual (or E-) Merchandisers work hard to know what will inspire their customers and trigger a purchase. They put together merchandise selections and displays that draw their shoppers to the items they are most likely to fancy.

Here is a typical mindmap of what's going on in the minds of many Visual (E-) Merchandisers (see Figure 6B.1).

Business Pressures on the Visual Merchandising Team

Merchandisers and Pricers own four of "the Ps" that make up an experience, as we covered at the beginning of the book, namely Product, Promotion, Placement, and Pricing.

1. Which Products are best to present for attracting people to the category?
2. How effectively are Promotions leading shoppers to these products, and what could be improved?
3. Where are the best Placements of content relating to their products?
4. How do we fine-tune Pricing, so it isn't above market but isn't too low either?

Know Your Customer

To win at their game, Visual Merchandisers pore over sales data. It is a very data-oriented profession. Data enables Merchandisers to know

MINDMAP Visual (E-) Merchandiser		
Proactively innovate & troubleshoot top-down		
CHALLENGES		
Our category sales goals are going up, but traffic is not—so how can I sell better?	I need to engage shoppers with my promotions, product & content placements, but how can I manage that if I can't measure success?	If prices are too high, shoppers won't buy. If they are too low, we lose margin.
QUESTIONS TO ANSWER		
Are promotions effective for sales of the targeted products?	Are there products with opportunities/issues?	Is my pricing too high/ low vs. market?
How can I bring quantitative data to negotiate the best placements for my category?		
SUCCESS CRITERIA		
Hit category sales goals	Increase add to-carts	Improve margin by improving pricing

Figure 6B.1 Typical Visual (E-) Merchandising mind map.

their customers, know which products they like to purchase, and what is trending.

Merchandisers also bring customer and sales knowledge into the function from physical store experiences. But does their qualitative expertise from the physical world always translate online exactly?

What's missing in most Visual Merchandisers' toolset is seeing how their online customers genuinely engage with the Product selections and Promotions leading up to purchases. What happens further up the funnel within pages before customers add to the cart and go to the cash register?

Web Analytics does not collect data about how customers engage within pages. When content within pages changes from shopper to shopper due to personalization, it increases the insights gap for Merchandisers. How are they supposed to know how digital customers decide what to purchase and what influences their decisions? It's as if you could only see which isles are visited by customers in a physical store but were completely dark on what happens within those isles.

Hit Category Sales Goals

Merchandisers share the burden with their Ecommerce colleagues on hitting their sales goals at the product category level. So how can Merchandisers best promote their category to achieve their goals?

And how can they get shoppers to try new products that they might not have known before? For example, a statistic from a GlobalData consumer survey in 2018[2] showed that online grocery shoppers have been more likely to purchase staples and familiar brands. But they have been less likely to try premium brands and products that they are not yet familiar with. There is an untapped opportunity there for increasing sales and margins.

Online vs. Offline Grocery Dynamics

Percentage of online and offline grocery shoppers who say they have done each thing when shopping for everyday grocery items in the past few months (see Figure 6B.2)

Manage Site Real Estate Across Competing Product Categories

There is only limited real estate on any page and site. Since different Visual Merchandisers are in charge of different product categories, they often compete for the best real estate—online, just like in stores. Everyone has incentives to hit their category sales goals, but they have to justify why their category should earn the more prominent placement on the site and app. For example, what will be the value of adding their product categories and pushing down other product categories instead?

To win their argument, Merchandisers need to bring data about how the placement of their category is driving sales. But without Experience

	Online grocery shoppers (%)	Offline grocery shoppers (%)
Actively look at new brand	39.7	61.4
Purchase influenced by packaging design or POS material	16.3	37.2
Consider buying a brand not usually purchased	22.8	53.5

Figure 6B.2 GlobalData consumer survey, Online Grocery & Food Shopping Statistics, 2018.

Analytics there is no data trail to connect product placement with customer exposure, engagement, and resulting sales.

Visual Merchandising Challenges and Use Cases

Let's now step into a typical day in the life of Merchandisers working on improving their category sales. Let's see how they use Experience Analytics to understand their digital customer better and overcome challenges.

- Challenge 1: Are Promotions effective for sales of the targeted products?
- Challenge 2: How can Placements of Products be improved based on performance?
- Challenge 3: How can Prices be fine-tuned relative to the market?

Challenge 1: Are Promotions Effective for Sales of the Targeted Products?

Promotions aren't just nice to have; they represent key initiatives to direct shoppers to categories that are trending, high margin, seasonal, or just plentiful in stock and need to move. But do customers care?

The effectiveness of the promotions is key to the business. The selection of products, the timing, the design and placement of the banners, the price of the promotions make up the mix of elements that lead to a good sales outcome—or not. So, how can Merchandisers see whether their signposts and placements are being noticed, whether they are attractive, and whether they are effective for add-to-carts of the targeted products? What could be improved?

To answer these questions, we need to combine exposure data with an understanding of the product catalog and the resulting transaction basket. It's an advanced data set even for Experience Analytics.

Case Study : How a British, Multi-National Home Improvement Retailer Fine-Tuned a Promotion

Home improvement fans—just as professional contractors—always have an eye out for attractive deals. Promotions are as common in home improvement as anywhere in retail. Often, promotions during sales seasons lead to not just a single item on sale but to a range of discounted products in the hopes that there is something there for every shopper and their next project.

The Challenge

We know from Ecommerce data which of the promotional items are selling, but how could sales be improved by fine-tuning the display of items on sale?

Step 1: Start with Your Usual Generic Assessment of the Promotional Banner's Overall Sales Performance

Use the Content KPIs we've discussed in earlier chapters to understand whether customers on the page interact with the banner, tap on it, and purchase something in the end. KPIs such as Exposure Rate, Click Rate, Conversion Rate per Click, and Revenue give us the top-level performance data for the promotional display.

In our case study, the home improvement retailer compared their banner's performance to other sales seasons and found it to be on par.

However, the open questions for Merchandisers are

1. Whether and how category sales performance could be improved, and
2. Whether resulting purchases are actually of the items that they are targeting?

There are new campaigns running every week and the team feels under the gun to deliver the best sales results. But they are blind as to why campaigns aren't performing better and how to improve them. With limited people and so many campaigns to organize, there is no time to go digging for clues. That's where Experience Analytics comes in to surface more actionable data more quickly.

Step 2: Investigate Campaign Success Based on Products Displayed vs. Purchased

By combining content interaction data with resulting transaction data, Merchandisers at this home improvement retailer now reviewed cart-adds and baskets due to clicking on the promotion. This confirmed that the banner was not just driving sales but was effective at driving sales of the targeted items on sale.

To Learn More About Visual Merchandising Reports, Visit This Book's Online Supplemental Materials.

https://ExperienceAnalytics.Live/Figures

Select Merchandising for chapter 6.

Step 3: Investigate Whether There Are Promotional Products with Opportunities That Would Improve the Effectiveness of the Overall Sale

Next, Merchandisers dug deeper by reviewing which promotional items are best at engaging shoppers—if they are exposed to them by scrolling, using filters, and so on.

Here is when an opportunity jumped out (see Figure 6B.3). Namely, there were a couple of products that customers rarely viewed, but they were very attractive for add-to-carts if shoppers encountered them. So the opportunity became, how do we expose more shoppers to these most attractive items? That's what would likely increase purchases from the overall promotion as a whole.

Action and Value

The home improvement retailer added the best-performing products directly to the list page to increase their exposure and drive more traffic, something that took just ten minutes but drove thousands in additional sales per product per month.

Product displayed	Views	Click rate & No. of clicks	Attractiveness rate	Conversion rate & Revenue
Product XYZ	65	50.8% (46)	85.2%	6.06% $3,483
Product XYZ	48	60.4% (177)	54%	27.6% $12,337
Product XYZ	25	12.0% (3)	25.0%	0% $0.00

Figure 6B.3 Example of two products displayed in the same content zone on the same page. One (blue highlight) is performing well in that zone, the other (red highlight) is not performing well in that spot.

Challenge	Are Promotions effective for sales of the targeted Products?	
Surface	Review promotion performance to see whether it's being seen, clicked, and whether the products users view, add-to-cart, and purchase after clicking on promotions are the ones that were targeted?	
Understand	If promotion performance is off, look for common patterns.	
	Few clicks on the promo banner? Are users exposed to it? Is the banner attracting their attention? Do they understand it or hesitate?	Are products purchased not the targeted ones? Look for products with issues/ opportunities. Refer to Challenge 2.
Impact	Quantify volumes for potential value of changing placements/ promotions creative.	
Test	Develop & test new promotion banner designs and placements and designs.	Adjust placements and pricing of the products you push after users click on the promo.
Evaluate	Why did the changes help/hurt? What were the biggest success factors we can learn for future tests?	

Figure 6B.4 Cheat sheet: Improve the effectiveness of promotions.

C-SUITE Cheat Sheet for Solving the Challenge

In summary, Figure 6B.4 shows how Merchandisers go about better understanding and improving the effectiveness of their promotions and sales campaigns with the help of Experience Analytics.

Challenge 2: How Can Placements of Products Be Improved Based on Performance?

When shoppers see multiple products and categories, what can we learn from their behavior about which tend to be most attractive? For example, are there products with opportunities that we should rank higher? Conversely, are there products that aren't engaging shoppers at the same rates and should be downgraded?

Mini case study: A world brand in luxury, famous for its iconic handbags, uses Experience Analytics data to identify the color and materials that are most engaging to their fans. When shoppers are exposed to the same handbag model in varying colors and materials, which of these is best at catching their eye? Even if they might end up buying the bag in a different color or material in the end?

By understanding what's most engaging to their customers, the brand fine-tunes its digital displays to feature the most attractive product variations. They also advise their retail network based on this customer insight, so retailers can update their online and offline shopping windows.

So, Merchandising expertise doesn't only flow from Merchandisers in the offline world to the online. But, with Experience Analytics, here is an example where online data informs brick & mortar store Merchandisers.

Case Study: How Castorama Identified a Product Leading to Site Abandonment and Recovered 13,000 Euro Per Month

Since we already looked at a case study of improving the ranking of products with opportunities, let's now look at the opposite case where a product is unexpectedly causing site and app users to abandon their session.

Castorama is a French retailer of DIY and home improvement tools and supplies headquartered in France.

Challenge

As with any home improvement retailer, there are tens of thousands of products on the site and app. It would be impossible to manage an assortment of this size without data by just "keeping an eye" on the performance of products.

Step 1: Are There Frequently Viewed Products That Are Rarely Added to the Cart?

To systematically find underperforming products within their assortment, Castorama investigated frequently viewed products that are relatively rarely added to the shopping cart.

To do this, they combined exposure data with transaction data within their Experience Analytics (see Figure 6B.7). It's an advanced data set that requires capturing the entire transaction and integration of the product catalog. That integration is not something that would be available by default in most Web Analytics or Experience Analytics configurations.

Definition: Product Displayed, Pageviews

Sum of the pageviews where a given product was displayed inside a given zone

---

Definition: Product Displayed, Click Rate

How likely is the product to be clicked when it is displayed (see Figure 6B.5)?

Calculation

$$\frac{\text{Number of pageviews where the product was displayed in the zone and clicked}}{\text{Number of pageviews where the product was displayed in the zone}}$$

Figure 6B.5 Product displayed, Click Rate, calculation.

Definition: Product Displayed, Conversion Rate

How likely is the product to be purchased (see Figure 6B.6)?

Calculation

$$\frac{\text{Number of purchasing sessions that have clicked on the product when it was displayed in the zone}}{\text{Number of sessions that have clicked on the product when it was displayed in the zone}}$$

Figure 6B.6 Product displayed, conversion rate, calculation.

Step 2: Why Are These Products Not Added to the Cart?

After singling out products that suffer from relatively low add-to-cart ratios, it comes to answering "the why" behind the issues. Multiple potential reasons need to be checked. One could be that the price is too high relative to the market. We'll cover that use case in the following case study.

Product	↓ Sessions	↕ Conversion rate	↕ Number of conversions	↕ Revenue	↕ My price	↕ Market price
ALL PRODUCTS	93,016	15.3%	14,214	$1,239,940.47	--	--
Product ABC	4,094	0%	0	$0.00	$186.15	$89.95
Product XYZ	2,957	1.76%	52	$6,757.40	$129.94	$129.94

Figure 6B.7 An example of spotting products with opportunities (second highlight) and products with issues (first highlight) (Sample data, not from the case study customer).

In this case, Castorama reviewed sessions where customers recently viewed the products but didn't add them to the cart. What jumped out immediately is that the items were only available in very few physical stores. So basically, they were out of stock in most stores.

Step 3: What's the Impact of the Out-of-stock Experience?

It wouldn't have a significant business impact if shoppers went about their usual way and just bought something else. However, it would still likely be a frustrating experience.

But when Castorama used Impact Quantification to compare customers who viewed the out-of-stock product vs. didn't, it showed that this experience significantly lowered their session conversion rate. The incident likely prompted these shoppers to abandon and go back to the Internet to find the same product at another retailer.

Action and Value

Simply by downgrading the low-stock products, Castorama remedied the conversion rate. For just one of the products in this category, this represented a recovery of 13,000 Euro per month alone.

The Moral of the Story

Similar case studies come from other retail categories, such as fashion retailers. Here, it is common that a product is out of stock in popular sizes and is only available for the smallest or largest ones. When shoppers see these products, it can be a huge buzzkill. For example, this lowered the session conversion rate from the typical 3% to just 0.5% at one British department store.

Simply by using data to spot the frustration at the product level, it's easy to eliminate these leaks from the funnel.

C-SUITE Cheat Sheet for Placement of Products

Figure 6B.8 provides our cheat sheet of things to look for with Experience Analytics for better-promoting products with opportunities or downgrading products with issues.

Challenge 3: How Can Prices Be Fine-tuned Relative to the Market?

Price is a critical part of the customer experience. Terms such as "sticker shock" and "bargain hunting" are telltale of that.

Customers are well aware of market prices with price comparison engines at their fingertips. When they aren't adding a product to the cart, could it be because the price is too high relative to the market? Merchandisers and Ecommerce leaders need to know this, so they don't spin off expensive site optimization projects when the real culprit for under-performance is just the price.

Likewise, could prices be increased to improve margin? No need to go soul-searching for inventing new experiences to increase topline revenue when simple opportunities for increasing prices to market levels could much more easily increase bottom-line profits.

In retail, you have a whole function tasked with fine-tuning pricing, that is, the Pricers. They tend to have a lot of data at their fingertips about competitor pricing levels and sales data from their own company.

Challenge	Are there Products with opportunities or issues?	
Surface	Products with opportunities: Are there products with few views but high add-to-cart ratio?	Products with issues: Are there products with many views but low add-to-cart ratio?
Understand	Review the placements of these products with opportunities to understand why exposure is low.	Are products with issues out of stock e.g. in colors, sizes, locations available? Are they overpriced vs. market?
Impact	Quantify volumes for potential value of changing placements.	
Test	Improve placement of products with opportunities to help more shoppers find them.	Downgrade promotion of products with out-of-stock issues. Fix pricing issues.
Evaluate	Why did the changes help/hurt? What were the biggest success factors we can learn for future tests?	

Figure 6B.8 Cheat sheet: Optimize the placement of Products.

However, what's typically missing in their data set is behavioral data. As such, it is difficult for Pricers to see what behavioral effect prices have on their customers, that is, where there are issues and where there are opportunities.

Supplemental Case Studies and Cheat Sheets on the Book's Accompanying Website

To see a case study and cheat sheet on pricing optimization, check out the following case study on this book's accompanying website.

Case Study: European Retailer Reaps a Million Euro Opportunity By Identifying and Correcting a Price That Was Too High Above Market

https://ExperienceAnalytics.live/CaseStudies

Select the Pricing case study for chapter 6

Notes

1 Contentsquare Blog, RBS & Contentsquare—Reinventing a business model to provide world-class customer experience, 2017.
2 GlobalData, Online Grocery & Food Shopping Statistics, 2018, www.onesp ace.com/blog/2018/08/online-grocery-food-shopping-statistics/

Chapter 7

Solve Common Challenges at the Bottom of the Funnel

If the teams do a good job at the upper funnel, their efforts will compound traffic and create an avalanche of customers who want to complete their conversion or transaction.

But suppose the bottom of the funnel is leaky due to customer struggle and issues. In that case, the business is squandering some of the rewards they had earned by providing a great experience earlier in the customer journey.

The following teams are tasked with finding and fixing bad user experiences that hurt customers and transactions. They are not restricted in their efforts on the bottom-of-the-funnel section of the site and app. But since those parts of sites and apps tend to be the most interactive and transactional, it's also where a lot of the struggle and errors tend to creep into experiences. That's why these teams often find themselves spending a lot of their time on the bottom of the funnel.

Chapter 7A: Solve Customer Feedback Management Challenges

- Business Pressures
- Challenge 1: Improve the areas of the site and app that drive the most feedback
- Challenge 2: Increase actionability of feedback and prioritize what to improve

Chapter 7B: Solve Operations, Triage, and Technical Performance Challenges

- Business Pressures
- Challenge 1: Understand what's blocking customers from converting and quantify the business impact
- Challenge 2: Resolve customer service complaints
- Challenge 3: Proactively identify the biggest areas of the site for improvement

DOI: 10.4324/b23273-10

Solve Customer Feedback Management Challenges

The challenges with turning customer feedback into the goldmine it is supposed to be, have been well discussed earlier in this book. In fact, there is a massive opportunity to learn from feedback. Companies look at it as their first line of defense, that is, if something is wrong, their customers will be first to let them know via feedback.

The problem is that customers don't explain sufficiently what behaviors and issues led up to their complaints. That makes it difficult or impossible to understand what's causing their frustrations. For example, when customers leave verbal feedback such as "Blank page, can't proceed," it's not clear how they arrived at a blank page when everybody else seems to be seeing the site just fine.

Even worse, if we can't distinguish outliers from the real problems impacting many customers, we can't steer the boat in the right direction.

Figure 7A.1 provides a typical mindmap of what's going on in many Customer Feedback Management teams' minds. We see the perspective of troubleshooting bottom-up, that is, starting with each feedback that comes in. However, these teams also try to stem the tide of feedback by proactively scanning the site for the journeys that are most prone to triggering customer feedback. They aim to prioritize these sections of the site for a proactive overhaul.

Business Pressures

Here are the pressures when managing customer feedback.

Listen to Your Customers

In a world where businesses are supposed to be customer-obsessed, customers are king, and listening to their feedback is imperative.

MINDMAP Customer feedback management, i.e. Voice of Customer (VoC) Proactively innovate & troubleshoot top-down		
CHALLENGES		
How do we improve overall customer experience and satisfaction?	Such a big site/app, so much feedback. What are the journeys that lead up to the most feedback?	Which sections of the site or app should we suggest for a redesign?
QUESTIONS TO ANSWER		
What are the most frequent journeys before customers leave feedback?	Why/when does it happen? Which users?	How can we recreate issues so we can understand and fix them?
What's the business impact and priority of potential improvements? How can we get buy-in for action?		
SUCCESS CRITERIA		
Improve customer satisfaction metrics.	Get ahead of the issues, stop the bleeding.	Align Product, Business + technical teams.

MINDMAP Customer feedback management, i.e. Voice of Customer (VoC) Prioritize & resolve the biggest issues, working from bottom-up	
CHALLENGES	
Customer feedback is a potential goldmine but often it's not clear what actually happened and why.	So much feedback. What feedback should we act on?
QUESTIONS TO ANSWER	
How can we recreate the steps leading up to feedback to see what happened?	How can we distinguish outliers from the common issues that impact many?
What's the business impact and priority of potential improvements? How can we get buy-in for action?	
SUCCESS CRITERIA	
Prioritize and fix the issues that matter faster.	Align the teams to protect the brand and customer lifetime value.

Figure 7A.1 Typical Customer Feedback Management Team mind map.

Quick, Quick, Quick to React

Feedback comes in continuously about many areas of the site and app. We want to understand and act on it quickly. We want to take advantage of the opportunities that customers highlight. We also want to fix issues as fast as possible before more customers run into the same problems and more revenue and customers are lost.

We Need to Prioritize What to Address

The issues customers complain about can't possibly all be at the same priority level. So we need to prioritize by understanding which problems are hurting experience and business outcomes the most, and precisely for which customer segments.

The Most Disgruntled and the Biggest Fans Are Most Likely to Leave Feedback

Feedback tends to come from the most frustrated users or the biggest fans. The majority of site users, perhaps 99% or more of sessions, are not going through the effort of leaving feedback. They may include many "silent sufferers," as my colleagues sometimes call them.

So, we need to understand their digital happiness and implicit feedback based on their behavior and experiences. We want to know "how they vote with their clicks" by either staying with the brand and coming back often or taking their business elsewhere.

Customer Feedback Management Challenges and Use Cases

Let's now step into typical days in the life of the teams working on customer feedback. Let's see how they better understand their customers with Experience Analytics and overcome challenges.

- Challenge 1: Improve the areas of the site and app that drive the most feedback
- Challenge 2: Increase actionability of feedback and prioritize what to improve

Challenge 1: Improve the Areas of the Site and App That Drive the Most Feedback

To make better sense of customer complaints, businesses have combined session replay with Voice of Customer feedback for more than ten years by now. However, what's relatively newer is a bird's-eye view of experiences associated with positive vs. negative feedback and the business impact. So let's see a case study for that.

Case Study : How Beerwulf Closes the Gap Between Customer Feedback and UX Insights

In our first case study, we will visit Beerwulf, the online beer shop with a tempting range of beer cases, beer kegs, and beer taps. Beerwulf keeps a keen eye on the Net Promoter Score (NPS) metric for growing their fan base. After all, NPS is highly correlated with future customer growth. Beerwulf uses Voice of Customer solution Mopinion to collect anonymous feedback from their customers, including an overall rating of their shopping experience.

The Challenge

Customers provide feedback on their overall experience enabling Beerwulf to measure an NPS score. However, to make the most of that feedback, Beerwulf needed to understand which common website journeys, groups of pages, and funnels were most influential in shaping the customers' feedback. Especially when it comes to customers that didn't rate their experiences as perfect.

Step 1: What Are the Journeys Leading Up to Feedback?

A very popular bird's-eye view on feedback is to look at the most typical journeys leading up to feedback. When feedback is unsolicited, that is, customers choose when and where they click the icon to provide feedback, it's great on the one hand because we are ready to listen wherever customers want to give us their opinion. But it's also a challenge because we want to narrow down what the journeys are that put customers over the edge and willing to go through the time and effort of giving that feedback.

The Experience Analytics visualization of choice here is Journey Analysis, and in this case specifically a Reverse Journey Analysis for the most common paths leading up to an interaction with the survey page.

Definition: Reverse Journey Analysis

Journey Analysis is a visualization of all customer paths at a glance. This can, for example, be a traditional path diagram or a Sunburst visualization, as seen below.

While regular Journey Analysis shows paths starting from a page, Reverse Journey Analysis shows paths leading up to a given destination page. To read a Sunburst visualizations for Reverse Journey Analysis, you start with the innermost ring. Here, it represents the destination of the journey. Every sequential ring outward from the middle is each previous page that the user navigated from in their journey through to reaching the destination.

How to Configure Reverse Journey Analysis Leading Up to the Feedback Form

The feedback solicitation form is ultimately just another page on the site—or a screen within apps. By choosing this page or screen as the destination, Reverse Journey Analysis will surface the most common paths leading to submitting feedback.

Beerwulf found in their Reverse Journey Analysis that most interactions with the Mopinion form were submitted after completed transactions, that is, from customers who achieve their goals but must have experienced sufficient obstacles along the way to want to provide feedback (see Figure 7A.2).

That is partially great news, that is, customers could succeed in the end. But it provides a new challenge for the customer feedback

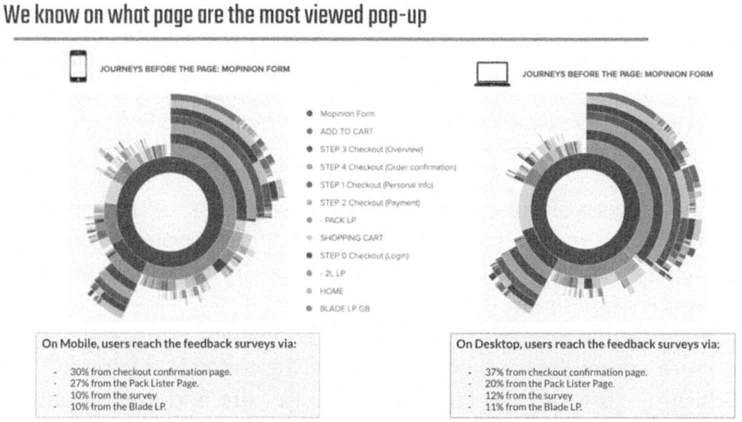

Figure 7A.2 Beerwulf's Reverse Journey Analysis leading up to the feedback form.

management team to understand where earlier in their journey these customers encountered experiences that prompted them to leave feedback many pageviews later.

Step 2: How Did Customer Profiles and Journeys Differ Between Positive vs. Negative Feedback?

Based on the NPS methodology, we distinguish

- Promoters that rated their experience highly and are therefore likely to contribute to brand equity, e.g., via word-of-mouth;
- Detractors that rated their experience poorly and are less likely to promote the brand.

Beerwulf has far more Promoters than Detractors, which means a very positive NPS. Yet, the way to improve your NPS further is to understand what can be improved for Detractors to win them over as fans as well.

So, Beerwulf's next step was to compare—the completely anonymous—customer profiles and the journeys of Promoters vs. Detractors.

How to Segment by Promoters vs. Detractors

As covered earlier in the book, Voice of Customer solutions can be integrated with Experience Analytics in multiple ways. The most common integration method enables session replay for each feedback received. However, an additional beneficial integration is to import feedback ratings submitted during a session so they become available also within the Experience Analytics. That integration enables users to segment journeys and in-page analytics for sessions that rated the experience highly vs. poorly.

What Beerwulf found, in this case, was that Detractors were more likely to be returning customers. Additionally, Journey Analysis showed their behavior to be quite different from first-time customers (see Figure 7A.3).

The Journey Analysis highlights that the biggest Promoters viewed a more comprehensive array of pages. In contrast, Detractors, as returning customers, seemed to know the site and go straight for the goal. Their behavior shows that they know what they want and that they are much more likely to add-to-cart straight from the listing page (e.g., see "- 2L LP" in Figure 7A3). The Journey

Detractors are mostly returning visitors who have high expectations

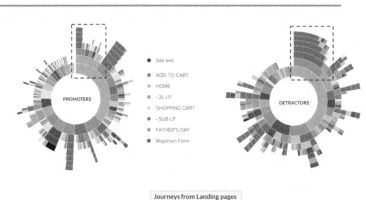

Journeys from Landing pages

Figure 7A.3 Beerwulf's analysis of journeys starting from landing pages on the site (innermost ring), comparing Promoters vs. Detractors.

Analysis shows how they afterward spend a lot more effort on the add-to-cart page to adjust their cart, that is, viewing the cart page repeatedly.

Essentially, returning visitors seemed to have higher expectations based on knowing the site, that is, the expectation to find the products they knew they wanted to purchase quickly. Yet, this expectation was not met therefore leading to lower feedback ratings.

But why?

Step 3: Why Did the Site Not Meet the Expectations of Detractors?

Now that we know where Promoters and Detractors differ in their journeys, we can zoom in to understand why. That's where we switch to in-page analysis to understand experiences and behaviors within pages.

Comparing the behavior of Promoters and Detractors within the Listing Page, Beerwulf found that Detractors spent less time actively engaging on the listing page and were less likely to scroll. Once again, their behavior suggested that they seemed to know what they were looking for. Plus, they expected the products they needed to be in front of them without much effort for scrolling.

But scrolling and engaging less means that they were likely not exposed to other product offerings and package sizes that might have been an even better fit for their needs.

As a result, the team hypothesized that Detractors might not have found the ideal products and packages that would have made their quick purchase journey as easy as they were hoping. Detractors did not want to scroll and spend time searching. So the Beerwulf team hypothesized that by providing better search filters on the listing page, they should be able to meet their expectations better, that is, make it effortless to zero in onto the products that fit their taste.

Step 4: Why Are the Listing Page Search Filters Not as Ideal as They Could Be?

Following this "smoke" to find the "fire," Beerwulf continued their in-page analysis with Zone-based heatmaps to study the interaction with search filters on the listing page. What jumped out from the data was that users were clicking multiple times per page on the filter options. Customers were spending more effort than expected in using the filters. And, again, this was especially pronounced for Detractors.

These Experience Analytics insights prompted Beerwulf to set up a specific survey on the filters screen within the list page to discover why this was happening. The survey would come up when customers spent more than a certain amount of time on the filters and would ask them: "Are you facing any issue with the filters? Which?"

The "Aha" and Action

This joint analysis between Beerwulf's Experience Analytics and Voice of Customer unearthed the filter options most likely to cause extra effort for returning customers. The biggest set of those issues was related to country-specific filters.

Work is underway as of this writing to test out improvements made to the filters based on this insight toward improving NPS and conversion rates.

Supplemental Images on this Book's Accompanying Website

See how the company adapted their search filters by checking this book's accompanying website.

https://ExperienceAnalytics.Live/Figures

See the Beerwulf case study example for Chapter 7A

The Moral of the Story

There is a symbiotic relationship between the Voice of Customer and experience insights. Experience Analytics contextualizes the feedback coming in. Experience Analytics also helps pinpoint where to invest in triggered surveys by pointing out specific moments in the journey where the business needs to understand better what their customers are feeling and thinking. After all, we don't want to interrupt customers unnecessarily. But just like in physical stores, if we see an area of confusion, we want to learn the problem and offer our help.

C-SUITE Cheat Sheet for Solving the Challenge

In summary, Figure 7A.4 shows common ways in which Customer Feedback Management teams identify the areas of the site that are most prone to feedback to recommend having these overhauled.

Challenge	Improve the areas of the site and app that drive the most feedback
Surface	Run a Reverse Journey Analysis for the most frequent paths leading up to providing feedback.
Understand	Look for common patterns.
	Compare journeys of good vs. bad feedback to look for telltale signals of where struggle or confusion is happening, e.g. looping behaviors, deviation from the ideal path, or heretofore undiscovered intent.
	Review in-page metrics and/or session replay on these pages to understand why struggle and dissatisfaction are happening.
Impact	Quantify volume of these behaviors and assess the impact of potential improvements.
Test	Design and test improvements to reap the benefits.
Evaluate	Why did the changes improve experience and success rates? What were the biggest success factors we can learn for future efforts?

Figure 7A.4 Cheat sheet: Stem the avalanche of feedback proactively.

Challenge 2: Increase Actionability of Feedback and Prioritize What to Improve

Now, let's switch to the most classic use case between Voice of Customer and Experience Analytics. Namely, feedback is coming in about specific page experiences. Here, customers aren't just showing you how to create a better site or app—they are literally trying to tell you! But it's often not clear why it's happening and what they mean. That's where Session Replay and Impact Quantification capabilities are the heroes of the day.

Case Study 1: How a Big Box Retailer Resolved the Mystery of the Blank Page

Our first case study is from a large grocery retailer. As peculiar as this example may seem, it's not that rare, actually. In earlier years, the same situation also happened to a large big-box retailer for home improvement goods.

The Challenge

Our grocer is using Voice of Customer solution Momentive. Feedback has been coming in with comments such as "Why aren't my items displaying so I can choose?" "Unable to access the page," and "Blank page. I cannot go to my account." Yet, the team could not see why this was happening by looking at their site.

Step 1: Replay the Sessions Leading Up to This Feedback

The customer feedback management team replayed the sessions leading up to feedback. The replays show users coming across a blank page while accessing their local supermarket's starting page. They reload the page, which remains empty several times. All that is showing on the page is the feedback icon. That's what they eventually tap to report what happened.

An analysis of this segment showed a commonality. Namely, they were all using a specific browser, that is, Internet Explorer in this case.

Step 2: Quantify the Magnitude of This Issue to Prioritize Action

While the experience is undoubtedly something that needs to be fixed, the question is always how urgently the team should prioritize this ticket relative to other issue tickets. The Customer Feedback Management team needed to quantify how often this issue happens.

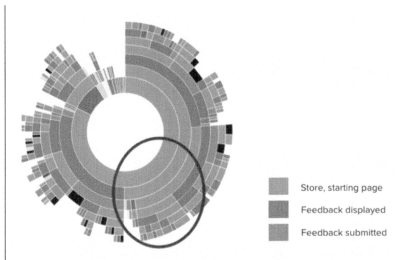

Store, starting page

Feedback displayed

Feedback submitted

Figure 7A.5 Journey Analysis visual helps quantify struggle with the store starting page.

Since the occurrence was tied to a particular journey rather than in-page behavior, a good way to quantify in this case was by using Journey Analysis. Figure 7A.5 shows the supermarket's Journey Analysis filtered on customers that used Internet Explorer, reached a store starting page, and submitted feedback. We can see these customers struggling and reloading the store starting page multiple times, sometimes more than seven reloads.

Step 3: Quantify the Impact of This Issue on Customers' Goals and Revenue

Impact Quantification analysis showed the issue happening to almost 10% of Internet Explorer sessions. Unable to start shopping, these users abandoned their journeys, sometimes after submitting feedback. The quantified business impact amounted to a loss of roughly 40,000 dollars per month.

Internet Explorer users per month: 50,000
Percent of those experiencing the issue: 10%
The regular conversion rate at that point in the journey would have been 8%
Lost conversions per month: 400
Average order value: 100 USD
Lost revenue per month: 40,000 USD

Step 4: Submit Issue Ticket for Resolution

Attaching the session replays with the impact quantification was a sure way to get this issue prioritized as a P0 top priority problem to resolve. The technical team quickly identified that the culprit was an incorrectly coded personalization for users with this browser. Namely, somebody forgot to add a closing bracket for a comment within the code, so everything that followed remained commented out.

The Moral of the Story

Voice of Customer, session replay, and impact quantification go hand in hand. It would be silly for a digital business to fight in the dark without these insights in this day and age when so much potential revenue leakage is at stake.

Supplemental Case Studies Online : How a Telecom Resolved the Mystery of Why Customers Aren't Finding What They are Looking For

To drive the typical routine home, here is another mystery case study available on the book's accompanying online website.

https://ExperienceAnalytics.live/CaseStudies

Select the Telecom case study for Chapter 7

C-SUITE Cheat Sheet for Solving the Challenge

In summary, Figure 7A.6 shows how Customer Feedback Management teams go about contextualizing feedback to understand why complaints are coming in and how to prioritize the issues.

Challenge	Increase actionability of feedback and prioritize what to improve
Surface	Replay the sessions leading up to feedback to see why customers complained.
Understand	Is it an outlier or a common problem experienced by many users?
	Review in-page metrics (e.g. via Zone-based heatmaps) on these pages to quantify how often others struggle with the same issues.
	Compare journeys of these customers to understand impact on the rest of their session.
Impact	Quantify the impact on conversion rate and revenue from these issues by comparing sessions to users that didn't experience the complaints at the same point in their journey.
Test	If you are prioritizing this issue for resolution, design and test improvements to improve the experience for all customers.
Evaluate	Why did the changes improve experience and success rates? What were the biggest success factors we can learn for future efforts?

Figure 7A.6 Cheat sheet: Contextualize feedback to make it actionable.

Solve Operations, Triage, and Technical Performance Challenges

As the digital channel is mission-critical for almost all brands today, nobody can afford to let experience issues linger. So, Operations and Technical Performance teams are responsible for eradicating friction points and ensuring that the site is performing optimally, as designed.

Larger businesses also have a triage team, sometimes called mission control, that processes incoming issue reports to assess which are the most critical to address and how. The triage team often sits in the Ecommerce organization, somewhere between business and Dev Ops. Figure 7B.1 provides a typical mindmap for these teams' business imperatives, questions, and opportunities.

Business Pressures

According to a study by the Qualtrics XM institute, bad customer experiences are putting $4.7 trillion in global consumer sales at risk.[1] Unfortunately, every business has its fair share of this problem. So, here is the pressure on the shoulders of the Operations, Triage, and Performance teams to reduce the burden.

Experience May Not Be Enough to Win a Transaction, But Bad Experiences Can Lose a Transaction

It's hard enough to acquire and win a customer. The business is spending lots of money to bring traffic to the site. No business can afford bad experiences blocking site and app users from completing their conversion goals.

It Doesn't Matter Whether Friction Is Due to Errors, Speed, Or UX Problems

Customers are struggling on every site, every day, regardless of whether it is due to errors, confusion or UX problems, or slow performance.

MINDMAP Operations & Triage Teams Proactively troubleshoot top-down		
CHALLENGES		
How do we ensure the site and app are performing as designed?	Such a big site, where are all the undiscovered blockers and leaks impacting revenue?	We need to find and fix the issues that matter, regardless of whether the cause is an error, UX struggle, or performance.
QUESTIONS TO ANSWER		
Top-down, which struggle, errors, performance are costing us money?	Why/when does it happen? Which users?	How can I effectively inform and enable the right team to fix it?
What's the business impact and priority of potential improvements? How can we get buy-in for action?		
SUCCESS CRITERIA		
Resolve issues proactively, stop the bleeding.	Separate outliers vs. the real issues.	Align business + technical teams.

MINDMAP Operations & Triage Teams Prioritize & resolve the biggest issues, working from bottom-up	
CHALLENGES	
I have tons of reported issues (e.g. VoC or contact center, etc.)—how can I understand, prioritize, and file a ticket for resolution quickly?	
QUESTIONS TO ANSWER	
How can I recreate each issue and identify the root cause?	Which issues are outliers? Which issues impact revenue and experiences for many?
How can I create an effective ticket to resolve the issues quickly?	
SUCCESS CRITERIA	
Prioritize and fix the issues that matter before it's too late.	Align the teams to protect the brand, revenue, and customer lifetime value.

Figure 7B.1 Typical mind map for Operations, Triage, and Technical Performance teams.

Frequently it is happening even where the site is working exactly as designed, but customers are confused or frustrated anyways.

Technical and triage teams need to identify all of these and prioritize them for resolution by the various responsible groups, DevOps, Product, or Business teams.

Quick to React

Every day that goes by without fixing reported problems, traffic leaks from the funnel, and revenue is lost. During peak holidays, every hour and minute counts.

Experience issues can hurt customer satisfaction so badly that consumer surveys regularly report affected users will turn their back on brands altogether. In addition, word-of-mouth about dissatisfaction can deter others from considering the brand in the future. Therefore, speeding up the meantime to resolution is critical.

Be Agile with Releases But Find Issues Proactively Before Customers Complain

Even better than resolving complaints quickly is finding and fixing issues before customers experience them. Especially so when Product teams release new experiences. The more agile a business is with releasing, the more critical it becomes to scan new releases for new issues quickly before customers—and the brand—get hurt.

Too Many Minor Issues That Together Add Up to Bleeding Too Much Revenue

If there was one huge problem that caused the site or app to be down for all users, the team would find and fix it immediately without needing analytics. But the reality is that most sites and apps thankfully work fine for most users. However, there are always many smaller pockets of customers that experience friction in one area or another. So, where Experience Analytics is mission-critical is for identifying these many points of friction that would fly under the radar otherwise.

Too Many Issues, Can't Fix Them All

In the end, there are always too many issues to address. Problem reports come in from Error Analysis, contact center complaints, or anecdotal problems where somebody tried something that didn't work. Product managers and technical teams have a long backlog of items they could be improving. So how can all teams prioritize their limited time to focus on the issues that matter most?

Challenges and Use Cases for Operations, Triage, and Technical Performance

The solution for speed to revenue recovery is not just about finding, recreating, and understanding issues. It also requires effectively aligning business and technical teams around the customer problems that hurt the worst. Let's now walk through the most typical challenges and related case studies.

- Challenge 1: Understand what's blocking customers from converting and quantify the impact of the issue
- Challenge 2: Resolve customer service complaints
- Challenge 3: Proactively identify the biggest areas of the site for improvement

Challenge 1: Understand What's Blocking Customers from Converting and Quantify the Impact of the Issue

Escalations and complaints come in every day that some customers are experiencing hurdles to complete their journeys. The first step is to understand what's leading up to these issues and why they are happening, for which customers, and how often.

While technical teams typically have access to APM tools (Application Performance Monitoring) and error logs, more data is needed to understand the problem because:

1. Issues are often related to UX problems and not errors or performance. In other words, struggle happens even though the site or app is working and performing as designed.
2. Understanding the issues requires the ability to segment experiences based on behavior.
3. Prioritizing the resolution requires assessing the overall business impact.

These are the questions that Experience Analytics answers. DevOps teams then use their favored APM tools and error logs to get deeper into the root cause and find the best way to fix the prioritized problems.

Case Study 1: How a Big Box Retailer Resolved Mysterious Complaints About a Gray Screen

The sites and apps of big-box retailers often generate billions in revenue per year across millions of successful customer transactions. But hidden among the successes are often small leaks. Given the high traffic volume on these sites, even rare issues due to some browser, device, or behavior-based combinations can quickly add up to millions of lost revenue. Here is just one of many case studies of this nature, in this case, from a US big-box retailer.

Challenge: Voice of Customer Complaints During Checkout

This big-box retailer was occasionally getting comments in their Voice of Customer tool such as: "Trying to checkout online, but it keeps getting stuck on gray when I click on 'Payment.' I guess you don't want my money." For months, this had been going on, but the team could not recreate the issue.

Step 1: Replay the Experience to Recreate the Problem

When the big-box retailer integrated Experience Analytics with their Voice of Customer tool, they could finally get to the bottom of the complaints. The replays show customers completing their checkout forms perfectly and clicking on Place Order. Yet, their screens turn gray instead of getting a purchase confirmation, and nothing more happens.

Session replays also provide the first clues into the source of the issue, for example, in this case, a problem with malfunctioning API calls.

Step 2: Quantify the Business Impact for Prioritization

Only some customers complain. How many others experienced the same bug? The triage team assessed the revenue leak's size by segmenting on customers who clicked the Place Order button but didn't reach the confirmation page.

> #### How to Segment on the Click of a Button
>
> In-page analytics doesn't just show pretty heatmaps of in-page behaviors but also needs to answer questions about specific in-page behaviors. For that purpose, Experience Analytics tools enable users to create segments based on these in-page behaviors.

A Zone-based approach to in-page analytics makes this particularly easy to do. Every HTML element is captured and assigned a zone, e.g., the "Place Order" call-to-action is ultimately a content zone. Segmentation capabilities include interaction events on zones. So, it's easy to define a segment based on users that did or didn't click or hover on the zone.

In some tools that don't provide a Zone-based approach, this kind of segmentation typically can be defined as an "on-click" event. However, that may usually require customizing the data collection tag or events for the page to send an additional event flag to the Experience Analytics when users click on the element of interest.

For an example of a segment definition screen based on in-page behavior see this book's accompanying website.

https://ExperienceAnalytics.Live/Figures

See the Segment example for Chapter 7B

So, in this case, the big-box retailer could create a segment based on clicks on the Place Order zone but without reaching the order confirmation page. Through that, they sized the leak to be $2.7 million monthly. And it had been going on for several months already.

Step 3: File and Prioritize an Issue Ticket for Resolution

The Operations and Triage teams cannot usually fix the problem themselves. So that's why the next step was to create an issue ticket with the appropriate high priority. Attaching the session replays to this issue ticket enabled the team to make it easy for DevOps to identify the root causes behind the bug and fix it.

The Moral of the Story

As we see in the nimble interplay between multiple teams in this case study, it takes a village. The triage team is like the traffic police on a busy roundabout in the village where new issue reports are coming in constantly. These issues must be understood quickly and routed in the right direction. Otherwise, the village roundabout will turn into a giant traffic jam.

Case Study 2: Resolving a Mystery Issue with Promotion Codes

Retailers constantly log incidents with customers getting messages about invalid promo codes. After all, it's common for shoppers to try using a promo code copied off of the Internet, just in case it works. Unfortunately, this happens so frequently that Ecommerce teams can be blasé about it, that is, they expect promo code errors when shoppers use bogus codes.

However, in this case, the team discovered an unexpected issue with promo codes, causing a drop-off during checkout. This case study is from the same big-box retailer as the previous one.

Challenge: Customers Complaining They Did Not Use Promo Codes

Among the many sessions with promo code validation errors, a few customers left feedback complaining that they got an error message even though they weren't trying to use any promo code.

That seemed weird; why would that be?

Step 1: Replay the Sessions

Replaying the sessions of these incidents, the triage team could indeed see that these customers did not interact with the promo code field during checkout at all. But these customers had a browser extension that auto-filled promotion codes for them during checkout. Many of these customers didn't even notice that this was happening.

In this segment of customers with the browser extension, 65% did not interact with promo code fields but did receive the "Invalid Promo Code" error message during checkout.

Step 2: Quantify the Magnitude of the Problem

They quantified how many customers 1. got a promo code validation issue, but 2. did not interact with the promo code field, and 3. abandoned their purchase. They did this by creating a segment in their Experience Analytics.

In the previous case study, the team had used a segment for users clicking on a particular content zone (i.e., the Place Order button). In this case, the team used the same segmentation capability but for customers who did not click into or interact with the promotion code field.

With that, the leak was sized at $2.1 million per month.

Step 3: Address the Issue and Recover the Revenue

With the problem identified, the team stopped the revenue loss by redesigning the promo code field to address the issues from auto-fill.

The Moral of the Story

We've now seen multiple case studies that all follow the same flow. Sometimes the issues are due to errors and bugs. Sometimes the leaks are due to confusion and UX problems. It doesn't matter what the cause of the problem is; the Operations and Triage teams need to get to the bottom quickly and prioritize resolution based on impact.

C-SUITE Cheat Sheet for Solving the Challenge

In summary, here is how teams typically go about understanding what's blocking customers from accomplishing their goals in a given reported problem area (see Figure 7B.2).

Challenge	Understand what's blocking customers from converting and quantify the business impact
Surface	For a given conversion problem, replay the related sessions of customers that abandoned their journeys to understand what's behind the problem, when and why it happens.
Understand	In the session replays, look for hints of UX problems and also study the event stream to see whether any errors are causing struggle.
	Using in-page analysis (e.g. via Zone-based heatmaps) on these pages, identify content elements commonly associated with the friction.
	Using Speed Analysis, identify whether performance issues are present and to what degree sessions with slower speeds correlated with lower conversion rates.
Impact	Quantify impact on conversion rate by comparing sessions of users that did vs. didn't experience the friction that you identified.
Test	If prioritizing this issue for resolution, design and test improvements to reap the benefits.
Evaluate	Why did the changes improve experience and success rates? What were the biggest success factors we can learn for future efforts?

Figure 7B.2 Cheat sheet: Identify and remedy conversion blockers.

Challenge 2: Resolve Customer Service Complaints

We already covered Customer Feedback Management teams earlier. However, often issues don't come in as feedback but as customer service cases via the contact center. Experience Analytics can help resolve tickets faster in these situations as long as it captures 100% of sessions for session replay. That is needed for finding the individual customer's session. A user identifier is also required—based on opt-in permission from customers. That way, the session can be searched and retrieved.

Case Study : Why Are Ferry Customers Buying Tickets for the Wrong Dates?

This case study is from a UK ferry operator popular with commuters on their way to work.

The Challenge

Every day countless customers successfully travel with the ferry service. Yet, the customer service team occasionally would log cases of customers calling into the contact center and complaining that the website messed up their ticket purchases. For example, instead of the dates, they purchased the ticket for, the issued ticket showed different dates.

But why would this be happening? Was it a user error or maybe a bug on the site?

Step 1: Find the Sessions of the Affected Customers to Replay Them

The triage team at the ferry service started their investigation by retrieving the session replay for the customers in question. This was possible for customers who logged into their account during their session and allowed permission to capture their account information.

Definition: How to Identify Individual User Sessions

There are multiple ways to identify sessions of individual registered customers where permission is present. Namely, an anonymous user identifier can be supplied into the Experience Analytics tool via its tag. When it becomes necessary to find a customer's session, users can search by that anonymous identifier.

By nature of being an anonymous number, the identifier is meaningless without a translation key. That translation key can be stored securely inside the company's CRM data for use when needed.

In other cases, the customer's email address can, for example, be used as that identifier if the email address is also the user name for logging into the website. No other translation is needed in that approach. Data is encrypted, and the decryption key is restricted to authorized customer service personnel only.

A third approach is to take an identifier such as the email address or account user name but to hash it to be mapped to an anonymous number stored within Experience Analytics. This way, the data stored about customers is entirely anonymous by itself, protecting privacy should there ever be a data leak. However, authorized and trained customer service personnel can search for sessions by the user identifier. The same hashing is applied to the search keyword in that search process to match the anonymous data.

Step 2: Replay the Sessions and Understand the Issues

Replaying these sessions, it became clear that no bug or error was present. The issue turned out to be a UX problem.

Customers would begin their ticket search on the homepage of the ferry service by completing their desired travel dates. But when customers clicked to close the overlaying calendar view, they clicked into the space on the page next to the calendar. That space looked empty, but actually, it was part of a promotion for discounted tickets during a promotion period (see Figure 7B.3).

So, these were accidental clicks on the promotion. Yet, the customers didn't notice that their travel dates changed to the promotion period instead of what they had just selected on the calendar.

Step 3: Quantify the Customer Service Problem

Besides the customers who complained, how many others experienced the same issue? To understand this, the team segmented on travelers on the home page that 1. started interacting with the calendar, 2. then interacted with the promotion, and 3. abandoned their search on this page.

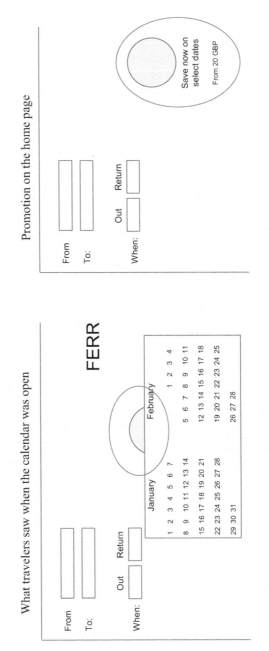

Figure 7B.3 A visual recreation of what caused the UX confusion.

It turned out that an incredible 38% of travelers who experienced this confusion abandoned their purchase altogether. That amounted to a loss of 1 million pounds per year.

Step 4: Redesign to Remove the Confusion

The team moved the location of the promo banner and made it more obvious how to close the overlaying calendar view. This removed the experience problem and confusion.

The Moral of the Story

Similar to Customer Feedback Management, Customer Services also brings the opportunity to resolve issues for all customers. Individual customer struggles can be clues to problems that affect the experience of many and cause a revenue leak.

Supplemental Case Studies Online : How an Investment Brokerage Firm Resolved a Spike in IT Error Messages Within 24 Hours

IT teams usually have many safeguards set up to alert them about bugs. What can be more challenging is understanding what leads to these errors. Check out a striking example from a US Investment Brokerage firm in this book's online materials.

https://ExperienceAnalytics.live/CaseStudies

Select the Investment brokerage case study for chapter 7

C-SUITE Cheat Sheet for Solving the Challenge

In summary, Figure 7B.4 shows how Triage teams go about understanding customer service cases to identify and resolve the underlying issues.

Challenge 3: Proactively Identify the Biggest Areas of the Site for Improvement

So far, we've covered use cases where Experience Analytics enables Operations, Triage, and Performance teams to be more like Sherlock Holmes and resolve mysteries faster. But even Sherlock Holmes gets bored sometimes and proactively searches for new cases to take on. It's

Challenge	Resolve customer service complaints
Surface	Find and replay the sessions relating to the customer's account to understand what were their steps leading up to the concern and what was their experience.
Understand	In the session replay, look for UX problems and also study the event stream whether any errors are causing the customer's concern.
Impact	Quantify whether the experience is an outlier or a common problem experienced by many. Find how many other sessions behaved in the same way or experienced the same concerns. Then compare their conversion rate vs. customers that did not run into the issues.
Test	If the issue is a common problem that you prioritize for resolution, design and test improvements to reap the benefits.
Evaluate	Why did the changes improve experience and success rates? What were the biggest success factors we can learn for future efforts?

Figure 7B.4 Cheat sheet: Accelerate customer service issue resolution.

similar for Operations and Performance teams. The only thing better than resolving issues faster is proactively identifying areas of struggle, bugs, and slow performance—before leaks grow or customer complaints come in.

Case Study 1: How The Conran Shop Proactively Resolved a JavaScript Error During Checkout

This case study is an excellent example for businesses with high average transaction values. Here, even the most minor issue impacting only a handful of customers can quickly add up to hundreds of thousands in lost revenue per year.

The Conran Shop is based in the UK and is the home of considered design and curated living. Offering a unique and distinctive blend of design classics and future collectibles, its innovative edit has inspired and excited visitors for generations. With a heritage spanning over 50 years, the Conran name has established itself as a brand synonymous with all areas of design.

The Challenge

While the vast majority of customers on Conran's website achieve their goals and checkout effortlessly, if there is even the most petite pocket of customers seeing any issue on their way to cart and checkout, we'd like to know and remedy the problem.

Step 1: Review Error Analysis Proactively

Error Analysis reporting is used to highlight issues on the site and prioritize them by their impact on lost conversions. These could, for example, be client-side JavaScript errors, functional errors (e.g., out of stock), and server-side API errors.

Reviewing their Error Analysis, The Conran Shop spotted one JavaScript error correlated with lost transactions (e.g. see Figure 7B.5). The issue impacted just a few hundred sessions over a fortnight. But the conversion rate of these shoppers was lowered by approximately 25%. Since the average transaction on The Conran Shop is quite sizable, this was worth investigating further.

Step 2: Replay the Sessions to Understand and Validate the Impact of the Error

Session Replay of anonymized sessions enabled the team to see when and where the error happened. There tend to be so many JavaScript errors present at all times on virtually all sites. Most of them are not even noticeable. So, it's essential to see with your own eyes that this particular JS Error is really to blame for a bad experience and the loss of conversions (see Figure 7B.6).

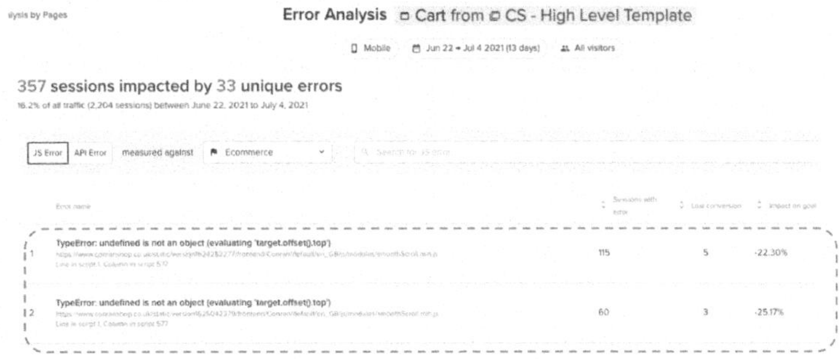

Figure 7B.5 Error Analysis report with conversion metrics.

Figure 7B.6 Session replay example with the Event Stream highlighting the error.

The team at The Conran Shop found that this JS Error caused friction on the cart page when shoppers tried to remove items from their baskets. These customers had a higher tap rate on the X for removing items, often leading to rage clicks. Some of them gave up and abandoned their journey.

Step 3: Profile Which Customer Profiles Are Running into This Error

Client-side errors tend to be very specific to devices and browsers used for accessing the site. So, we need to discover which technical profiles run into the problem.

When the team profiled browsers with this error, it turned out this issue affected mobile devices exclusively, specifically iOS (see Figure 7B.7).

Step 4: Quantify the Impact On Conversion

The Error Analysis showed how many sessions saw this error and their reduced conversion rate. But, when putting together our case for prioritizing this issue, it's important to monetize the leak and business case as succinctly as possible.

Figure 7B.8 illustrates how the team did that, putting together a simple table of transactions lost during the two weeks of the analysis:

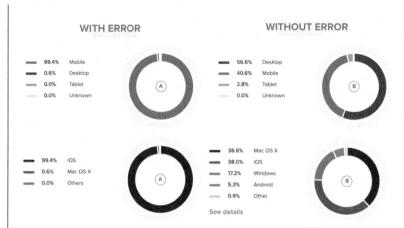

Figure 7B.7 Segment discovery for the technical profile associated with the issue.

	Sessions	Conversion rate	Number of Conversions
Users saw error on Cart page	382	15.70%	60
Usres didn't see error on Cart page		22%	84

Figure 7B.8 Impact Quantification for users that saw the issue over 15 days.

In other words, only about 50 customers per month abandoned their shopping journey after running into this issue. But with a high average order value on The Conran Shop, this meant tens of thousands in lost revenue every month.

Step 5: Fix the Problem and Recover the Revenue Leak

With the session replays and technical profiles in hand, the team was able to draw up an effective issue ticket so that the site's developers could resolve the bug quickly.

The Moral of the Story

It's just another great example that if an issue impacted most customers, it would be spotted immediately—no need for analytics. But, the many minor problems that fly under the radar also amount to losing too much revenue.

Case Study 2: How a Multinational Insurance Company Surfaced Why Some Online Applications Are Abandoned

Pretty much any online conversion on any site requires completing forms at some point. But while most industries can aim to simplify their forms as much as possible, there is one industry that's got the problem from hell to worry about—namely, insurance companies. You just have to ask for so much information to quote the right insurance offer. That's why insurances need to be super professionals at form optimization. And that's a perfect use case for Experience Analytics.

The Challenge

This multinational insurance company offers auto insurance as one of its many products that customers can price out and purchase online. While this process seemed to be humming along perfectly for most potential customers, the team needed to be proactive with identifying any remaining pockets of issues. So, were there still any customers experiencing any friction along the way?

Step 1: Automatically Scan the Experience for Signs of Frustration and Lost Conversion

Rather than manually analyzing challenges, automated frustration scoring speeds up the process. Automatic scanning needs to cover both UX issues and technical errors because both can lose a potential customer.

The insurance company noticed multiple field interactions on the auto insurance flow in this case (see Figure 7B.9). Many applicants had to try numerous times to complete a field. This friction point lowered the conversion rate by 32% for customers who raised this friction signal.

Step 2: What Is the Problem That Users Are Encountering?

The quickest way to understand this problem was to replay the actual experiences leading up to the multiple attempts. This revealed a surprise.

Customers are at the step where they should enter their profile as a driver and then provide their home address before clicking on the call-to-action to continue. But the call-to-action remains grayed out. Customers are going crazy trying to solve the issue, clicking

Figure 7B.9 The insurance company's Opportunity Report based on Frustration Scoring.

multiple times, toggling their consent checkbox, reentering their driver's license information. But nothing is helping. It breaks your heart to watch them struggling on the replays.

What these customers were supposed to see on the page were three additional form fields for entering their home addresses. Yet, these fields were simply not showing up for the customers in question (see Figure 7B.10).

Since the form fields for home addresses weren't present for the customers that ran into this issue, they couldn't complete them. That's why the call-to-action for going to the next step remained grayed out for them.

Step 3: Impact Quantification

An impact quantification from the session replay confirmed the magnitude of the problem to a pocket of 50 customer applications per week. This segment of customers tap on the call-to-action but don't arrive at the next step in the application process and then drop out.

Figure 7B.10 Session replay of actual experience vs. intended experience.

Step 4: Write Up an Effective Issue Ticket and Stop the Leak

With this insight, the session replays, and the technical profiles of these sessions in hand (e.g., browser, devices, etc.), the Operations team wrote up an effective issue ticket for the Developers to investigate. So they resolved the problem swiftly.

The Moral of the Story

It may sound outlandish that required form fields would just not show up for some customers. But issues relating to missing content elements are commonplace. You just can never know what you don't know. But what you don't know will still hurt you.

Mini Case Study: "How can I purchase this product?"

At one US big-box retailer, the team was getting Voice of Customer feedback occasionally about how to purchase a particular product, i.e., there was no way to buy the product. When they replayed these sessions, to their amazement, they saw that the add-to-cart button was simply not present for these customers on these particular products.

Supplemental Case Studies on the Book's Accompanying Website

As we already know, the slower the performance of an experience, the more visitors abandon and the more revenue is lost. So, even if an experience is designed to be very intuitive, and there are no errors, just slow speeds by themselves can be enough to spoil everything. Therefore, speed analysis and optimization must be done proactively, especially before new experiences are released.

Check out a typical case study on this book's accompanying website.

Case Study: Major Fashion Brand Increases Revenue by Improving Performance on Mobile

https://ExperienceAnalytics.live/CaseStudies

Select the Fashion brand case study for chapter 7

C-SUITE Cheat Sheet for Solving the Challenge

In summary, Figure 7B.11 shows tips for surfacing issues automatically.

Challenge	Proactively identify the biggest areas of the site for improvement in regards to friction and frustrations		
Surface	Score experiences automatically for signs of struggle.	Review Error Analysis for errors impacting conversion.	Review Speed Analysis to identify areas of sub-par performance.
Understand	Replay examples, understand causes of friction & errors.		
	What behaviors are commonly associated with the friction leading to exits?	Which errors are happening when and where?	How can speed of the pages be improved?
Impact	Quantify the impact i.e. potential value of improving the experiences.		
Test	Fix the issues, and/or test improving the design of the experiences.		
Evaluate	Why did the improvements win/lose? What were the biggest success factors we can learn for future tests?		

Figure 7B.11 Cheat sheet: Surface the biggest areas of the site to improve.

Note

1 Qualtrics, Bad Customer Experience Puts $4.7 Trillion in Global Consumer Sales at Risk, 2021, www.xminstitute.com/blog/bad-experiences-risk-sales/

Chapter 8

Solve Common Challenges at the Flip Side of the Funnel

All the talk about "the funnel" is only a highly simplified look at actual customer journeys. The purpose of a funnel-centric view is to generalize an understanding of customer journeys and goals so that teams can draw out common bottlenecks, opportunities, and next-best actions.

Once the team has taken advantage of all that a funnel-centric view can yield, the first step toward a more mature customer relationship model is to realize that the customer lifecycle is more like an hourglass. Namely, after the customer acquisition, the real work begins to serve, delight, and grow customer relationships.

In this chapter, we will visit two teams on the existing customer side of the business, namely Customer Service & Support and Customer Marketing. We'll see the Experience Analytics use cases that help them better take care of their customers.

Chapter 8A: Solve Customer Experience, Service, and Support Challenges

- Business Pressures
- Challenge 1: Understand and improve the digital experiences that drive up contact volume for customer service and support
- Challenge 2: Increase customer success and satisfaction with self-service help

Chapter 8B: Solve Customer Marketing Challenges

- Business Pressures
- Challenge 1: Manage my content marketing assets based on their value for engaging and inspiring customers
- Challenge 2: Improving customer marketing campaign results
- Challenge 3: Gaining permission to market and improving the targeting of campaigns

DOI: 10.4324/b23273-11

As with any model, even the hourglass model is just a simplification of course. In reality, customer journeys are in many of these stages simultaneously. A customer might be in the market for one product but already be a satisfied customer of another product while struggling with customer support on a third one. They may go back and forth between journey stages such as awareness and consideration.

The better customer marketing teams can leverage real-time signals of the current intent of a customer, the better they can serve them "in the moment" instead of making model-based assumptions. In the third part of the book, we'll look into those emerging use cases for personalization based on customers' digital body language.

Solve Customer Experience, Service, and Support Challenges

Goals and expectations for the Digital Customer Experience (CX), the Service and Support team in the business will differ based on the business model. Common to probably all companies is that customer service and support represent a cost that the business would ideally like to keep from creeping higher than it needs to be. Enabling as much self-service success as possible via the digital team is the best way to keep costs under control.

However, service and support also represent a huge opportunity to grow customer lifetime value and loyalty. So, rather than focusing only on "call avoidance" to lower contact center costs, modern enterprises also have the mantra of "right-channeling." Namely, we encourage the right customers to speak with a live representative in the right situations.

Figure 8A.1 is a look at the CX, service, and support goals mind map regarding the interplay of digital experiences with contact center support.

Business Pressures

Let's step into the shoes of customer service and support teams to feel some of the business pressures they feel.

Customer Obsession

Where are better customer relationships and loyalty going to come from? It's by declaring customer love as a top goal and mantra. And, it's by putting our money where our mouth is, that is, making the customer perspective part of every decision process.

Besides strategy, it requires a CX team that watches over journeys and identifies those that need improvement or reimagining to meet customer wants and needs.

MINDMAP **Customer Experience, Service & Support** **Proactively Innovate & Troubleshoot Top-down**		
CHALLENGES		
How do we improve customer satisfaction and loyalty while keeping services costs under control?	Too many avoidable contact center requests. Need to bring down costs by improving self-service.	Which journeys should we suggest for improvement?
QUESTIONS TO ANSWER		
What are the unsuccessful journeys causing pain and prompting customers to seek help?	Why/when does it happen? Which users?	Recreate issues so teams can understand and fix them?
What's the business impact and priority of potential improvements? How can we get buy-in for action?		
SUCCESS CRITERIA		
Hit goals for increased self-service.	Reduce contact center volume.	Align Product, Business + technical teams to increase customer satisfaction.

MINDMAP **Customer Experience, Service & Support** **Prioritize & Resolve The Biggest Issues, Working From Bottom-up**	
CHALLENGES	
I have tons of reported issues (e.g. VoC or contact center, etc.)—how can I understand, prioritize, file a ticket for resolution quickly?	
QUESTIONS TO ANSWER	
Why is my customer seeing issues or why are they confused?	How many others also get stuck on the same issues?
Resolve the customer's request but also prioritize action to reduce future call volume. Tell our story visually to get "buy-in" for actions.	
SUCCESS CRITERIA	
Resolve the individual customer's service needs swiftly.	Align the teams to protect the brand, revenue, and customer lifetime value.

Figure 8A.1 Typical mind map for Customer Experience, Service, and Support goals regarding customers' digital experiences.

Meet Business Goals for Cost Control

The digital team and customer service team share a goal toward reducing contact center costs. Toward shifting more and more support to the self-service channel, digital teams get tasked with meeting ever-higher targets for self-service journey adoption and completion.

That doesn't just help the customer service and support team with their goal of managing costs. It also serves customers' wishes that prefer to resolve their questions without needing to stand in line for live help.

Drive Customer Success and Value with the Brand's Products

Typically today, product documentation is online. It includes information in written and video formats. In some cases, products are even entirely digital, for example, think about software and streaming video services. Enabling customers to get more value from their products by finding the right help isn't just a customer service goal; it's part of a good product and brand experience. The more successful customers are, the more likely they will keep using the products. It may also lead to purchasing additional product options and recommending the brand to others.

Customer Support and Service Challenges and Use Cases

These business pressures translate into many challenges where Experience Analytics helps. How can the team learn from their customers how to provide them with better service and support? How can Experience Analytics help with getting customers the investment in CX they need and deserve?

- Challenge 1: Understand and improve the digital experiences that drive up contact volume
- Challenge 2: Increase customer success and satisfaction with self-service help

Challenge 1: Understand and Improve the Digital Experiences that Drive Up Contact Volume

The contact center's systems keep track of the account management tasks and transactions that are handled by live agents. Typically, customers can accomplish many of these tasks themselves in the self-service website or app, but they request live help nonetheless. Why is that happening, and how can the company increase self-service journey completions?

Case Study 1: How a Retail Bank Increased Self-Service Success for Loan Processing

In the first case study, we visit an American retail bank offering deposit and loan products. They are a pure online bank. They want to enable customers to accomplish most of their goals without needing live help from bankers.

Customers can apply for loan products on the site and upload the supporting documentation required for processing their loan requests. This process often includes situations where the bank needs to request additional documents from its applicants.

In this case study, this step in the customer service journey is also online. The customer receives a notification that they have a message waiting for them in the secure message center. The customer connects to the site or app to view the note instructing them to upload documentation.

The Challenge

In reviewing their data, the bank found that many of these applicants either abandoned their loan application entirely or called the contact center at the point of the journey where additional documents were requested. There appeared to be a significant pain point and "leak" in the self-service journey at this stage.

But why was it happening? Is it that most of these applicants are simply unable to provide the additional documents? Or was there something about the self-service journey they could improve?

Step 1: Where Are the Bottlenecks in the Self-Service Journey to Upload the Requested Documents?

The analytics team at the bank started their investigation with Journey Analysis. It turned out that only 9% of the customers that entered this flow for additional documents completed it successfully. The most significant drop was already at step one of the flow. Most applicants did not even click through to see which additional documents the bank requested.

So, here we know that the "leak" in the funnel doesn't have anything to do with applicants that are unable to provide the required documentation. In this first step, applicants do not even know yet what additional information is needed.

Step 2: Why Are Customers Not Continuing to See Which Additional Documents Are Required?

The analytics team drew on In-page Analysis to investigate this question, that is, Zone-based heatmaps. Most applicants were viewing their messages on their mobile devices. It turned out that the design of the page included a rookie mistake. The call-to-action was not prominent enough on mobile devices because it was barely visible above the fold. For customers on desktop devices as well, the Hover Rate metric showed that few customers noticed the call-to-action button, let alone clicked it (see Figure 8A.3).

Definition: Hover Rate

The percentage of pageviews on desktop devices in which visitors hovered over the zone with their mouse cursor at least once (see Figure 8A.2). This metric determines which zones are consumed the most.

Calculation

$$\frac{\text{Number of pageviews with at least one hover over the zone}}{\text{Total number of pageviews}}$$

Figure 8A.2 Hover Rate, calculation.

Step 3: Improve the Design and A/B Test

The Product team improved the layout of the message page to eliminate white space and make the CTA more prominent.

Results and Value

Micro conversions from this step to viewing the required documents increased by 400%! While not everybody who viewed the necessary documents uploaded them immediately, application completion improved by 10%.

That's a massive win for the bank from a tiny improvement to make. Think about how much additional marketing spend would be needed if the bank wanted to reach 10% additional prospective customers to increase loan applications by the same amount.

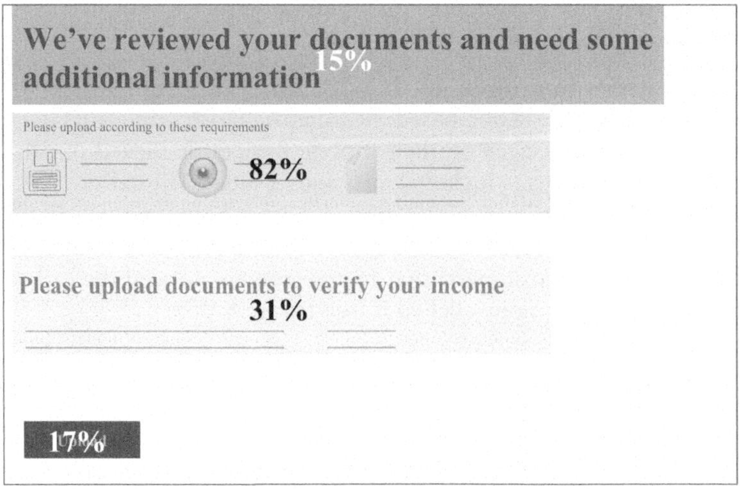

We've reviewed your documents and need some additional information 15%

Please upload according to these requirements

82%

Please upload documents to verify your income
31%

17%

Figure 8A.3 Zone-based heatmap with Hover Rate metric.

The Moral of the Story

An ineffective CTA may sound like a silly rookie mistake. In the past, customer service journey flows often didn't receive the same degree of design and attention that customer acquisition journeys typically receive. However, that is a bias that is becoming outdated now, given that the world is increasingly digital.

Case Study 2: How an Insurance Company Right-Channeled Cases for Third-Party Claims

If there is an industry that's known to be cost-conscious, that is insurance companies. So, they usually love for their customers to handle customer service questions themselves via the site and app to reduce costs. But in cases where an auto insurance claim comes into the insurance from a third party, it's a different story. Here, insurance companies would love to talk to their customers. They can better understand the situation and devise to which degree the third-party claim is justified.

It's a case for right-channeling. Encouraging their customer to speak with live customer service saves the insurance more than avoiding the call.

The Challenge

The insurance company's service data showed that live interactions were occurring for third-party claims, but not consistently. How could the right-channeling be improved?

Step 1: Why Are Customers Not Calling In?

Journey Analysis showed that customers reach the service page that encourages them to call in. The call-to-action on this page is also easy to see above the fold on all devices. It is right in the top banner. So, what A/B test would most likely improve the page goal?

Step 2: Review In-Page Analytics to Understand User Behavior

Reviewing the page with Zone-based heatmaps, what jumped out is that designers and product managers had placed additional options for getting in touch under the fold, that is, specifically "request a callback." After all, the product managers knew that

1. Not every customer would be reading this message in a moment when they are free to call.
2. Customers might think it's a hassle to wade through the contact center phone menu.

However, putting all of the different contact options into the top banner seemed too much clutter. So they placed it lower on the page instead (see Figure 8A.4).

As expected, scrolling and exposure heatmaps showed that most customers weren't scrolling enough to be exposed to this additional contact option.

Step 3: Improve the Design and A/B Test

With the data in hand, the Product team did invest in an A/B test to move the additional contact options into the top banner. It was worth trying to see whether the additional information would help, even if the visual looks more cluttered.

Results and Value

The test was successful. Clicks and taps on the contact options increased by 130% leading to 60 additional "right-channeled" calls per week.

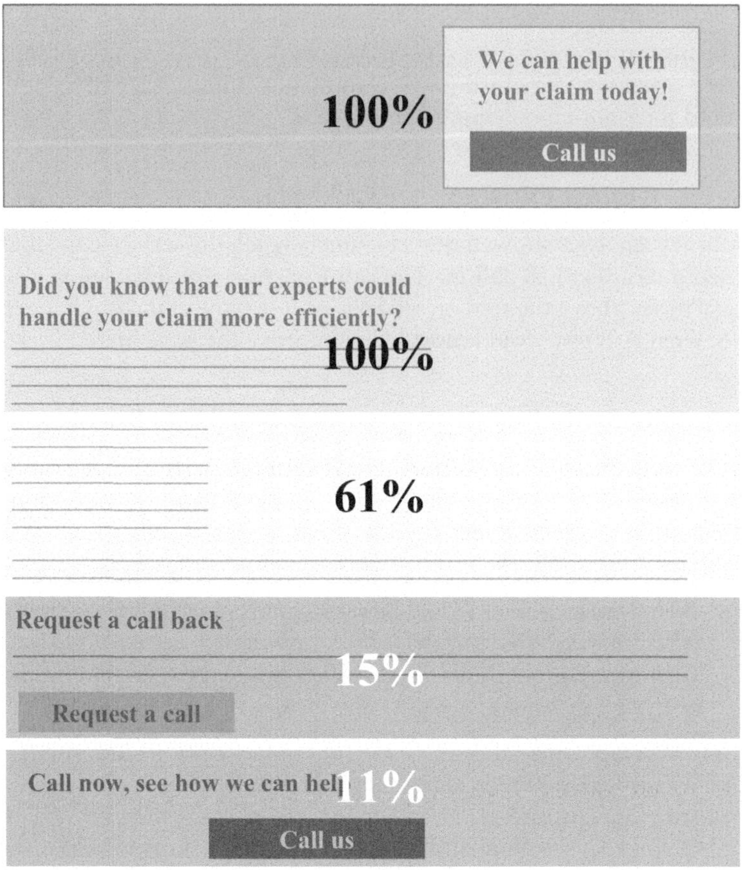

Figure 8A.4 Secondary call-to-action under the fold line. The Zone-based heatmap displays an Exposure Rate metric.

The Moral of the Story

Everybody knows that placing content above the fold will get more eyeballs on it and actions. But not all content can possibly be above the fold. There just isn't enough real estate. So it's a matter of knowing what goes up and what can be deprioritized.

C-SUITE Cheat Sheet for Improving Self-Service Journey Completions

In summary, Figure 8A.5 shows the typical steps for investigating and improving self-service journey completions.

Challenge 2: Increase Customer Success and Satisfaction with Self-Service Help

Providing the best customer self-service experience isn't just a matter of reducing contact center costs. It's also business-critical for customer satisfaction and loyalty. When customers are happy, the brand can grow via word-of-mouth.

From account management and documentation to the configuration of the products, digital customer self-service is part of the brand experience. It needs to be a good experience for brands to succeed.

Challenge	Find + improve the self-service journeys that drive up contact volume		
Surface	Review Journey Analysis to pinpoint where customers abandon self-service journeys.	Review Error, Form and Speed Analysis for signs of confusion, struggle, bugs.	Score experiences automatically for signs of friction.
Understand	Review in-page analytics to understand what's happening and why, especially Zone-based heatmaps and session replays.		
	What behaviors and what context (e.g. browser) are commonly associated with success vs. abandonment?	Which content elements are helpful vs. not for success?	What's the root cause, i.e., UX, errors or speed?
	What enhancements would help more users find the golden journeys? What issues should be improved or fixed?		
Impact	Quantify the impact, i.e., potential value of improving the experiences.		
Test	Fix any issues, and/or test improving the design of the journeys.		
Evaluate	Why did the improvements win/lose? What were the biggest success factors we can learn for future tests?		

Figure 8A.5 Cheat sheet: Proactively improve self-service journey completions.

Case Study : How a Software Provider Increased Positive Ratings By 20% in Just One Month

Back when most software used to be a one-time purchase model, all focus and attention at software companies was on the initial sales journey. Now that most software providers have switched to SaaS and subscription models, the growth of vendors depends on user adoption and success with the product. That's what leads to subscription renewals, add-on sales, and so on.

As a result, providing a good software user experience, including the usability of the product itself and its documentation, has become a primary success factor for software companies. That's great because it's a win-win for customers and providers alike.

The Challenge

The productivity software in our case study has been the leading product in its category. It was used by many professionals in the field. After dominating the market for professional users, the vendor expanded their market in two ways:

1. They additionally embraced the consumer market where the software however competes with free "built-in" tools that are included on many Smartphones and other services.
2. They switched from a one-time license fee to a monthly subscription fee model to make the price more palatable for consumers.

Both of these changes necessitated that the company's new target users be as successful with the adoption of the product as possible. If users aren't able to take advantage of all the advanced capabilities in the product, then they might as well be using a free tool instead.

As a result, the vendor focused on making their self-help documentation as helpful as possible. Are answers to questions easy to find and understand? If not, why not?

Step 1: Decide on Customer Success KPIs

The team embraced the focus by deciding on the following KPIs as a measure of their success

- Improve customer experience
- Increase app usage
- Increase customer satisfaction
- Decrease customer effort
- Reduce live support contacts.

Their product documentation and online tutorials were critical to this initiative. This was under the assumption that

- If users can quickly solve their own problems, satisfaction increases and assisted support contacts decrease.
- If users can achieve their desired level of competency on their own, app usage rates increase.
- If users find what they need quickly, customer effort decreases.

Step 2: Understand and Improve Every Step of the User Journey

The team started their project at the first step of the customer journey, that is, reading documentation for installing the software. Before using Experience Analytics, their efforts for making this documentation effective would have included motions such as checking the accuracy of the documentation. With Experience Analytics, they investigated the usability of the documentation.

How are users seeing the page for installation instructions and engaging with it? That's where in-page analytics revealed a surprise.

Namely, one of the images on the help page was a screenshot of the software installation, including a button on that screen. To the surprise of the documentation team, many users were trying to click the button within the screenshot. Of course, clicking the screenshot did nothing. It was just an illustration of what users would see on their computers during the installation. Yet, their heatmaps showed recurring clicks and frustration.

Step 3: Hypothesize a Better Information Design and A/B Test It

The team changed the screenshot styling to clarify that the page element isn't something meant to be clickable.

Results and Value

They continued to measure their KPIs and found in the first month of testing the change that

- The click frustration stopped;
- Positive ratings of the installation experience (via Voice of Customer feedback) went up by 7 points from 35 to 42%;
- Average active time spent on the help page was reduced by 13 seconds;
- Calls into the contact center for help with the installation were reduced slightly.

Rinse and Repeat

The CX team continued improving every step in their self-service documentation with this same approach. It led to adjustments in navigation for finding the right help documents at the right time. It also led to a change of layout for help pages and more. It, of course, also included design changes to adapt the usability for mobile devices.

Based on very early results, they found that

• Customer satisfaction began to increase;
• Retention slightly increased;
• New customer conversion was holding steady.

At the time of writing, the impact on the following key metrics was still to be determined.

• App usage
• Customer effort
• Assisted support contacts significant reduction.

The Moral of the Story

With the wealth of information that needs to be provided within the customer self-service sections of sites and apps, is it any wonder that their optimization is helpful? It requires just as much focus and attention as improving acquisition journeys. Yet, the potential rewards for the business and its customers are mission-critical, especially in competitive markets.

Mini Case Study: Another Software Company

A large software company found a similar user experience problem in their help section. In their case, an image on a customer service page was supposed to convey that support is available via multiple channels. It showed icons for various channels such as phone, chat, email, etc. But to the surprise of analysts, clickmaps showed that users were confused by the image and tried clicking the channel names. They were apparently hoping that this would, for example, open up a live chat. Yet, the image was purely for illustration purposes.

C-SUITE Cheat Sheet for Increasing Customer Success and Satisfaction with Self-service Help

In summary, here are typical steps for investigating and improving support and documentation toward increasing customer success and satisfaction (see Figure 8A.6).

Challenge	Increase customer success, satisfaction, and product usage by improving self-service help and documentation		
Surface	Review Journey Analysis to pinpoint where customers give up or struggle for finding help, for example going in loops?		Which help articles are getting low feedback ratings?
Understand	Review in-page analytics to understand what's happening and why, during both search for the right help article and then the engagement with that article.		
	What behaviors, help search keywords, and what context (e.g. browser device) are commonly associated with success vs. not?	Which content elements and search filters are helpful vs. not?	What are underlying issues, i.e., UX, errors, speed?
	What enhancements would help more users find the right articles and engage with the content on them? What issues should be fixed?		
Impact	Quantify impact, i.e., potential value of improving and fixing issues.		
Test	Fix any issues, and/or test improving the design of journeys and pages.		
Evaluate	Why did the improvements win/lose? What were the biggest success factors we can learn for future tests?		

Figure 8A.6 Cheat sheet: Proactively improve self-service help journeys.

Solve Customer Marketing Challenges

Existing customers and fans of the brand are a company's biggest asset, and hardest to earn. New customer acquisition is expensive. So, the loyalty and retention of existing customers is the name of the game. Serving them well is mission-critical.

The Customer Marketing team has the opportunity to re-engage them for repeat and additional business. With the opportunity come great challenges. Figure 8B.1 is a mind map for customer marketers as it pertains to experience insights.

Decades worth of thinking on customer-centric marketing has gone into how best to serve and grow customer relationships. CRM, Multichannel Marketing, 1:1 Marketing, Cross-channel, Omnichannel marketing are just some of the mantras that are top of mind for marketers. As a source of insights into customers' current wants and needs, Experience Analytics can enrich everything that customer marketers are already doing to engage and inspire their customers. We will cover the value of Experience Analytics data for these teams in Part III of the book.

Business Pressures

With their great power (of being allowed to speak to existing customers) come great responsibilities and business pressures for the Customer Marketing team.

Hit Ever-Growing Sales Goals for Repeat and Upsell

Just like all sales and revenue goals are going up every year, so are the ones for the Customer Marketing team. How can Marketing improve their campaigns so that more revenue is generated *per customer*? That requires earning and keeping permission to market (e.g., opt-in to receiving messages, loyalty programs, and data collection). And then it requires making the most effective use of that permission given.

MINDMAP Customer Marketing Proactively innovate & troubleshoot top-down		
CHALLENGES		
Revenue goals are going up and up. How can we do more with our customer base?	Need to tell our brand and campaign story effectively to gain permission to market, and re-engage customers.	Need to understand and target different customer segments effectively.
QUESTIONS TO ANSWER		
Why is traffic bouncing on campaign landing pages? How can we improve that?	Is the Content strategy working for engaging and persuading customers?	What content & placements work best for which segments?
What's the business impact and priority of potential actions?		
SUCCESS CRITERIA		
Gain and maintain permission to market.	Reduce campaign bounces, improve journeys.	Hit revenue and retention goals.

Figure 8B.1 Typical Customer Marketing Team mind map.

Retain Customers at Risk and Increase Lifetime Value

The more the world shifts to digital, the more competitive it becomes. On digital, alternative brands are just a click away. And for Millennials and Gen Z, brand loyalty does not seem to be as strong as it might have been for earlier generations. For customer marketers, that means that the brand has to earn its business every time, not just bank on past credentials.

Target-relevant Communication and Avoid Contact Fatigue

When the biggest constraint on acquisition marketers is probably their budget, for customer marketers, the currency is the attention span and permission to market by their customers. Done well, it is nearly free to communicate with them. But done badly, no amount of throwing coupons at them will achieve the goal.

Customer Marketing Team Challenges and Use Cases

Let's see how customer marketers use Experience Analytics to help with their challenging goals. What can we learn from our customers about the golden paths that work well for them (and us), and what's annoying and ineffective that we should just stop doing?

- Challenge 1: Manage my content marketing assets based on their value for engaging and inspiring customers
- Challenge 2: Improve customer marketing campaign results
- Challenge 3: Gain permission to market and improve the targeting of campaigns

Challenge 1: Manage My Content Marketing Assets Based on Their Value for Engaging and Inspiring Customers

To bring their customers back to the site, app, and stores, customer marketers target content and offers to their audience. Which of these is best at engaging customers and persuading them to take the desired actions? Where are the best placements of these items so that customers see them? Let's review a case study for video analytics, where this question is burning hot.

Case Study: How Well Are Videos and Their Placements Working for Engaging Our Telecom Customers?

Other than live events, videos are probably the most engaging content marketing asset type for customers. However, they are also the most expensive and challenging to develop. So, it's critical to manage that investment toward success by understanding which videos work best, when, and where in the customer journey.

That's exactly the question raised at the Telecom company in our case study here.

The Challenge

The team has invested in videos for various topics such as helping new customers get started quickly, trading in previous mobile phones when adding a line, configuring parental controls, WIFI, etc. Which of these videos were seen and watched by customers? How did that behavior then impact conversion goals?

Step 1: Configure Videos for Experience Analytics Data Collection

When specific videos are embedded in web or app screens, inter-action with the videos by tapping the "play button" is captured automatically by Experience Analytics. Without any additional tagging, we can see:

- How many users scrolled far enough to be exposed to the video?
- How attractive is the video, i.e., what ratio of customers that are exposed to the video tape to start watching it?
- How many users hit the stop button to interrupt the video before it finishes?
- What's the influence of all this, i.e., how does watching vs. stopping the video change downstream journey completion?

However, additional data is needed to answer customer marketers' more challenging questions so that they can manage their content marketing program. Namely,

- How long is each video played and viewed on average?
- Where in the video do customers give up and tap to stop watching it?
- If videos embedded in a player window on a given page aren't static but dynamic, for example, in a video streaming service, then which videos are users watching?
- What's the influence of this finer-grained behavior on down-stream journeys and conversion?

The video player needs to integrate with Experience Analytics to send the additional data items to capture this finer-grained detail. Ask your Experience Analytics provider to configure this integration.

Step 2: Which Videos Are Popular on Mobile vs. Desktop?

The customer marketing team first sought out to identify their most popular videos for users on mobile vs. desktop devices. It turned out that interest in videos was quite different between devices.

Funnily enough, the video on trading in the customer's old mobile phone was very popular when customers browsed from desktop devices. However, it was much less common for users to watch this video from their mobile phones. Instead, the most popular video on mobile was the quick start tutorial.

This information enabled the customer marketing team to target the right content to visitors on each type of device. That's already a much better experience than listing a long list of videos and potentially losing audiences because of TL;DR (too long; didn't read).

Step 3: Which Videos Are Not Engaging Enough or Are Too Long?

Ok, but how do we do better? So, the follow-up question by the customer marketing team was about how to improve the videos themselves by understanding where customers stop watching.

Definition: Video Completion Rate

The percentage of users that watch the video to the end (see Figure 8B.2).

Calculation

$$\frac{\text{Number of pageviews watching the video and completing it to the end}}{\text{Number of pageviews watching the video}}$$

Figure 8B.2 Video completion rate, calculation.

Definition: Video percentage watched

The portion of the video length that users watch on average (see Figure 8B.3).

Calculation

$$\frac{\text{Average number of seconds that users watch the video}}{\text{Total length of the video in seconds}}$$

Figure 8B.3 Video percentage watched, calculation.

The telecommunication company found that their instructional videos were the most successful by these metrics. Most customers that watched them completed them to the end.

In comparison, some of the promotional videos were less engaging. The average video percentage watched was only 46%. Those are the videos to revisit potentially.

Step 4: What's the Impact of Watching a Video?

Now, we come to the "So, what?" Which investments in videos are moving the needle for customer success and persuasion?

Definition: Video Impact Quantification

Contrast completion rates for targeted journeys for customers that did vs. didn't watch or complete the video.

In our case study, the video on trading in the customer's old mobile phone had the highest incremental impact on completing the checkout journey. Both for customers on desktop and mobile (see Figure 8B.4).

Page name	Title of video completed	Incremental impact on reaching checkout
Mobile Device Trade-In	Trade in your current mobile phone.	7%

Figure 8B.4 Example for reporting the impact of watching videos on conversion rate.

Step 5: Putting It All Together to Drive Action

Now, when we combine the fact that the video for trading in the old mobile phone has a high impact but isn't seen by customers on their mobile phones, we have actionable information at our hands. Namely, we need to either help more mobile customers find and play this video by improving its placement. Or, we need to provide this information in an alternative format if a video isn't the way that customers want to consume it on their mobile devices.

The Moral of the Story

While this case study was focused on video content, the same train of thought can be applied to any customer marketing content elements embedded within pages on the site and in the app. It's all about letting customers' behavior show you how they would like to be engaging with the brand.

C-SUITE Cheat Sheet for Solving the Challenge

We've already covered a general cheat sheet for helping marketers understand whether the content strategy is working and how to improve it, namely as part of the chapter on Brand and Content Marketing teams. Please refer to that cheat sheet for Customer Marketing purposes as well.

For that reason, in this C-SUITE cheat sheet, let's dive one level deeper to look at the common algorithm for improving video-based content marketing assets with the help of Experience Analytics (see Figure 8B.5).

Challenge 2: Improve Customer Marketing Campaign Results

Another mainstream use case is to improve results from customer campaigns by understanding what journeys work best for engagement and conversion, which don't, and how can we improve these. Just as

Challenge	Manage my video format content marketing assets based on their value for engaging and inspiring customers		
Surface	Which videos are not played as often as hoped?		Which videos lead to higher CVR vs. not?
Understand	Review success factors for both mobile and desktop devices.		
	In Journey Analysis, see whether traffic is reaching the pages with the video.	Using In-page Analysis, understand why customers do or don't play the video.	Where do they stop watching? What's the impact of that on conversions?
	How can you help more customers find and play the video or get the information in an alternate format?		How can you improve the video or shorten it?
Impact	Quantify the impact, i.e., potential value of improving videos, signposts, and placements.		
Test	Fix any issues, and/or test improving the design of the journeys.		
Evaluate	Why did the improvements win/lose? What were the biggest success factors we can learn for future tests?		

Figure 8B.5 Cheat sheet: Improve ROI on video-based marketing assets.

in acquisition marketing, the challenge for customer marketing is ultimately to increase exposure to marketing messages, reduce bounces, and improve results.

Case Study 1: How a UK Department Store Increased Loyalty Sales by 76% Per Campaign Day

Most major retailers provide loyalty programs as a win-win for customers and the brand. The brand gets permission to market and track a customer's purchases across channels. The customer, in return, earns rewards or discounts. Brands capitalize on that opportunity by orchestrating regular campaigns to their customer base. These often span multiple channels, from email and direct mail to personalized offers on the site and app.

The Challenge

The department store in our case study is running major loyalty campaigns every quarter. A lot of effort goes into these campaigns by the ecommerce and merchandising teams to get the content and offers right. But how can the Customer Marketing team improve their campaign orchestration to increase conversion rates and sales from these campaigns? After all, the outcome of these campaigns makes or breaks their quarterly bonus for the team.

Typically, loyalty campaigns offer steep discounts to customers. A way to increase sales would be to offer even bigger discounts but this would cut to the bone by crushing margins. How can the retailer increase response to campaigns without hurting their margins?

Step 1: What Journeys Are Working—Or Not—for Customers Responding to the Campaign?

Loyalty campaign emails drive customers back to the site to see their personal offers and browse the products. Where are the opportunities and issues in these journeys for loyalty program customers?

The experience visualization that best answers this question is Journey Analysis with segmentation for loyalty campaign customers.

Definition: How to Segment for Campaign Customers

To focus on campaign respondents, we need to filter the Journey Analysis for this group of site visitors. There are many easy ways to do this in Experience Analytics. The specific method will depend on your campaign setup.

For example, in the most straightforward case where campaign messages send customers to a unique landing page, Journey Analysis can be filtered on customers that started browsing on that entry page. The entry page is a standard filter option available in probably all digital analytics tools.

But how can we do this for offline campaigns, e.g., direct mail? When no specific entry page is available, a different way to segment is needed. Over the years, many brands have configured frequently used customer segments in their web analytics tools. In this case, by passing CRM data into their analytics.

Instead of duplicating this setup within the Experience Analytics tool, the ideal approach is to simply import the customer segments you have already created from your web analytics tool. That way, both systems leverage the exact definition. Ask your Experience Analytics provider how to configure this for your setup.

In the case of our UK department store, journeys showed a typical pattern (see Figure 8B.6). After clicking through from the loyalty campaign message, most customers tried to log in to the loyalty program member area. This was to access their loyalty offers. But Journey Analysis showed that too many of these customers repeatedly tried to log in and gave up, exiting the site.

Step 2: Why Are Customers Struggling with the Member Login?

A shortcut to session replays for these customers showed that most of them had simply forgotten their passwords. Some tried multiple times. Many did not even bother with the password recovery journey. They just gave up.

Step 3: Hypothesize a Better Design and A/B Test It

The Customer Marketing team addressed this challenge by pushing back the login wall. Instead of driving campaign visitors to the

JOURNEYS AFTER THE PAGE: MEMBER LOGIN

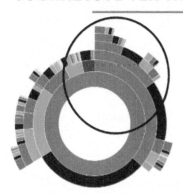

● Site exit

● Member Login

Figure 8B.6 Journey Analysis filtered on loyalty campaign customers.

member area, they directed them into the shopping flow to first engage and fall in love with the products. As is common practice in retail, they left the login for the bottom of the funnel after customers had committed themselves and added products to their bag.

Results and Value

As a result of this improvement and many other refinements that the team made over time, the Customer Marketing team increased their loyalty sales quarter by quarter. These improvements added up to:

- A 76% increase in loyalty sales per campaign day
- + 61% sales conversion rate on desktop
- + 22% sales conversion rate on mobile.

The Moral of the Story

It doesn't scale to increase sales by throwing more coupons at customers. But when customer marketing teams step into the shoes of their audiences, they can let customers show them how to fix leaks and reap the benefits.

Case Study 2: How a Retail Bank Increased Mobile App Downloads by 40%

Banking is the proverbial relationship business. These days, it goes without saying that a bank's mobile app is perhaps the top "branch" through which customers interact. Traffic on a bank's mobile app is often much higher than traffic on the bank's website. Both channels remain key, with the website driving most customer acquisition. But for customer marketers, the app is where their best and most loyal customers are to be found and served.

The Challenge

When new customers join the bank, driving them to download the mobile app is crucial in the customer life cycle. For the bank in our case study, the app was very successful. The more their customers adopted the app, the more loyal they became. In fact, at this bank, their app users have the highest NPS (Net promoter score) of all their digital channel users.

But how can the Customer Marketing team drive more new customers to download the app and do so earlier in the customer relationship? Despite heavy investment in content to drive interest in the app, actual downloads remained flat.

What's more, as with most financial institutions, any changes to the site's pages require legal approval. So, the team could not just run A/B tests randomly and hope that one of those A/B tests would bear fruit. They had to pinpoint the A/B test that would be most likely to move the needle on app downloads to focus internal efforts on getting permission for that test and nailing it.

Step 1: Are We Reaching Our Target Customers When Promoting the App?

As with many businesses, the bank in our case study has a web page that is the destination for encouraging customers to download their app. A call-to-action from the page goes to the Google and Apple app stores where customers can get the app.

The first question for troubleshooting their lackluster KPI for downloads is to confirm that traffic is reaching this page in sufficient numbers. The bank's Adobe Analytics confirmed that this was indeed the case, i.e., all the customer marketing efforts to bring customers to this page were successful.

So, why do they not download the app then?

Step 2: What Works vs. Doesn't for App Downloads from the Promotional Website Page?

The Customer Marketing team needed to answer the next question: What behaviors on the page lead to a successful click-through to the app store? And why are so many customers leaving the page without going to the app store? The Experience Analytics visualization of choice here is in-page analytics.

Step 2a: Do Customers See and Notice the Call-to-Action on the Page?

The first question for In-page Analysis is whether customers even see and notice the call-to-action for clicking through to the app stores. It's great that they reach the website page, but are they engaging with the page and spotting the call-to-action?

The Customer Marketing team looked at Exposure Rate (i.e., Scrolling) heatmaps to answer that question.

Definition : Exposure Rate

This metric identifies how far down the page the average visitor is scrolling. Understand which sections of the content are seen.

As so often, the call-to-action placement was not ideal and could be improved to increase exposure. But that's just the beginning of the story.

Step 2b : Is the Call-to-Action Attractive?

The next question before redesigning the page is whether customers that scroll far enough are attracted to the call-to-action and click on it? The Attractiveness Rate metric answers that question.

Definition : Attractiveness Rate

This metric translates the attractiveness of an element. It calculates the percentage of visitors who clicked on a zone after they are exposed to it (see Figure 8B.7).

Calculation

Number of views with zone displayed
and at least one click

Number of views with zone displayed

Figure 8B.7 Attractiveness Rate calculation.

It turns out they weren't attracted to it. The call-to-action was relatively small in size on the page (see Figure 8B.8).

Step 2c : Is Any of the Other Content on the Page Persuading Some Customers to Click the Call-to-Action?

The call-to-action was surrounded by lots of rich content to explain the merits of using the app. The customer marketers had poured out their soul to promote the app with lots of imagery and value statements. But were customers noticing and finding inspiration in this content? That question is answered by metrics such as exposure time

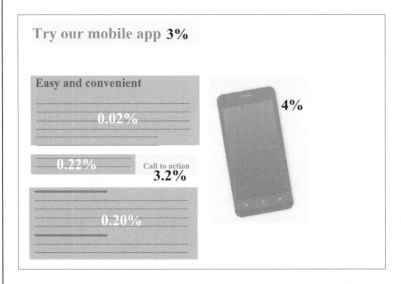

Figure 8B.8 Zone-based heatmap showing low Attractiveness Rate all around, including the call-to-action.

> **Definition : Exposure Time**
>
> It's the time that the mid-height pixel line of the zone is visible when displayed. This metric allows you to identify content zones and sections of pages viewed the longest during a pageview.

And what did the data show? Customers didn't engage with any of the other content. If they scrolled at all, they scrolled quickly and left. It was all "TL;DR."

Step 3: Hypothesize a Better Design Based on the Data and A/B Test It

The data revealed that customers didn't care for lengthy explanations about the mobile app. So, the Customer Marketing team put one and one together and cleaned up the page. They removed most of the content and instead featured the call-to-action much more clearly and prominently. This was the A/B test for which they sought legal approval.

Results and Value

Guess what, app downloads went up by 40%.

The Moral of the Story

Sometimes less is more. And today's customers are digitally savvy. They know what the app is for, expect the bank to provide one, and expect to find the app effortlessly.

C-SUITE Cheat Sheet for Solving the Challenge

In summary, Figure 8B.9 provides a cheat sheet for typical use of Experience Analytics to increase results from customer marketing campaigns.

Challenge 3: Gain Permission to Market and Improve the Targeting of Campaigns

Whenever customer-centric marketers learn about Experience Analytics data, what they get most excited about is its potential for enriching the

Challenge	Create more uplift from the customer campaigns that we are working on		
Surface	Segment on customer campaign traffic and …		
	Review whether engagement within the related landing pages and its impact on conversion is as planned and hoped.	Review journeys to look for signs of friction.	Score experiences for signs of frustration.
Understand	Look for common patterns:		
	What behaviors and engagement with content elements commonly lead to converting on the campaign offer vs. not?		Replay examples, understand points of friction.
	What enhancements will help more customers find the ideal path?		What would resolve the struggle & issues?
Impact	Quantify impact, i.e., potential value of improving.		
Test	Improve & test the enhanced campaign experiences.		Fix any bugs or issues.
Evaluate	Why did it win/lose? What were the biggest success factors we can learn for future tests?		

Figure 8B.9 Cheat sheet: Improve customer marketing campaign results.

targeting capabilities in their programs. After all, customer marketers have been turning data into predictive scores for targeted and personalized marketing for decades already. They score customers' propensity to purchase various products, next-best actions for engaging each customer, and churn risks. They do this based on the best data available to them. We'll cover examples and use cases in the third part of the book on emerging use cases.

Establishing Data Relationships

However, there is a classic use case and challenge for customer marketers that is a prerequisite for being able to target customers with campaigns outside their web and app sessions. Namely, it's about gaining permission to market via opt-in to messaging and tracking. By earning the trust of customers, by providing value and a good experience, brands have the opportunity to increase site registrations and opt-in to loyalty programs.

That's always been the case but as of this writing, the challenge has become top of mind for the industry. That's partially because of the GDPR data privacy laws in Europe that require opt-in to website cookies. But it's also because Google has announced that it is phasing out third-party website cookies from its Chrome browser by the end of 2024. Third-party cookies have been used for anonymous retargeting of visitors with relevant display ads based on their earlier behavior on the site. But if they get phased out, then retargeting and personalization beyond the current session on the site and app will require first-party registration and permission marketing.

That's why the entire digital ad tech industry is focused on customers' first-party registrations now.

Supplemental Case Studies on the Book's Accompanying Website

Check out the following case study on this book's accompanying website. It's an illustrative use case for Experience Analytics in the drive to first-party, loyalty program registrations.

Case Study: How a US Fashion Retailer Optimized Their Registration Drive for the Loyalty Program

https://ExperienceAnalytics.live/CaseStudies

Select the Fashion brand case study for chapter 8

Chapter 9

Solve Challenges Across the Entire Customer Journey

Among all the teams within Digital, there are at least two that are responsible for experiences across all stages of the customer lifecycle. Namely, the Product team is responsible for the experience anywhere in the journey, whether it's the home page or the conversion funnel, or the secure customer section of the site. Likewise, the Conversion Rate Optimization, Experimentation, and Analytics teams help understand and improve metrics anywhere in the journey.

For that reason, these teams share many use cases with other teams that we've already discussed earlier. However, this chapter will illuminate a few additional common challenges that keep these teams up at night. So let's step into their shoes to solve these challenges with them.

Chapter 9A: Solve Product Management and UX/CX Challenges

- Business Pressures
- Challenge 1: Let customers show you the way to innovate and prioritize roadmap
- Challenge 2: Find and fix experience issues faster to speed up release cycles and free up time for innovation

Chapter 9B: Solve Conversion Rate Optimization and Analytics Challenges

- Business Pressures
- Challenge 1: Democratize access to data for decisions
- Challenge 2: Find and eliminate bottlenecks for journey completion
- Challenge 3: Optimize form completions
- Challenge 4: Inform A/B test strategy
- Challenge 5: Understand customers and predict trends

DOI: 10.4324/b23273-12

Solve Product and UX/CX Challenges

If you were around back at the dawn of the World Wide Web in the early 1990s, you would still remember how most sites used to be static HTML pages, that is, electronic brochures. Today, sites and mobile apps are built on a complex stack of technologies enabling customers to accomplish their goals. Therefore, many digital businesses today think of their Web and app channels as a *product*, and Product Management is one of the hottest rising occupations within digital.

User Experience (UX) teams are often part of the Product organization. They enable Product teams to design products that provide meaningful and relevant experiences to users, as the Interaction Design foundation[1] defines it.

Customer Experience (CX) typically has a broader mission that goes beyond just the digital channel. CX ideally rolls up centrally across channels to a Chief Customer Officer or a Chief Experience Officer. The word *experience* is ingrained in UX and CX. So, it goes without saying that Experience Analytics is indispensable.

Figure 9A.1 shows a typical mindmap of what it's like to be in Product and UX teams. Both from the perspective of proactive innovation and enhancements, and also from the perspective of reacting to issues more quickly.

Business Pressures

Increasingly, Product teams pride themselves on driving product-led growth, that is, "a go-to-market strategy that relies on using your product as the main vehicle to acquire, activate, and retain customers," as author Wes Bush defines it.[2] That's a lot of pressure on the Product and the Product Team to "get it right." Even if most mainstream sites and apps benefit from traditional marketing efforts as the primary vehicle for acquisition, the activation and retention of their acquired customers heavily depend on the digital "Product." Based on all the stories we've

MINDMAP Product Team Proactively innovate & troubleshoot top-down		
CHALLENGES		
So many roadmap ideas but few resources—how do we prioritize?	The more agile and faster we release, the more we also introduce new issues by accident.	Most A/B tests fail to move the needle.
QUESTIONS TO ANSWER		
What content/features lead to success and we should help more users find them?	What frictions & bugs put customers off.	What's the intent and experience of different user segments?
Quantify impact to prioritize action. Tell our story visually to get "buy-in"		
SUCCESS CRITERIA		
Uncover opportunities to inform and prioritize roadmap.	Resolve issues proactively.	Enable agile product design.

MINDMAP Product Team Prioritize & resolve the biggest issues, working from bottom-up	
CHALLENGES	
For reported issues and complaints, how can we understand their impact and prioritize which ones to resolve faster?	
QUESTIONS TO ANSWER	
How can the team recreate the issues and identify the root cause?	How many others also get stuck on the same issues?
How can we separate outliers from the issues that really impact customers and the business?	
SUCCESS CRITERIA	
Prioritize and fix the issues that matter before it's too late.	Free up time to innovate more.

Figure 9A.1 Typical Product/UX Team mind map.

already covered, it's clear that Experience Analytics has a mission-critical role to play.

Millions of Ideas, But Only Enough Capacity to Work on a Few of Them

There is no shortage of ideas, but there is always a shortage of capacity. Product Managers usually prioritize their potential roadmap by the expected impact on goals vs. effort. Then, when it comes time to implement the top roadmap ideas, they usually get told, "OK, so which three of your ten most mission-critical, must-have, can't-live-without, P0 items do you want us to address? Because that's all that we've got people and time for." That hurts!

This challenge is exacerbated by the fact that capacity is typically divided between fixing and enhancing existing experiences vs. having time left over to create new ones. Not to mention that periodic re-platforming and acquisitions, and mergers of new brands into the business often require integrating new systems, eating up additional time and bandwidth.

Everybody Has an Opinion, But How Can We Let Customers Speak, Not Just the HIPPO

Everybody has an opinion on what's wrong with the product (i.e., website and app) and what would be great to improve. Everybody feels like an expert. And when it comes to the Highest Paid Person's Opinion (HIPPO), it naturally sways the boat's direction (e.g. see Figure 9A.2). After all, that's what they get paid for. But without data, it should be "just another opinion."

Figure 9A.2 Dilbert on Product Management woes. Not funny, if you are a product manager or UX professional[3]. DILBERT © 2013 Scott Adams, Inc. Used By permission of ANDREWS MCMEEL SYNDICATION. All rights reserved.

So, how can Product teams let data speak? And how can they let that data demonstrate how customers would like to interact with the brands and their digital channels, not just what the employees assume they do?

That's even more mission-critical for UX professionals. They can often sense where the issues are. But they need data to quantify the business impact to get buy-in for their solutions.

Product Teams Want to Manage Roadmap by Outcomes, But They Need a Way to Measure the Impact of Their Work

The Product Team's challenge is to build a product that will help customers, and the business, achieve their goals while providing the best experience. To do that, they need a way to assess the impact of potential enhancements and ideas. So, of course, they need first to understand their users, their intent, and their pains. They also need a way to quantify issues and potential benefits. Traditional Web and Product Analytics capture click-based behaviors, but they leave a blindspot to all the behavior and problems between clicks. As a result, they don't provide insight into intent, pains, and experience.

Product and UX/CX Team Challenges and Use Cases

It's already clear from the business pressures that being in the Product team is not just a hot and exciting job but also highly challenging. So let's look at typical use cases in the days of life in the Product and UX/CX Teams.

- Challenge 1: Let customers show you the way to innovate and prioritize roadmap
- Challenge 2: Find and fix experience issues faster to speed up release cycles and free up time for innovation

Challenge 1: Let Customers Show You the Way to Innovate and Prioritize Roadmap

Let's start with the most difficult but potentially the most beneficial use case, that is, proactively innovating the best new ideas to improve outcomes. Even where there is no customer friction or issue, what redesign, A/B test, or new launch is most likely to move the needle in a lasting way?

Case Study 1: How Juniqe's Product Team Improved Acquisition by Reducing Bounce Rates for Targeted Segments from 55% to 9%

Juniqe is an online art retailer operating out of Berlin, Germany. They are on a mission to help customers "turn their four walls into a home by adding their personal touches in the form of wall art and decor." "Art with character, a community passionate about design, and finding inspiration at every corner—this is JUNIQE's founding philosophy. As long as our customers are happy and excited, so am I," as Juniqe founder Lea Lange says.

In that sentence, you see the ideal customer-oriented attitude for letting customers show the way to create a better experience. The only thing more important to Juniqe than their passion for art and artists is to make sure that their customers are happy and excited.

The Challenge

Juniqe's website was designed with a passion for art and artists, giving both ample real estate on their product pages because the assumption is that both are equally critical to their customers when they are designing their home.

Very typical for many businesses, customers enter the site not necessarily on the home page but land on a Product Display Page coming in from a Web search. And very typical for most businesses, Juniqe had a 55% bounce rate on this traffic, that is, very much in line with industry benchmarks.

However, reducing this bounce rate posed a massive opportunity for increasing flow into the shopping funnel. It's the ideal traffic, organic, and looking for art or an artist. So what should the Product team invest in to capture these potential customers' interest?

Step 1: Look at What's Working vs. Not for Engagement

Saúl Trujillo Suárez leads the Product team at Juniqe. As almost always in these situations, his team started analyzing the blocks of content on the landing page. What's driving engagement on the PDP, and what is being ignored? Are there any golden paths for customers that we can learn from?

We need to dive into an in-page analysis for customers arriving on the PDP as their entry page for this question. A great metric to use when addressing questions about bounce rate is Attractiveness Rate.

Definition: Attractiveness Rate

What content gets customers clicking if they are exposed to it? (It's the opposite of bouncing, after all.)

Definition: How to Segment on Incoming Traffic

Most digital analytics tools can filter analysis based on entry or exit page. In this case, Saúl's team filtered their analysis on the PDP as the entry page.

What jumps out in Figure 9A.3 is that the content above the fold is very attractive. However, when it comes to content under the fold, some elements are more attractive to customers than others. Specifically, the section "Similar products we recommend" has a

Figure 9A.3 Juniqe, Zone-based heatmap with Attractiveness Rate.

much higher Attractiveness Rate (26.12%) than some content higher up on the page. However, the product recommendations were so far down the page that most customers weren't scrolling far enough to notice them.

Step 2: Understand What Customers Are Saying Through Their Behavior

It seems that a significant portion of the traffic landing on the site via search is open to exploring similar art by other artists. They are not yet in the moment of their journey where they want to deep-dive into the specific artist's work that they landed on. They are still "window shopping."

The premise is that if we can help customers achieve their goals and purpose for visiting the site, it will be a win-win-win for the customers, the artist community, and of course, Juniqe.

Step 3: Innovate and A/B Test Based on the Hypothesis

Saúl and his team designed a variation based on the insight above and additional analysis of behaviors). The PDP test variation provides customers with many avenues to continue their exploration via an added secondary navigation and featuring product recommendations very high up on the PDP (see Figure 9A.4).

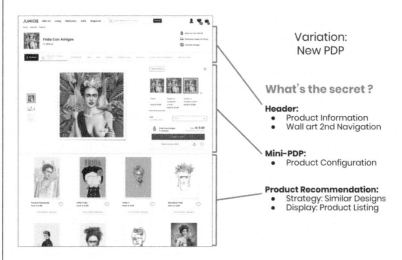

Figure 9A.4 Juniqe's new PDP design for A/B testing.

254 Solve Business Challenges Faster with Experience Analytics

The Result and Value

There are a million things that Saúl's Product team could have tried in A/B testing the PDP. But by letting customers show them their intent and desired way to browse the content, they hit gold.

Bounce rate reduced from 55% to 9% for large targeted segments throughout their testing efforts. It's easy to imagine how much that means to the business!

The Moral of the Story

It takes a mature product organization to let the voice of customers speak, as represented through their data. It seems much faster for a customer-centric strategy to do what we believe is right for serving customers based on our assumptions and opinions. But as Sun Tzu is quoted, that would be an example of "Strategy without tactics is the slowest route to victory."

Case Study 2: How Beerwulf's Product Team Improved Flow from the PLP by Understanding Their Customers' Intent

We already encountered Beerwulf earlier in the book. They are an online beer shop with a tempting range of beer cases, beer kegs, and beer taps. Beerwulf features over 600 beers from 150+ craft brewers from 20+ countries to choose from. The website provides fans with detailed and exciting stories about every beer and brewery.

The Challenge

As all Product teams can relate, the Beerwulf team prioritized enhancements based on value for customers and the business. So what does the data say about customers' wants and needs?

Step 1: Review Customer Journeys for Opportunities

As so often when nothing is particularly wrong, the Beerwulf Product team started with Journey Analysis to understand opportunities for further improvements.

The team saw that many visitors were showing a looping behavior between the product list and product detail pages. For example,

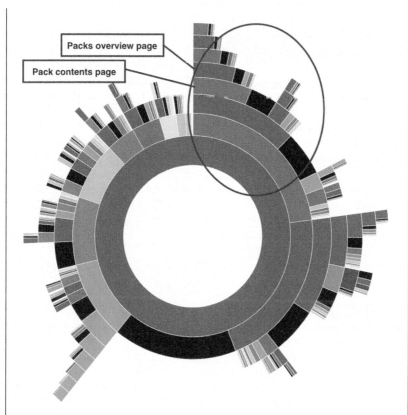

Figure 9A.5 Journey Analysis showing a looping behavior between the PLP and the PDP.

people were going back and forth to try and compare the contents of the pack displayed on the product detail page (See Figure 9A.5).

Beerwulf's packs are one of their most emblematic product categories, so it provides a lot of value to customers to ensure that this page is working well.

Step 2: Hypothesis on Customer Intent and Action

The Beerwulf Product team deduced that customers were going into these loops to compare the contents of various packs to choose one. So the hypothesis became that if Beerwulf can make it easier for customers to see and compare the contents of the packs, this would give customers a much better experience.

Figure 9A.6 The test variation with the ability to view the contents of packs was adopted by 8% of shoppers.

Step 3: A/B Testing and Value Achieved

What the Beerwulf Product team decided, as a result, is to enable shoppers to see the contents of a pack with a tap right from the PLP. This solution was easy to use on mobile devices too. Instead of going from the PLP to the PDP for the pack, they could immediately compare the contents of packs right on the PLP (See Figure 9A.6).

The test was very successful: 8% of the users on the PLP adopted the new feature leading to a 2.4% overall conversion rate increase from the PLP. That's a major win!

The Moral of the Story

Customers reward the business for the right investments in experiences. Opportunities are always there, waiting to be discovered even where there is no friction or struggle. We just need to put opinions aside and let customer data guide us.

Supplemental Case Studies Online : How the Mobile App Product Team at a European Retail Group Increased Sales by Half a Million Per Month

Whatever challenge Product teams may have with managing their Web channel, that challenge is tenfold on their apps Apps are a no-joke, legitimate software development project that requires brands to be as good at development as any full-time software company. So check out this typical case study in the book's online materials.

https://ExperienceAnalytics.live/CaseStudies

Select the Mobile App case study for Chapter 9

C-SUITE Cheat Sheet for Solving the Challenge

In summary, here is a visual overview of common ways in which Product teams inform and prioritize roadmap based on better understanding their customers, what makes them happy, and what frustrates them (see Figure 9A.7).

Challenge 2: Find and Fix Experience Issues Faster to Speed Up Release Cycles and Free Up Time for Innovation

As with Ecommerce and Ebusiness managers, Product and UX teams are also equally invested in finding and fixing struggles and errors that are hurting their desired outcomes. The faster those friction points are found and resolved, the quicker potential losses are recovered, and resources are freed up to focus on innovation. After all, innovation is where the real upside opportunity is found.

It doesn't matter whether the struggle is due to UX issues or technical errors and performance. Whatever the root cause, anything causing frustration needs to be identified, prioritized by impact, and resolved.

We've already covered examples of finding and fixing technical errors and performance issues in the section for Operations teams. We've also covered Voice of Customer use cases in the section on Customer Feedback Management teams. So, in this chapter, we'll focus instead on case studies for UX issues.

Challenge	Letting customers guide better roadmap decisions and prioritization			
Surface	Compare goals for your product experiences vs. actual user journeys. See whether you are hitting expectations for micro-conversions. For example, on landing pages, are bounce rates low and traffic is flowing into the site/app at high rates?			
	Do journeys show signs of opportunities, e.g., high engagement?		Do journeys show signs of friction, e.g., high effort, looping, or premature exits at certain pages?	
Understand	Look for common patterns within those pages.			
	Do in-page behaviors reveal a previously undiscovered intent?	In-page, look for deviations from the "ideal path" you designed content for.	Which content elements/ behaviors are associated with success vs. not?	Compare successful vs. unsuccessful engagement with the content elements.
	What new experience would better serve this intent?	What changes will help more users find the ideal path and move the needle?		
Impact	Quantify business impact, i.e., potential value of improving.			
Test	Prioritize, develop & test the new designs.			
Evaluate	Why did the test win/lose? What were the biggest success factors we can learn for future tests?			

Figure 9A.7 Cheat sheet: Prioritize roadmap based on the potential impact.

Case Study 1: How the Mobile App Product Team at a Sports Retailer Reduced App Abandonment on the Home Screen to One-Sixth

As a modern retailer serving a hip target audience, the Product team at this Sports retailer took inspiration from one of the best experiences on the Internet, that is, Google Search. They designed their app's home page to feature a prominent search bar at the top to help users quickly find what they are looking for. Menus are less popular with mobile users anyways, so this seemed like a good idea. They relegated the menu to the bottom of the screen instead. It's an approach that you can see with other apps too, for example, Amazon's app.

Step 1: Use Journey Analysis to Identify What's Working/Not

The design launched with big expectations. But a quick look at Journey Analysis showed the Product team that much to their dismay, they had a problem. The app now had a higher exit rate from the home screen than before (See Figure 9A.8).

Even more puzzling, some users viewed the app's home page multiple times in a row and then still exited the app anyways.

Step 2: Answer Why Users Are Exiting with In-Page Analytics and Session Replay

Zooming into this problem with in-page analysis, the retailer saw that less than a quarter of users interacted with the search bar (See Figure 9A.9). Given that this was supposed to be the number one

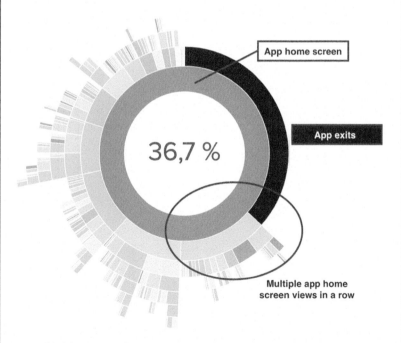

Figure 9A.8 Journey Analysis shows a high exit rate from the App's home page, i.e., 36.7% bouncing.

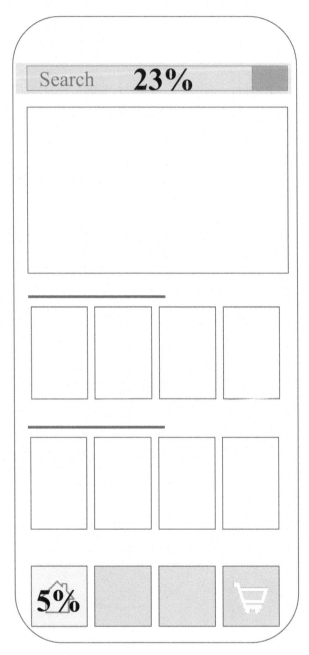

Figure 9A.9 Zone-based heatmaps showing a 23% tap rate on the search bar and a 5% tap rate on the home button.

way they designed for all shoppers to begin their journey into the app, it was clear that too many users did not understand what they were meant to do.

Additionally, session replays for users that bounced showed them quickly scrolling up/down on the home page, and some of them were eventually clicking on the "home" button while they were already on the home screen. That explains why some users viewed the home page multiple times in a row.

Users were perplexed about the innovative design of this app's home page.

Step 3: Redesign

Seeing this, the retailer redesigned the home screen simply by making the traditional menu options at the bottom of the screen much easier to spot by coloring it with much bolder colors.

Step 4: A/B Test and Value Achieved

The fix was very successful. Abandonment of the app went down to one-sixth of the earlier bounce rate. In addition, the conversion rate from the home screen increased by an incredible 23%.

Interestingly, interactions with the search bar also increased by 20%. Once users understood how the home page functions, they were back in their comfort zone. They knew that they had both search and a traditional menu at their fingertips and tapped whichever they preferred.

The Moral of the Story

Innovation is hard. You are going where no brand has gone before. You are doing it because your brand is unique, your target audience is unique, and you are trying to differentiate via your digital channel.

Frequently, however, the best thought-out ideas don't work out the way that the Product team imagined. The ability to quickly troubleshoot when and why this is happening is mission-critical so Product teams can course-correct rapidly. Innovation and troubleshooting go hand in hand. The more agile you are with improving your site and apps, the faster you need to troubleshoot these experiences.

Why does that matter? App users are a brand's most valuable customers. For that reason, experience issues that hit app users hit the business where it hurts the most.

Case Study 2: How Škoda Increased Test Drive Visits by 40%

Škoda is a Czech automobile manufacturer founded over a hundred years ago in 1895. Today, they are a wholly-owned subsidiary of the Volkswagen Group. As with many car manufacturers, that is, OEMs as they call themselves, Skoda.com serves a central role in driving demand for the brand.

Škoda's goal was to optimize customer experience with their brand online. The particular focus in this case study from 2020[4] was on booking test drives via the website. Test drives are vital in progressing the customer's car purchase journey. With much pre-purchase research taking place online, Škoda's website is also the perfect place for prospective customers to visualize how their dream car might look and feel. On-site tools such as the Škoda Toolkit (including a Car Configurator and Finance Calculator) facilitate this.

The Challenge

Škoda UK wanted to encourage visitors to request a test drive by increasing the number of interactions with ŠKODA's Toolkit. The Toolkit provides potential drivers with a range of functionality, including test drive bookings, a Finance Calculator, Find a Retailer, and the Car Configurator.

Step 1: Understand Journeys Leading Up to Using the Škoda Toolkit and Booking Test Drives

A journey anomaly jumped out, indicating potential areas of confusion to improve. Namely, a portion of users was looping between the Homepage and New Cars page.

Step 2: Understand Why Users Experience Friction and How to Improve

As always, when trying to answer why a behavior is happening, in-page analytics are the go-to visualization. In this case, the Click Rate metric in Zone-based heatmaps showed that very few users were clicking the Toolkit. It was located at the bottom of the page. The Exposure Rate metric showed that less than 20% of users on the page scrolled far enough to see the toolkit (See Figure 9A.10).

When site users didn't see the toolkit, they lacked clarity on where to take their journey from there.

Figure 9A.10 Analysis of a car model page with the Exposure Rate metric on the Škoda site. Only 19.6% of users reach the toolkit content.

Figure 9A.11 Test variation informed by data in Fall 2020.

Step 3: Design an Improved Product Display Page

This data led the team to highlight the visibility of the toolkit by implementing a "sticky tools" navigation on the right side of the page (see in green on Figure 9A.11).

A/B Test and Value Achieved

The enhancements informed by customer behavior drove a +40% increase in test drive visits. They also generated improvements to the other call to action in the toolkit, that is, a +10% increase in visits to the Finance Calculator, +12% visits to Find a Retailer, and +3% to Car Configurator.

The Moral of the Story

There is always talk about customer-centric business. In this case, the original design of the page was no doubt aiming to be conscious of customers' mindset, that is, provide information first and then show the call to action afterward. Surely drivers will want to see the information first before they are ready to engage with the toolkit?

But we repeatedly see that we cannot guess what digital customers' behavior will be. So we need to measure their experience and let the data tell us what will work best for our customers.

Supplemental Case Studies Online : How a Luxury Fashion Retailer Discovered a Surprising Confusion with Their New Gift Packaging Options

As we said, the faster you release as a Product team, the quicker you want to scan the new experience for any unexpected signs of struggle. Your early customers on the new experience are not supposed to be guinea pigs. But, their behaviors can still guide how to improve the experience for all users that follow them.

Check out this supplemental case study online where a luxury fashion retailer uncovered a surprising confusion with their newly released gift packaging options.

https://ExperienceAnalytics.live/CaseStudies

Select the Luxury Fashion brand case study for chapter 9

C-SUITE Cheat Sheet for Solving the Challenge

In summary, Figure 9A.12 highlights common ways in which Product teams troubleshoot their products by revealing unexpected points of confusion and friction, regardless of whether it is due to UX gaps or outright defects.

Challenge	Find and fix experience issues in (new) Product experiences to speed up release cycles and free up time for innovation		
Surface	Review whether engagement inside related pages and impact on conversion is as planned and hoped.	Review journeys across the experiences to look for signs of friction.	Score new experiences for signs of frustration.
Understand	Look for common patterns.		
	What behaviors and content interactions commonly lead to engagement with the product and its call-to-actions vs. not?	What leads to higher CVR & LTV*?	Replay examples, understand points of friction.
	What enhancements will help more users take advantage of the ideal path and increase CVR & customer LTV*?		What would resolve the issues?
Impact	Quantify impact, i.e., potential value of improving.		
Test	Re-develop & test new designs.		Fix any bugs or issues.
Evaluate	Why did the investments win/lose? What were the biggest success factors we can learn for future tests?		

Figure 9A.12 Cheat sheet: Understand what puts customers off (* CVR = Conversion rate, LTV = Customer lifetime value).

Solve Conversion Rate Optimization and Analytics Challenges

It's the age of data. The opportunity is for companies to compete on analytics. Using data is everybody's responsibility. But there is one team that is 100% tasked with providing data-driven intelligence that facilitates better decisions and outcomes throughout the business. That team goes by many names. Nowadays, in digital business units, this team is increasingly called Digital Intelligence & Insights. But you may more simply find them referred to as Analytics, Conversion Rate Optimization (CRO), Experimentation, or ultimately Business Intelligence (BI). In short, we'll simply refer to this team as Analytics in this chapter; here is a typical mindmap of what it's like to be in their shoes (See Figure 9B.1).

Business Pressures

With such a broad mission, the pressures are endless. So let's highlight just a few top-level ones here.

Turn Data into a Competitive Weapon for the Business

The Analytics team owns the responsibility to be clear, clever, and creative with turning data into intelligence that will enable the business to grow and prevail in its marketplace. That is a broad mission that requires beating their peers at other companies at their game.

Enable Data-Driven Decisions for All

Analytics teams are often at the mercy of never-ending report requests from the rest of the organization. Naturally, they hate when others see them as "report squirrels." But, if they don't democratize access to data for their colleagues so that they can answer more simple questions by

MINDMAP
Analytics Team
Proactively innovate & troubleshoot top-down

CHALLENGES		
Compete on analytics.	Better understand customers. Create uplift more often from A/B testing.	Free up time by democratizing access to data.

QUESTIONS TO ANSWER		
Where are our bottlenecks for conversion and growth? Why? How do we solve them?	How do we inform our A/B test strategy?	What are our customers' wants and needs?
Quantify impact to prioritize action. Tell our story visually to get "buy-in."		

SUCCESS CRITERIA		
Improve conversion proactively.	Inform/prioritize roadmap and A/B testing.	Inform customer centric strategy.

MINDMAP
Analytics Team
Prioritize & resolve the biggest issues, working from bottom-up

CHALLENGES
For reported issues, and unexpected behaviors, how can we understand why they are happening, what is their impact and, what should we do about them?

QUESTIONS TO ANSWER	
How can we recreate the issues and behaviors to identify the cause and intent?	How can we separate outliers from the issues that really impact customers and the business?

SUCCESS CRITERIA	
Prioritize and fix the issues that matter before it's too late.	Free up time to innovate more.

Figure 9B.1 Typical Analytics Team mind map.

themselves, analysts will never have time to answer the million-dollar questions that only they can figure out. Besides, they will go insane!

Just like the customer experience is too important to be only some teams' responsibility, data is also too important to be the responsibility of only the Analytics team.

Tell Compelling Stories with the Data

It's the dream of Analytics teams to become the hero of the business. Yet, to achieve that, it's not enough to find insights. They also need to persuade everyone else in the company to take action. So, it's mission-critical to build an effective narrative with the data. They need to show in a convincing way what is happening, why it is happening, what the impact is on customers and the business, and what they should do about it.

That requires access to deeper data and impact metrics besides just surface-level statistics. And it requires the ability to produce intuitive visuals that enable colleagues to step into their customers' shoes.

Challenges and Use Cases of CRO and Analytics Teams

Data is a formidable opportunity but also a fierce challenge. That's why this chapter for CRO and Analytics teams has a longer list of challenges than we've covered for other teams. And even this list just scratches the surface really for Analytics teams.

- Challenge 1: Democratize access to data for decisions
- Challenge 2: Find and eliminate bottlenecks for journey completion
- Challenge 3: Optimize form completions
- Challenge 4: Inform A/B test strategy
- Challenge 5: Understand customers and predict trends

Challenge 1: Democratize Access to Data for Decisions

Democratizing access to data is essential. An analytics practitioner in Germany once phrased this challenge in a particularly German manner of saying things: "I need to enable my colleagues to answer the stupid questions themselves, so I don't have to do it for them."

Experience Analytics can help alleviate this challenge because, unlike tabular reporting and bar charts, Experience Analytics can provide intuitive visuals and metrics that everybody can understand and act on. Let's see a case study of that.

Case Study: Why Do People Seem Not to Like Free Beer?

In this case study, we visit the Marketing team at the company I work at, namely Contentsquare. As a B2B2C company, Contentsquare's Marketing team works to engage prospective clients for their opportunity to improve experiences for their customers. Let's see how Marketers at Contentsquare used data for answering a challenge with one of their campaigns.

In the words of my colleague Catlin Roberge, she told the story in her blog post.[5]

> Contentsquare's marketing team ran a campaign in summer 2020 offering a custom consultation with UX experts over a cold beer—delivered straight to the home of the prospective customer. Because who can say no to the offer of refreshing yourself and your website at the same time? As it turns out, quite a few people.

The Challenge

> The marketing team had gifted brews in the past and knew just how popular the opportunity for free beer can be. Surprising people with beer was one of the highest performing direct-mail campaigns that Contentsquare ran in 2019. Showing up to the office and receiving an unexpected box filled with eight different craft beers delighted many people enough to take the time to chat.
>
> That insight, of course, comes from a pre-COVID era. Quite a few things shifted in 2020. So, instead of sending beers to the office world to charm people into taking meetings, we started offering digital consultations over a cold one. On the marketing campaign landing page, we asked prospects to sign up for a quick chat with the promise to get beers delivered straight to their home to enjoy during the meeting or after (see Figure 9B.2). The surprise may have been taken away, but the free beer remained, and that's all that mattered, right?
>
> Not exactly. Campaign results remained far behind the success of 2019 initially. Why and what could be done to turn the campaign around?"

Normally, you have to call in the Analytics team to the rescue. But thanks to democratized access to insights, Catlin and the team solved the mystery themselves.

Digital Consultation With a "cold one"

Refresh yourself
and your website

Your Name

Company

Email address

Submit

Scroll down for more info ⌕.

What's included with your free "hoppy our" consultation:

Figure 9B.2 Illustration of the "free beer" campaign landing page.

Step 1: What Is vs. Isn't Engaging Prospective Customers on the Campaign Landing Page?

The Marketing team activated their live browsing heatmaps to see what was working and, more importantly, what wasn't on the campaign landing page.

Definition: Live Browsing Heatmaps

Users can browse their website and overlay experience metrics (e.g. see Figure 9B.3). The purpose of this is to make access to Experience Analytics as easy as browsing your own website.

The data displayed are the same as in regular Zone-based heatmaps. But business users credit the easier accessibility with the greater daily use of Experience Analytics. For example, when a question comes up during a meeting, such as: "what was the most popular content for this campaign?" they use Experience Analytics to answer it immediately.

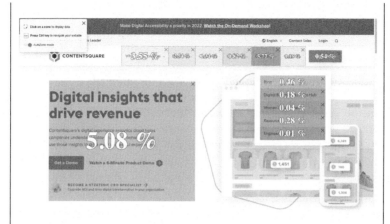

Figure 9B.3 Example of using a browser extension for overlaying experience metrics over a home page.

As the Marketing team confirmed, prospective customers were getting to the page. Unfortunately, they just weren't converting—but why?

> We started by investigating click-based metrics. Where were the hot zones on our page? Were any elements particularly frustrating to our landing page visitors?
>
> Our first move was clear. One of the highest clicked elements on the page wasn't even clickable! Rookie mistake. Namely, an arrow meant to signify that scrolling down would reveal more details about the offer was not relaying that message.
>
> We also checked our click recurrence and noticed that this element wasn't just getting clicked, but getting clicked multiple times! The frustration was visible.

Step 2: Remove Visitor Frustration

To start, we removed the arrow and replaced it with the copy, "Scroll down for more info 👇." Just like that, no more clicking frustration.

But when we checked our Exposure Rate, we were surprised to find that 50% of our header content (and the CTA!) still wasn't seen by almost half of our visitors. We may be offering eight hand-selected craft beers, but what good is it if no one sees the offer?

Step 3: Bring Essential Info Above the Fold

Next, we shrunk the top banner to make sure the most relevant content is above the page fold and entices visitors to scroll down to learn more.

One of our biggest quick wins was to make sure the submit button was visible when you loaded the page. So it was time to cut the dead weight in the contact form and bring that button further up the page. We turned back to our click rate and noticed that 2.58% of visitors clicked to add their postal code, but only 1.28% clicked to select their state. Did we need the state if we knew the postal code? No.

Step 4: Increase CTA Attractiveness

The last thing we checked was the Attractiveness Rate, or what percentage of visitors seeing the call to action (CTA) is likely to click on it. Turns out, our CTA at the very bottom of the page, or "Book My Hoppy Hour," was a very popular option for the people who actually reached the bottom of the page. So we had some good news, something was working as it should.

Results and Value

We saw immediate improvement once we made these slight tweaks to our simple landing page. Our page visitors were finding the information they needed to feel more confident booking a meeting, and the requests started rolling in.

People do still like free beer! But, it's not just about the result; it's about the journey they have to take to get there.

The Moral of the Story

Even at a technology provider for Digital Experience Analytics, masters are made, not born. So we all need to look at the data and take our direction from there. "Experience Analytics helps uncover exactly how prospects and customers navigate the digital experiences we create. And sometimes, a few small tweaks can have big results."

C-SUITE Cheat Sheet

We already covered a C-SUITE cheat sheet for landing page optimization in the chapter for Marketing teams. Refer back to that one when you are tackling campaign conversion questions.

Challenge 2: Find and Eliminate Bottlenecks for Journey Completion

The daily bread and butter of Digital Analytics teams are to find bottlenecks for conversion and prioritize them for resolution proactively. Here is a case study from the highly accomplished Web analytics team at a well-known shoe brand.

Supplemental Case Study Online : How a Famous Shoe Brand Identified and Removed UX Challenges for Their Shoe Shoppers

Everything was humming away pretty well on this shoe brand's regional websites. But as always, their analytics team was systematically investigating what could go even better at each journey stage.

That's when in this case study, they also took a look at the Product Display Page (PDP) and discovered an unexpected frustration for customers.

https://ExperienceAnalytics.live/CaseStudies

Select the shoe brand case study for chapter 9

C-SUITE Cheat Sheet for Solving the Challenge

In summary, here is a blueprint for common ways in which Analytics Teams identify bottlenecks, get to the bottom of what's happening, and prioritize what solution to recommend.

Analysts hardly need a blueprint for their work since they are curious and imaginative by nature. They will let the data and their intuition lead the set of questions that they will ask when they investigate a challenge. Nonetheless, the cheat sheet in Figure 9B.4 shows a typical structure for troubleshooting conversion issues.

Challenge	Proactively find and eliminate bottlenecks for journey completion		
Surface	Review Web Analytics drop-off reports to pinpoint leaks from the funnel.	Review Journey, Error, and Speed Analysis for signs of confusion, struggle, bugs.	Score experiences automatically for signs of friction.
Understand	Review in-page analytics to understand what's happening and why, especially Zone-based heatmaps and session replays.		
	What behaviors and what context (e.g., browser) are commonly associated with success vs. abandonment?	Which content elements are associated with the issues?	What's the root cause, e.g., UX, errors, or speed?
Impact	Quantify impact, i.e., potential value of improving.		
Test	Fix the issues, and/or test improving the design of the experiences.		
Evaluate	Why did the improvements win/lose? What were the biggest success factors we can learn for future tests?		

Figure 9B.4 Cheat sheet: Troubleshoot conversion bottlenecks.

Challenge 3: Optimize Form Completions

Improving form completions is a unique skill needed for conversion optimization. However, it's such an everyday use case that it deserves its dedicated section and case studies. After all, the conversion process ultimately requires completing a form on almost any site.

Form Analysis is a systematic way to troubleshoot form experiences. The Form Analysis toolset within Experience Analytics has come a long way over the years and helps analysts diagnose issues quickly.

Case Study I: How a Car Rental Company Made Their Forms Easier to Use

In our first case study, we will encounter all the traditional Form Analysis metrics used for a decade already to smoothen the form completion process. Our example here is from a car rental company. If online forms at Financial Services sites are the biggest troublemakers, those at travel and transportation sites are probably a close second in terms of complexity.

The Challenge

Completed bookings came in every day from the truck rental portion of this car rental company's site. But where were all those yet-to-be-discovered points of friction that were losing some potential customers? Moving is stressful enough, so how can we make life easier for customers about to rent a van?

Step 1: Top-Down Form Analysis

The first step in a systematic Form Analysis starts with the form funnel (e.g. see Figure 9B.5). This provides a bird's-eye view of where to look for issues in form completion. But, unfortunately, that's when the analysts found that only a painful 12.5% of potential customers on mobile successfully submitted the form after interacting with it.

Using the example in our case study, we can methodically troubleshoot the form with the help of the form completion funnel.

1. *How many customers don't even bother with the form?*
   Of the 100% of potential customers that arrive on this form page, how many exit without interacting with the form? In this case study, that was a huge 60.1%. Whenever this ratio is too high, Analytics teams want to investigate whether the form looks too daunting at first glance. Could it be too much asking customers to complete such a form so early in their journeys when they haven't seen value yet and have no reason to trust the brand?

2. *Of those that begin the form, how many drop out before submitting it?*
   Of the 39.9% that started interacting with the form, how many interacted but did not submit? In this case, that's 8.8%. When this number is too big, we want to look for friction and errors for users interacting with the form fields.

3. *Of those that try to submit, how many fail?*
   Of the 31.1% that submitted the form, how many tried but failed to submit? That's 18.6% in the example shown. We always want to bring this number as close to zero as possible. It usually suggests struggle and confusion with form validation errors, but it can also surface technical errors that prevent customers from proceeding.

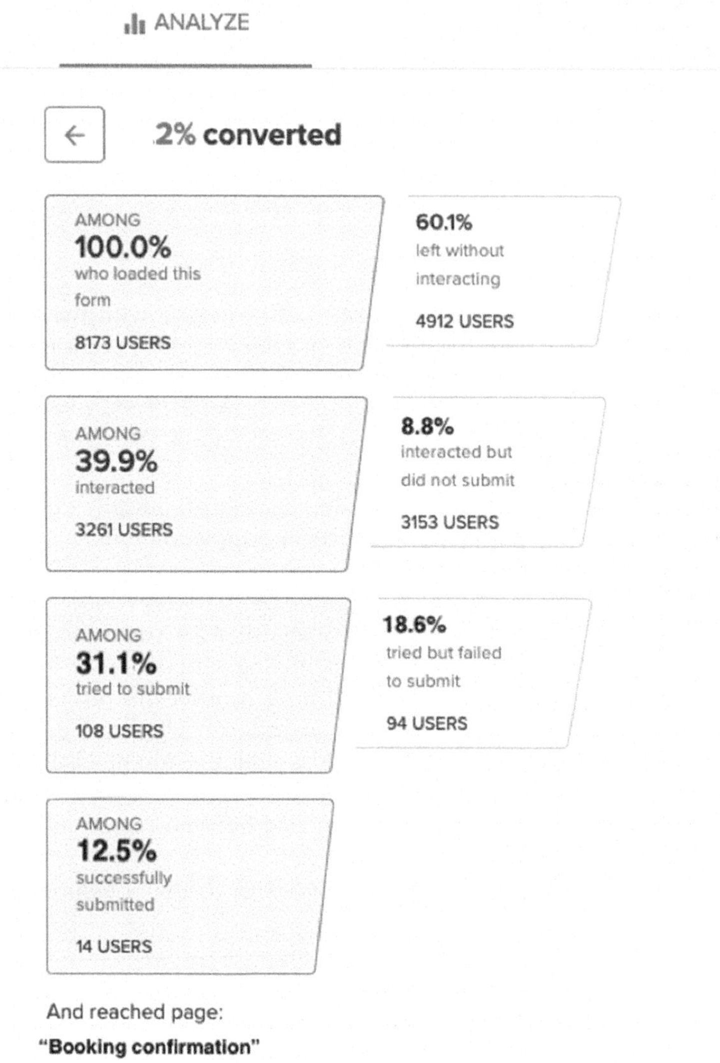

ılı ANALYZE

←   **.2% converted**

AMONG
100.0%
who loaded this
form

8173 USERS

60.1%
left without
interacting

4912 USERS

AMONG
39.9%
interacted

3261 USERS

8.8%
interacted but
did not submit

3153 USERS

AMONG
31.1%
tried to submit

108 USERS

18.6%
tried but failed
to submit

94 USERS

AMONG
12.5%
successfully
submitted

14 USERS

And reached page:
"Booking confirmation"

Figure 9B.5 A typical form completion funnel report.

But where were the problems for the truck rental form in our case
study? The form is compact and seems obvious.

So they needed to dig into interactions at the form-field level to
find out where all the dead bodies were buried.

Step 2: In Which Order Are Customers Interacting with the Form?

One behavior that often surprises product owners is that customers aren't necessarily completing their form fields in the expected order. Finding out about this can be a first hint to where the form is making customers think too much.

Definition: Time Before First Click/Tap

This metric identifies which elements users interact with first. It helps rank zones according to the time spent before users engage with the zone. It is calculated as the average time for the first click on the area in pageviews with at least one click on the zone.

That's exactly what the team found here. Many customers started interacting with the dates before tapping into the pickup and drop-off location fields (see Figure 9B.6). It's a first hint that these customers are in an exploratory mindset and not yet set on locations.

The time before the first click report shows the surprising order in which most customers completed the form fields.

Step 3: Drop-Rate Metric—Which Form Fields Are Leading to Abandonment?

A metric that pinpoints some of the biggest troublemakers in a form is Drop-Rate, that is, the last field before abandoning the form.

Definition: Drop-Rate

The percent of users who interacted with a field just before abandoning the page.

What the analytics team found to their surprise is that the drop-off location field was most frequently the last field where customers gave up. After interacting with this field, more than 15% of customers dropped off here.

That seemed odd. Drilling into session replays showed some of these customers trying to tap into the drop-off location field unsuccessfully. It seemed unresponsive. A relatively high average tap

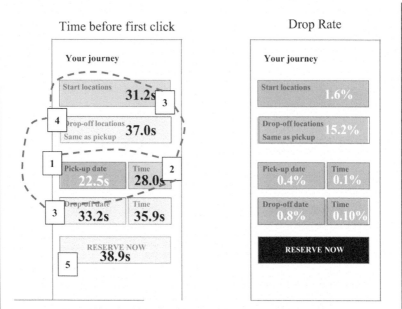

Figure 9B.6 Time before the first click and form field Drop-Rate reports.

recurrence on that field also demonstrated this problem. It provided a clue for colleagues in the Product team to investigate and fix the issues.

Step 4: Refill-Rate Metric—Which Form Fields Need Repeated Tries to Complete?

What are some form fields that are laborious or difficult for renters to get right? The metric that can pinpoint repeated effort is Refill-Rate.

> **Definition: Refill-Rate**
>
> The percent of users who refilled the field after an unsuccessful attempt to submit the form.

As suspected earlier, the car rental company saw that customers are trying multiple pickup locations. As a result, they explore various options to understand which one is the best.

Step 5: Blank-Rate—Which Form Fields Are Skipped?

Which fields seem so daunting or irrelevant that users try to submit without completing them? That's what we learn from the Blank-Rate metric.

Definition: Blank-Rate

The % of users who left the field blank when submitting the form.

For the truck rental journey, it turned out that pickup and drop-off dates are left blank by an incredible 25% of potential renters. Likewise, the drop-off location is also left blank by nearly the same percentage of customers.

Once again, we see that customers seem to be in a pre-planning mode and exploring their options.

Step 6: Impact Quantification to Get Buy-In for Investment

By segmenting on users that struggled with these items, the analytics team quantified that their bookings conversion rate was 98% lower than the average, that is, these customers in the exploratory mode were almost guaranteed to give up.

They also quantified that every 10% improvement to completion rate for these potential customers would improve revenue by $40,000 per year based on traffic volume.

Step 7: Design a Better Form

Through their behaviors, customers show how to create a better experience for their needs. Some directions for better experiences that jumped out from the data were the following:

- Providing customers with the option to select a range of days or a daily price finder rather than requiring specific dates and times.
- Improving the pickup location finder, e.g., by implementing a way to research by postal code or by suggesting popular locations.
- Setting the drop-off location as "the same as the pickup location" by default to reduce the manual effort.

Step 8: Inform A/B Test Strategy Most Likely to Improve Completions

At the time of this writing, the car rental company's redesign process is in progress. The metrics do, however, suggest clear ideas. In a world shifting to mobile, the low 12% completion rate on mobile devices cannot be satisfactory for anyone.

The Moral of the Story

An investigation that takes eight steps and many metrics is clearly something that is only in the realm of Analytics teams. In the hands of those teams, however, the metrics available for Form Analysis enable them to turn more lookers into bookers.

But, could there be a more automated way to troubleshoot form completions? There sure is.

Case Study 2: Why Are Credit Card Applicants Giving Up?

We saw the traditional way of troubleshooting a form in the previous case study. These days, frustration scoring can automate part of the process. Let's see an example at a retail banking institute.

The Challenge

Applications are coming in, but where are all the points of friction that we just haven't discovered yet? Of course, you know that they are always there. We just need to find them!

Step 1: Surface Friction Points with Automated Scoring

When scanning their site with automated frustration scoring, the top finding for areas of opportunity related to the bank's credit card application form (see Figure 9B.7). Specifically, automated scoring narrowed down frustration to multiple clicks on the button for submitting the credit card application form. These were associated with abandoned applications.

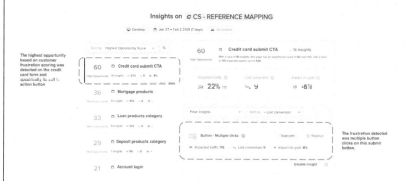

Figure 9B.7 Automated frustration scoring highlights the biggest areas of opportunity, namely multiple clicks on a button within the credit card approval process.

Step 2: Get a Quick First Impression with Session Replay

Replaying the sessions that struggled with multiple submit button interactions immediately showed many signs of confusion and friction. The analytics team was pained to see customers trying to submit again and again when they reached the bottom of the application form but to no avail.

Some customers resorted to scrolling up and down the form, which is when the session replays show how they discovered form validation errors indicated further up on the page. But these error messages were out of sight when users had scrolled down to submit the form. Many applicants never noticed the validation error messages further up and simply gave up after rage-clicking on the submit button.

Step 3: Quantify the Impact of the Issues

The analytics team quantified the impact of this UX problem by comparing the group of customers that clicked the submit button multiple times but didn't reach the next step vs. those that proceeded successfully.

The issue was quantified as a loss of 121 credit card applications per month, or nearly 1,500 per year.

Improve the Form and Reap the Benefits

In the end, form validation errors displayed out of sight for customers are rookie UX mistakes. Many companies have made that mistake at one point. The fix is well known. Namely, the best approach is to automatically scroll the form to the form fields where validation errors need the customer's attention.

C-SUITE Cheat Sheet for Optimizing Form Completions

Figure 9B.8 shows a cheat sheet for form optimization in a nutshell. It's a typical formula for optimizing form completions, no pun intended.

Challenge	Optimize Form Completions		
Surface	Review the Form Funnel report for each form to evaluate its current state and bottlenecks.		Automatically scan experiences for signs of struggle and errors across forms, form fields, and form submit CTAs.
Understand	Investigate depending on the type of bottleneck and friction.		
	If users aren't starting the form: • Does the form look too daunting? • Are users hitting the form too early in their journey?	If users start but don't submit. And for frustrations surfaced for form fields: • Identify the most problematic form fields and behaviors based on Drop-Rate, Refill-Rate, Blank-Rate metrics. • Which fields cause too much effort, hesitation + unusual order to complete?	If users submit but can't proceed. And for frustrations surfaced for the submit CTA: • Identify issues with form validation errors, e.g., via error reporting. • Identify bugs, and rage click behaviors, e.g., via error reporting.
	Replay the most problematic, frustrating, and unsuccessful sessions to understand when/why it's happening.		
Impact	Quantify impact, i.e. potential value of fixing or improving.		
Test	Fix the issues, and/or test improving the design of the forms.		
Evaluate	Why did the improvements win/lose? What were the biggest success factors we can learn for future tests?		

Figure 9B.8 Cheat sheet: Troubleshoot form completions.

That said, it is somewhat complex and typically something that Analytics teams get tasked with.

Challenge 4: Inform A/B Test Strategy to Create Uplift More Often

Experimentation is one of the best arrows in the quiver for Conversion Rate Optimization (CRO) teams. Yet, as we said early in the book, too many A/B tests fail to move the needle, that is, complete without apparent uplift or value. Said differently, their only value is eliminating yet another way that doesn't improve results. But they all cost a lot of time and effort to design and execute.

A more systematic way to inform the A/B test strategy is needed, unless CRO teams want to be working like Thomas Edison. He allegedly said that he found 10,000 ways that don't work for creating a light bulb before finally finding the one way that did.

However, CRO teams today are lucky to have a powerful partner that can help them, namely the wisdom of the crowds. With the help of Experience Analytics, they can let their customers show them the most likely tests that will create uplift.

Throughout this book, we've already seen many case studies where teams informed successful A/B tests based on customer behavior. Check out another great example from a US fashion retailer on this book's accompanying online portal.

Supplemental Case Studies Online: US Fashion Retailer Identifies the A/B Test Most Likely to Improve PLP Micro-Conversion Rates

https://ExperienceAnalytics.live/CaseStudies

Select the Fashion retailer case study for chapter 9

C-SUITE Cheat Sheet for Informing A/B Test Strategy

Since A/B testing is so critical to success, see Figure 9B.9 for a cheat sheet with the principles of how to inform a better experimentation roadmap with Experience Analytics data.

Challenge	Inform A/B testing roadmap with experience insights to create more uplift, more often			
Surface	Where are the biggest opportunities and issues?			
	Do journeys show signs of opportunities, e.g., high engagement.	Do journeys show signs of friction, e.g., high effort, looping, or premature exits?		Does automated scoring reveal points of friction?
Understand	Look for common patterns within those pages.			
	Do in-page behaviors reveal a previously undiscovered intent?	In-page, look for deviations from the "ideal path."	Which content elements/ behaviors are associated with success vs. not?	Compare successful vs. unsuccessful engagement with the content elements.
	What new experience would better serve this intent?	What changes will help more users find the ideal path and move the needle?		
Impact	Quantify business impact, i.e., potential value of improving.			
Test	Develop & test the new design.			
Evaluate	Why did the test win/lose? What were the biggest success factors we can learn for future tests?			

Figure 9B.9 Cheat sheet: Inform A/B test roadmap based on the potential impact.

Challenge 5: Understand Customers and Predict Trends

Conversion Rate Optimization only scratches the surface of what data and Analytics teams can do for their business and customers. The real strategic value comes from the opportunity to understand customers better. What is their intent? What influences their decisions? What makes them happy? How can the business anticipate their wants and needs and align everybody around them?

This challenge is perfectly aligned with the higher purpose of Experience Analytics. It will be primarily the subject of Part III in the book. Upfront here is an anecdotal example, however as an appetizer. For this case study, we are back in the car rental industry.

Case Study: Why Should We Change How We Rent Cars on Mobile Devices?

The team at this car rental company likes to say that "UX isn't enough to win a transaction, but bad UX can lose a transaction." So their focus has been to find and eliminate points of friction that stand in the way of their customers.

The Challenge

As with most businesses, traffic has been shifting to mobile channels. Increasingly, many travelers would be able to use their mobile devices to bypass the car rental counter and head straight to their rental car on the lot.

While that offers much better convenience for customers, it presents huge challenges for car rental companies. In this case, the car rental company's Web analytics showed this.

1. The conversion rate for new bookings on mobile devices is much lower. So how can they prevent business from going down just because of the shift to mobile?
2. Given the cutthroat race to the bottom on rental prices, much of the profit comes from ancillary sales, e.g., the prepaid gas tank or the extra insurance. Yet, ancillary sales on mobile devices were also much lower.

Question 1: Why Are We Struggling with Selling Ancillaries on Mobile?

The company's first pass at ancillary sales on mobile was simply a screen within the bookings journey listing all the ancillary options and descriptions. When studying this screen with Zone-based Heatmaps, the reason for low ancillary sales became clear. Travelers were not engaging with the options. Most were scrolling swiftly to find and tap the button to advance to the next step.

For illustrations of the app screen for choosing ancillary options before and after the case study, see this book's supplemental online materials.

https://ExperienceAnalytics.live/figures

See the Ancillary options case study for chapter 9.

Answer 1: How Can We Do Better with Selling Ancillaries on Mobile?

Seeing this, the car rental company strategized on a better way to sell ancillaries. After all, no agent at the rental counter would throw ten different ancillary options at their customer hoping that one of them would stick. Instead, they would have an intelligent conversation based on what options are most relevant based on the person in front of them.

So that's also what the car rental company translated to mobile now. Depending on the type of rental booking, for example, a weekend minivan for a family vs. a weekday rental by a frequent traveler, they identified and presented only the two most relevant ancillary options for that type of rental. They implemented this using the company's Adobe Target experimentation and personalization tool.

The result? A 21% increase in ancillary sales. A huge contribution to the bottom line.

Question 2: Why Are We Losing Potential Mobile Bookings?

The analytics team went on to study the entire mobile bookings journey to find and close all the leaks. They found many unnecessary screens that they were able to eliminate. Such as, why would they ask a known and authenticated frequent traveler for their home address when this is already on file anyways?

Most importantly, however, they found that travelers simply gave up when they reached the last step where they needed to enter their credit card to confirm a booking. Too many of them didn't even start interacting with the form. They were possibly on the move in the airport, and the prospect of having to pull out and enter their credit card on a mobile device was too much (this story predates today's browser credit card wallets).

Answer 2: How Can We Do Better with Renting Cars on Mobile?

The car rental company already knew from their Adobe Analytics that the credit card screen was the most significant drop-off from their funnel. But what Experience Analytics added was the insight that it wasn't a matter of simplifying the form or an error or friction. Instead, travelers weren't even considering interacting with the payment form.

With these data, visuals, and session replays in hand, the analytics team built the case for a radical makeover of their mobile rental process. Namely, to let customers on mobile reserve a car without a credit card to hold it.

You have to understand that this was a big gamble for the business. If no credit card is provided to hold the car, many vehicles might be reserved and not picked up. That would hurt the company's profits. This controversial proposal would have raised only a skeptical eyebrow without data and visuals in hands. "Really?"

However, with the data in hand, the analytics team did get the buy-in to test the new approach.

Value

The test was, of course, a resounding success for the digital conversion funnel, lifting car rental bookings by a total of 25%. But what happened when it came time for customers to pick up their rented cars?

It turns out that in some countries such as Germany, most travelers were conscientious enough to cancel their bookings if they didn't need the car after all. However, in some other countries, this wasn't the case. So the company kept the approach in places such as Germany and rolled it back elsewhere.

The Moral of the Story

Experience Analytics is the new eyes and ears of the business for seeing and understanding customers. While Conversion Rate Optimization and troubleshooting of experiences are highly lucrative, they seem very tactical benefits compared to the power that Experience Analytics gives to business leaders to better understand their customers and steer the business.

C-SUITE Cheat Sheet for Better Understanding Customers

Understanding customers' goals, pains, wants, and needs is a very human skill. It requires both listening carefully and watching how customers are truly behaving to comprehend. Yet, it's what managers in offline businesses have done intuitively for thousands of years.

Reducing that to a cheat sheet cannot be adequate. Nonetheless, Figure 9B.10 provides a cheat sheet that approximates what we are looking for when putting the Experience Analytics lens on customers to understand their wants and needs.

Challenge	Understand customers and their wants and needs	
Surface	What can I learn about my customers that I don't already know?	
	Do journeys show signs of likes and dislikes when customers engage with my brand, channels, content, and offering?	
	Do different target groups of customers differ in the way they engage, what they like/dislike?	
Understand	Compare customer intent vs. actual experience.	
	Do in-page behaviors reveal a previously undiscovered intent?	Which content elements/behaviors are associated with success vs. not?
	What influences customers for making their decisions? What new experience—online or offline—would better serve the way they think?	
Impact	Quantify business impact, i.e., potential value of investing in new and improved experiences to inspire customers based on their intent and make their experiences more seamless and rewarding.	
Test	Develop & test the best new and improved experience candidate.	
Evaluate	Why did the test win/lose? What were the biggest success factors we can learn for future tests?	

Figure 9B.10 Cheat sheet: Understand customer wants, needs, and opportunities.

Notes

1 Interaction Design foundation, User Experience (UX) Design, www.interaction-design.org/literature/topics/ux-design
2 ProductLed, Wes Bush, https://productled.com/blog/product-led-growth-definition/, 2022
3 DILBERT © 2013 Scott Adams, Inc. Used By permission of ANDREWS MCMEEL SYNDICATION. All rights reserved.
4 Case study, Contentsquare and Merkle, Increasing test drive visits by 40%, https://contentsquare.com/customers/skoda/
5 Contentsquare, Catlin Roberge, Contentsquare Data Says People Don't Like Free Beer, 2020, https://contentsquare.com/blog/contentsquare-data-says-people-dont-like-free-beer/

Part III

See Into the Future with Experience Analytics

We've walked in the shoes of nearly every role in the digital team and seen so many use cases of Experience Analytics. Yet, Experience Analytics packs a lot more power than merely to be used as a reporting tool for web and app experiences. In Part III, now let's have a look at emerging and future use cases.

Chapter 10: Target and Personalize Marketing Experiences Based on Digital Body Language

Chapter 11: Extending Experience Analytics to New Channels

DOI: 10.4324/b23273-13

Target and Personalize Marketing Experiences Based on Digital Body Language

Customer attention and response to marketing experiences will be higher the more relevant they are. That's been commonly accepted for decades already. Yet, in today's age of 24/7 constant overload with digital content and advertising, relevancy isn't just a benefit, it's an imperative. Customers have become experts at tuning out—or even blocking—irrelevant marketing messages. They easily drop off when a journey is not as expected.

And the new generation of customers that are growing up with Smartphones, on-demand TV and music, ad-free experiences, always multitasking on their devices, have no patience for experiences that aren't catching their fancy immediately.

So, marketers want to engage their customers as individuals. Yet there is a problem. How can they actually understand each customer closely enough to achieve this?

If It's Not Relevant, It's Scrap

For decades already, CRM has sought to embrace this opportunity by gathering as much customer profile data as possible. That's great, but it has its limits in a world that is increasingly privacy-conscious.

Depending on the maturity of a marketing team, these data lakes usually combine customers' transactions, account information, and marketing interactions from all mainstream channels. In addition, some behavioral data is included, especially from digital channels, for example, most recent products viewed or abandoned in shopping carts.

DOI: 10.4324/b23273-14

Supplemental Online Materials: Segment Definition Example

For an example of a Multichannel Marketing profile for customer marketers see this book's supplemental online materials at the following URL

https://ExperienceAnalytics.Live/Figures

See the Multichannel Marketing profile example for Chapter 10.

To call out one difference vs. mainstream digital marketing, it's personally identifiable information (PII). Whereas PII is becoming to seem like a dirty word in digital marketing, customers would not be amused if brands they regularly do business with constantly forget their name, address, and account history. In customer relationships, PII is expected.

That's great for "down the road" in customer relationships once the brand has earned the permission to track and market. But what about the top of the funnel, that is, earlier in relationships when no permission has been given yet? Should we just throw in the towel and hope that generic, one-size-fits-all experiences will do the trick there?

For the first time now with Experience Analytics, we have the opportunity to do the seemingly impossible. Namely, to understand customers as humans, at scale, and without compromising their privacy. Experience Analytics can provide an understanding of the digital body language, for example,

- What is the customer's intent in their current session?
- Are they engaged with certain products and content?
- Are they able to achieve their goals?
- How well is the experience serving them, e.g., are they confused or struggling anywhere?
- How can we best help them achieve their goal while they are here?

Definition: Digital Body Language

Liraz Margalit (Ph.D.) coined the term digital body language back in 2017 during her work at Experience Analytics vendor Clicktale. A Psychologist by training, here is how she defined it in an article on CSMWire:[1]

Digital body language is a combination of all the digital gestures and micro-signals made by customers, from which

> we can identify patterns and anomalies to determine their behavior, mindset, and intent. Being able to interpret digital body language is a must-have standard for the next wave of digital commerce.

With this data, digital stores should in the future be able to engage and serve customers even better than human salespeople. But how do we pass these signals into the various personalization and targeting tools?

Enriching the Marketing Technology Ecosystem with Experience Analytics Data

In the time since my book, *Multichannel Marketing: Metrics and Methods for On- and Offline Success*,[2] was published in 2007, it has become commonplace for traditional web behavior data to be included in customer profiles and marketing data warehouses. As a result, for example, abandoned shopping cart retargeting campaigns are ubiquitous these days.

The same exact mechanism that is used for including traditional, click-level web analytics in marketing databases can also be used to include Digital Experience Analytics data

Case 1: Anonymous Browsing Behavior

Site personalization and targeting tools are all built to take in external real-time information via their data collection tags on the site. They typically provide JavaScript tags for capturing additional information about the anonymous customer in the current session.

So, the trick is for Experience Analytics to invoke those tags for submitting insights on the customer's intent and their experience. For example, "the intent in the current session is a quick purchase" mode, and "this shopper is hitting an error on the cart page when they try to change the number of products."

The additional information is used in the decisioning logic to trigger the best personalization on-site before the customer leaves.

Case 2: Known-Customer Profiles

When customers have opted in through registration and authentication, their experience signals within a session on the site and app can also be associated with their customer account identifier. This makes it possible to send the data to the company's Marketing Cloud and Customer

Data Platform. They can then apply their decisioning logic and trigger a targeted action via additional channels, for example, email or any offline channel.

Refer to my Multichannel Marketing book on how this is done. We just need to export the data from the Experience Analytics and import it into the company's marketing database. Ask your Experience Analytics provider about data exports.

Use Cases for Digital Marketers

Everybody is familiar with how different our customer experience is when shopping at a big-box retailer vs. shopping at our friendly neighborhood store. While prices are excellent in big-box retail, it can sometimes be tough to find a store clerk to get help from. However, service is always on offer in the neighborhood store, and the team might even know and help us personally.

Brick-and-mortar stores have economic constraints; they can't offer both the lowest prices and the most customer service. But on digital, the opportunity is to make every digital experience more like that friendly neighborhood store—at scale. And that's where Experience Analytics data has its highest future potential.

Rescue Customers That Are Struggling on the Site

The most straightforward idea for real-time personalization with Experience Analytics data is to detect when customers experience friction and frustrations. Is a customer on the site rage-clicking? Did they encounter an error message? Are they going in loops and can't seem to find what they are looking for? It's a perfect moment to pop up an offer for live chat and assistance to rescue the situation.

Today, this is still relatively crude; however, for example, multiple clicks on a home page slider should be taken as a good sign of engagement, whereas multiple clicks on a call-to-action button are not. So the frontier for pinpointing actual struggle requires that Experience Analytics tools understand the context, that is, the purpose of content elements on pages.

Personalize Experiences for Customers in the Moment

The ultimate use case for digital marketers is to engage customers as individuals, just like a live store salesperson would do. Enable sites and apps to tailor experiences to each customer's intent and interests. Enable them to detect when a customer is losing interest and re-engage them with the right content at the right time.

An excellent analysis completed by a railway operator shows where this could lead to future digital experiences.

Case Study: Anticipate a Customer's Intent and Tailor Their Experience

As with most travel operators, their mobile app is popular with their customers. It offers everything from researching travel destinations to booking and managing trips. The brand's best and most frequent travelers are the app's top users. As a result, Marketing is always interested in engaging these customers with additional offers and inspiration for their next trip.

Step 1: What's the Intent of Our App Users?

When the company compared user journeys in their app, it became clear that users took different journeys in the app depending on their travel plans (no pun intended). (see Figure 10.1)

1. Is the customer booking a trip for three or more months out? Journeys show them researching multiple alternative destinations and dates. They are unlikely to complete a booking within the same session. They might not even have decided yet whether they will go by train at all.
2. Are they looking to book a trip for the same or the next day? Journeys show them going through the booking journey swiftly while ignoring all distractions.
3. Do they have an existing booking and their train is leaving shortly? They are most likely to look up their current trip to see whether their train is on time and what gate it is departing from.

Step 2: What Would Be the Most Human Experience Based on Users' Intent?

With these insights in hand, the company's marketing masterminds thought of more human ways to engage their customers. Instead of always showing the same banners in the app of happy people playing on the beach, wouldn't it make sense to tailor the experience based on predicted intent?

1. For journeys three months out, customers are likely to appreciate inspirational content. So, offering them links to travel

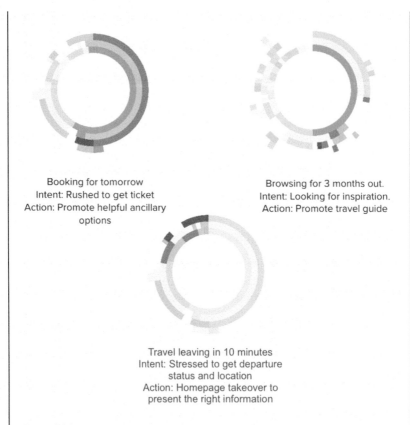

Booking for tomorrow
Intent: Rushed to get ticket
Action: Promote helpful ancillary
options

Browsing for 3 months out.
Intent: Looking for inspiration.
Action: Promote travel guide

Travel leaving in 10 minutes
Intent: Stressed to get departure
status and location
Action: Homepage takeover to
present the right information

Figure 10.1 Journey Analysis segmented by travel dates shows different intent.

brochures and destination guides would be the most human and relevant way to engage them.

2. When users are booking a journey for the same or the next day, they already know what they want. So instead of offering irrelevant brochures, they would appreciate any help to make their trip better, e.g., by getting offers for a rental car at their travel destination.

3. When users with an existing train ride about to leave the station are opening the app, they would be frustrated if they had to wade through irrelevant cross-sell content and complex app navigation menus. Instead, they just want to know when and where that train is leaving. So why not take over the home screen with that information and maybe present an offer to upgrade their booking to first class?

Step 3: A/B Test Personalized Experiences

The brand tested some of these ideas by implementing them via their rules-based personalization engine.

Results and Value

Results showed a 12% increase in bookings and a 25% reduction in undecided behaviors for window shoppers.

The Moral of the Story

We don't always need to know the customer personally for personalizing experiences during the session. Customers can stay within their comfort zone if they wish to lean back and remain anonymous.

It's just like in brick-and-mortar businesses where we've always spoken with store clerks without first showing them our passport.

Use Cases for Customer Marketers

Once the customer has given permission, marketing can span across channels. Experience Analytics data can improve upon the promise of making cross-channel marketing a 1:1 experience.

Response Attribution in Customer Marketing Data

There are many reasons why customer-centric marketers keep close attention to marketing treatments vs. responses. It's not just that they need to measure the success of their programs. But for marketing to feel more like a dialog, less like a campaign blast, marketers need to listen to what customers are saying through their actions in response to the marketing treatment. Otherwise, it's only a one-sided monologue.

Just putting it that way makes it clear that Experience Analytics can help customer-centric marketers listen much more closely by understanding the digital body language of their customers as part of response attribution.

Definition: Response Attribution by Match Back

Response attribution by match back works by keeping a list of customers that received a marketing treatment, for example, an offer or message. Then, you check off which of these customers responded, for example, by clicking through to the website or completing a transaction offline.

This response information can trigger the next action in the dialog, for example, a retargeting message or a follow-up or thank-you message.

The term "dialog marketing" already implies that the "conversation" will stretch over multiple marketing treatments, responses, and channels. Same with ideas such as "drip marketing." So how will Experience Analytics help here?

Before Enriching with Experience Analytics Data

Response tracking is a somewhat flat view of customer responses. For the digital channel, it can typically include flags for email opens, clickthroughs, views of website pages, and transactions. But unless they completed a purchase already, it's unclear whether the customer is interested or confused. Even if they converted, was it a good experience? Are they likely to come back?

After Enriching with Experience Analytics Data

The customer's digital body language shows their mindset and experience. For example

- Are they in a "window shopping" mindset or already in the consideration phase?
- What is important to the individual buyer, for example, are they studying an offering's terms and conditions and technical details?
- What prompted them to abandon the journey, i.e., did they simply stop browsing, or did they run into a point of friction or even an error?

These insights can then help the customer-centric marketer with what they will be saying next in the dialog. See the following section for next-best-action marketing.

Next-Best-Action in Customer Marketing Programs

Next-based action refers to selecting the best next offer or marketing message to an individual customer that they are most likely to find relevant and convert on.

Definition: Next-Best-Action

Here is how Wikipedia wisely defines it:[3]

> It's a customer-centric marketing paradigm that considers the different actions that can be taken for a specific customer and decides on the "best" one. The next-best-action (an offer, proposition, service, etc.) is determined by the customer's interests and needs on the one hand and the marketing organization's business objectives and policies on the other.

For example, in financial services, for a customer of a certain age who already has the institution's deposit and loan products, maybe the next best offers would be wealth management and retirement planning accounts.

For decades already, this has been automated by what customer-centric marketers call their "next-best-action engine." This is essentially a predictive analytics process that draws on all available customer profile information to score customers' propensity for responding to a set of available offers.

Supplemental Case Studies Online : Financial Services Institution in the Netherlands

One of the most mature next-best-action programs ever has been implemented at a Dutch financial services institution during the heyday of Enterprise Marketing Management. Read about it in this book's online materials, and how Experience Analytics could help them go further today.

https://ExperienceAnalytics.live/CaseStudies

Select the Financial Services case study for chapter 10

Supplemental Case Studies Online: Automobile Manufacturer Improves Lead Scoring for Potential Buyers

Car manufacturers—or OEMs as they refer to themselves—are partnered with a dealership network of independent businesses. The role of the OEM's website is to drive demand for the brand and generate leads for their network. Check out this case study on how one of the large US auto manufacturers improvised lead management based on digital data, and how Experience Analytics could help them go further today.

https://ExperienceAnalytics.live/CaseStudies

Select the Automobile-Manufacturer case study for chapter 10

Predict Churn Risk for Retention Marketing

Keeping a customer and growing their wallet share in relationship-oriented businesses is just as important—if not even more—than gaining new customers. Famously, in Telecom, everybody already has one or more cell phones. Acquiring new customers is challenging and expensive. That makes retaining and growing customer relationships a top priority.

Definition: Churn Risk

The propensity of a customer to close their account and leave.

Definition: Retention Marketing

Trigger-based campaigns and targeted offers to make things better for (profitable) customers who are at risk of churning.

For example, when you are about to close your credit card account that carries an annual fee, sometimes the call center agent can magically waive the annual membership fee. But, if they offered this to all customers by default, it would be a big hit on revenue.

So, how can a marketer identify customers at risk of churning and retain them with an offer before it is too late?

Supplemental Case Studies Online: Behavior-Based Retention Marketing at a US Telecom

This US Telecom company was one of the first to include website behavior data in their churn risk calculations. Their rationale was a no-brainer. If a customer is about to leave, there is probably some behavior during their website visits that differs from the behavior of happy customers. Read their case study online, and how Experience Analytics could help them go further today.

https://ExperienceAnalytics.Live/CaseStudies

Select the Telecom case study for Chapter 10.

An Extended Maturity Model for Targeted Marketing

Experience Analytics does not change the principle of what customer-centric marketers are trying to accomplish. In one way or another, they always focused on getting closer to something similar to the ideal of 1:1 marketing, as defined by Don Peppers and Martha Rogers in their seminal 1993 book, The one-to-one future.[4]

But as Figure 10.2 indicates, Experience Analytics enables marketers to get several steps closer to this ideal by

1. Better understanding what makes each customer click, e.g., what is their intent and interest in the current interaction?
2. Seeing what obstacles they encountered along the way, i.e., areas of confusion, frustrations, and errors.
3. Understand customers earlier in their journey, before they register and authenticate, but without compromising their privacy.

The Trend to Privacy-First

Privacy is part of the customer experience. It's a human right.[5] It's the law.[6] All marketers have to adapt. We need to make the most out of opportunities even when interactions are entirely anonymous. Alongside, we need to work on earning each customer's trust to gain their permission to market and build a data relationship.

Experience Analytics is part of the solution here in multiple ways.

Step 1: Provide the Best Possible Generic Experiences That You Can

Build trust by providing value to the customer. What's in it for them in return for registering? Your brand needs to lead by providing value while the relationship is still entirely anonymous.

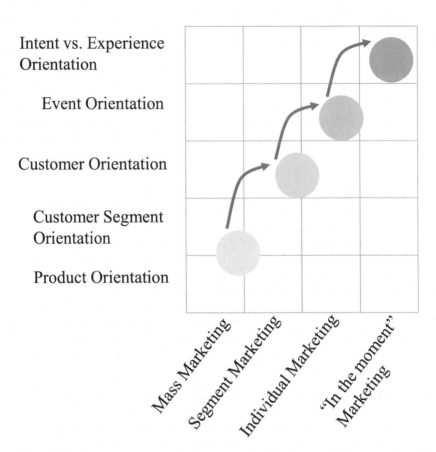

Intent vs. Experience
Orientation

Event Orientation

Customer Orientation

Customer Segment
Orientation

Product Orientation

Mass Marketing

Segment Marketing

Individual Marketing

"In the moment" Marketing

Figure 10.2 A new maturity model for targeted marketing. Inspired by a traditional model from customer marketers at Telefonica.

The use cases for Experience Analytics throughout this book help you provide that value by making the digital experience as good as it can be. Understand how customers want to be interacting with your brand and innovate your web and mobile experiences for that. Eliminate all areas of confusion and friction proactively.

Step 2: Personalize Based on Intent

Even when the relationship is still wholly anonymous, the opportunity with Experience Analytics is to help personalize same-session experiences in real-time based on the customer's digital body language.

Step 3: Ask for Permission in the Most Effective Way

When it comes time to ask permission from the user by registering on the site or app, use Experience Analytics to make that registration process as seamless as possible. Find and eliminate all areas of friction. Place the registration options in the most effective locations within pages and the customer journey.

Step 4: Use the Permission Wisely

Even after permission to market is established, marketers can still lose it all too quickly. Use Experience Analytics continuously to make sure that marketing contacts remain as relevant as possible and that experiences remain as seamless, rewarding, and inspiring as possible.

The resulting customer lifecycle model looks more like an ellipse than a circle. Customer relationship marketing is here to stay but works best for customers that are already closest to the brand and have given their permission to market. But at any moment, there is an even larger audience who choose to stay anonymous while they discover the brand and do their "window shopping from a distance." With experience optimization and personalization based on intent, we've got a better chance to inspire them and win them to the brand.

Supplemental Online Materials: The Customer Lifecycle Ellipse Model

For a visual representation of the customer lifecycle ellipse model see this book's supplemental online materials at the following URL:

https://ExperienceAnalytics.Live/Figures

See the Model example for Chapter 10.

The Digital Store of the Future

As the Chief Product Officer at Contentsquare, Lucie Buisson, often says: "No brick and mortar store clerk needs to ask a customer's name and address before they can help them achieve their goals in the store. And brick & mortar conversion rates are stellar compared to today's average digital conversion rates."

With the help of Experience Analytics data and AI, the digital store of the future has the opportunity to be even more engaging and attentive than human salespeople. Digital stores will be able to listen to customers' digital body language and understand them even better—and at a greater scale—than human salespeople can. All without always needing to know who each customer is.

Notes

1   Liraz Margalit: Read Digital Body Language to Deliver Brilliant Customer Experiences, on CMSWire, September 2017, www.cmswire.com/digital-exp erience/liraz-margalit-read-digital-body-language-to-deliver-brilliant-custo mer-experiences/
2   Multichannel Marketing: Metrics and Methods for On- and Offline Success, Wiley/Sybex, 2008.
3   Wikipedia, Next-best-action marketing, https://en.wikipedia.org/wiki/Next-best-action_marketing
4   Don Peppers and Martha Rogers, The one-to-one future, 1993.
5   United Nations, Universal Declaration of Human Rights, www.un.org/en/about-us/universal-declaration-of-human-rights
6   Wikipedia, Privacy Law, https://en.wikipedia.org/wiki/Privacy_law

Chapter 11

Extend Experience Analytics to New Channels

We've focused on digital experiences via desktop, mobile, and apps throughout this book. But already today, digital is much bigger than that. When I watch my kids on their phones and smart speakers at home, they are already having conversations with digital devices in a way that was only the realm of Sci-Fi a few years ago.

It's already visible today that the increasing sophistication of AI and 5G Internet connectivity of devices will revolutionize the world of everything that we interact with. These coming new digital devices and channels will require Experience Analytics even more than traditional digital channels do today.

A Day Without Digital?

Imagine a day without digital.

Gulp.

You would probably find that:

- You can't call anyone, not even your kids. Of course, your cell phone has their phone numbers memorized, but do you?
- Forget ordering online. You don't even know which store in town is open, which products are the right ones for your needs, and where you will find them in stock. Did you still keep the traditional old yellow pages and phone books around?
  - You can't travel anywhere anymore. You could not buy tickets anyways, most travel agents are long gone. Your car wouldn't work without computer chips. But what's more, do you still have any printed maps handy these days?
  - Brands can't reach their audiences anymore. TVs are all connected, smart devices. Yet, there is no Internet. How many households are still getting printed newspapers? It's back to bill-board advertising, then.

DOI: 10.4324/b23273-15

- Dating has just taken a big hit.
- Better not have any medical emergency. Where is that closest urgent care doctor again?

This only shows how much our lives have already become digital and how mission-critical Experience Analytics is. But now, consider the coming rise of more sophisticated AI.

The Rise of More Sophisticated Artificial Intelligence

Today, nobody could fault you for being skeptical about supposed AI qualities in many B2B software products. Many providers are promoting AI in their software in a way that is more reminiscent of Wild West-era snake oil salesmen. Perhaps some of these technology providers should be tarred and feathered, similar to the Western era.

But there is no doubt that the sophistication of AI is on the horizon. That future is already visible everywhere. Along with it comes a need for Experience Analytics like never before to ensure AI-supported experiences meet the mark.

Chatbots

Live chat has been an integral part of the contact center for a while already. It comes in many flavors, whether through a chat option on the website or part of messaging apps such as WeChat in China. It's been said that new businesses in China first open their WeChat presence, before they think about starting a website.

Increasingly, businesses aim to scale chat by automating as much of the interaction as possible via chatbots. When customers interact with a chatbot, they navigate a potential set of journeys that the chatbot can help with. In a sense, it's not too different from navigating a phone menu where users can branch into one of the multiple branches by choosing options.

Either the chatbot can provide the information or transaction that the customer is looking for. Or the chatbot reaches a point where it doesn't understand or cannot help anymore so that it transfers the interaction to a human agent.

Opportunities for Experience Analytics are everywhere here. It's pretty similar to those for web and app channels.

Journey Analysis and Optimization

What is the user flow through the chatbot? What are the golden journeys that lead to success? Where are customers going in loops or abandoning

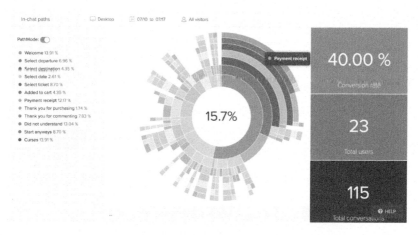

In-chat paths   🖳 Desktop   📅 07/10 to 07/17   👤 All visitors

PathMode: 🔘

- Welcome 13.91 %
- Select departure 6.96 %
- Select destination 4.35 %
- Select date 2.61 %
- Select ticket 8.70 %
- Added to cart 4.35 %
- Payment receipt 12.17 %
- Thank you for purchasing 1.74 %
- Thank you for commenting 7.83 %
- Did not understand 13.04 %
- Start anyways 8.70 %
- Curses 13.91 %

Payment receipt

40.00 %

Conversion rate

15.7%

23

Total users

115

❓ HELP

Total conversations

Figure 11.1 Journey Analysis for chatbot interactions.

unexpectedly? Where are they branching into unintended directions and having to back out (e.g. see Figure 11.1)?

Find and Fix Friction, for Example, with Natural Language Processing

Where do customers misunderstand the chatbot? And where is the chatbot misunderstanding what the customer is saying? Is it buggy or too slow at some stages? What's happening in the background causing these points of friction and errors?

Intent Analysis and Innovation

What is the intent of customers in their interactions? What are some unexpected customer goals for which the chatbot experiences should be extended?

Sentiment Analysis and Improvement

Where are customers happy vs. unhappy with the interaction? Why is it happening, and how can it be improved?

Voice Assistants

Gen Z and Generation Alpha are growing up very comfortable with talking to smart speakers and voice assistants. Watching them feels like seeing a Sci-Fi movie. By the time these kids grow up, they might find that

Figure 11.2 No comment.

half of their daily conversations are with intelligent beings not made out of flesh and blood.

We can honestly use the word conversation here. Today, most interactions with voice assistants still feel more like controlling a device by voice instead of typing or pressing buttons. But you can already have some fun talking to voice assistants, for example, see what happens when you wish them a good day. Today, the responses are "coded in." But there is no doubt that, eventually, this will evolve to a level where a conversation can perhaps even feel therapeutic. It will, in small parts, sometimes, serve as a "stand-in" for a human connection.

Optimizing those experiences requires everything we've covered for Experience Analytics under chatbots above, plus:

Voice Recognition Analysis and Optimization

Where is the voice assistant incorrectly hearing what customers are saying? How can it be improved (e.g. see Figure 11.2)?

Sentiment Analysis and Improvement

While already covered under chatbots, it's worth highlighting how much more need, opportunity, and value there is in sentiment analysis when interactions are via our voices rather than written only. So how do users *feel* about the interaction experience?

Cognitive Analysis and Optimization

Hey, even humans go through school and make it through puberty before we consider them fully mature. (And even then, you have to wonder sometimes.) So, no doubt improving the cognition of machines will require an incredible amount of Experience Analytics to help them reach maturity.

Call-center AI

Another area at the frontier of AI is call centers. They are, of course, staffed with flesh and blood humans. But technology providers are working hard to augment the capabilities of our old-fashioned human workers with the help of automated voice recognition and sentiment analysis. This technology aims to support sales and call center agents with AI running in the background.

Some of this technology focuses on gathering aggregated metrics on the most common topics that drive customers to call in. Analysts can then use that data to identify where self-service experiences should be improved. But the opportunity is also for the AI to offer possible replies to questions and concerns, for example, when a customer is agitated and at risk.

The movie RoboCop[1] comes to mind, which features a machine-augmented law enforcer. Now, we'll have machine-augmented Sales and Customer Service representatives. Watch your wallet!

This opens the path toward call center Experience Analytics. We're already used to being prompted to take a survey after interacting with a call-center agent. That's the equivalent of asking for participation in surveys on websites. We are also used to getting told about calls being recorded for training purposes, and that's the equivalent of session replay for websites and apps. But just as surveys and session replays aren't enough for providing excellent website experiences, neither are their equivalents for call centers.

We need to compare what customers are saying in their feedback and the actual behavior and experience. And we need a way to quantify that at scale.

For Experience Analytics to help here, it will need all the capabilities we've already covered under chatbots and voice assistants earlier. However, it will need these capabilities at a much higher degree of sophistication because live conversations are far more complex than chatbot interactions.

In-store Experience Analytics

In-store analytics are already a growing industry. Funnily enough, it started pretty similar to web page traffic counters that preceded web analytics in the mid-1990s. Namely, foot traffic counters measured how many people walked through the store's door. But nowadays, insights available for in-store analytics go much further and are reminiscent of digital intelligence. For example:

In-store Journey Analysis

How is customer traffic flowing through the store? Where are the areas that are crowding up vs. getting ignored? When are queues building up in front of the checkout? And how can store employees be alerted and guided in real-time?

In-store Heatmaps

What are the areas of the store that are perpetually crowded vs. empty? And how does that correlate to sales of the related product categories, that is, conversion rate (e.g. see Figure 11.3)? There are many opportunities for improvement that can be derived from comparing the two data

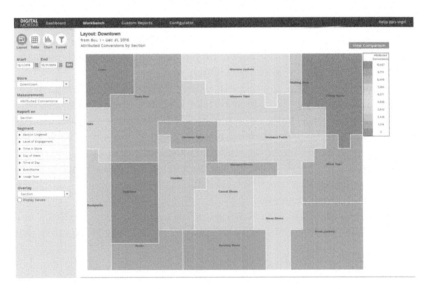

Figure 11.3 Brick-and-mortar store heatmap by Digital Mortar, providing in-store analytics.

Source: https://digitalmortar.com/

elements. The use cases seem very analogous to the ones we've covered for websites and apps in this book.

In-store Shelf Analysis

Typically meant for grocery stores, which shelves are emptying up so store personnel should replenish them? A depleted shelf is neither good for keeping sales going, nor is it a good customer experience.

Smart Devices

Almost every kind of device that exists is undergoing an evolution, with manufacturers innovating potential smart versions. Not just Smart TVs, cars, kitchen appliances, doorbells, HVAC controls, and vacuum cleaners. But these days, even light bulbs are available that are WIFI connected and become part of a Smart Home.

Previously, learning how to use these devices only required understanding their physical buttons and capabilities. Sometimes, that can be trouble enough. But now, there is a whole cyber world of things to learn and interact with. Therefore, the customer experience with using these devices would already benefit from digital Experience Analytics.

Funnily enough, crash testing for cars has always been a critical factor in the product's safety experience. Software crash testing is now also an indispensable factor of their user experience and safety.

Wearables

Fitness trackers have become ubiquitous. Smartwatches are taking over. Smart glasses had a false start, for example, with products such as Google glasses being pulled back out of the market again in 2012. But, personally, I can't wait for them to have their second coming when their AI capabilities mature.

These wearables turn us into digitally and AI-augmented beings. Imagine the smart glasses of the future that tell ignorant husbands like me when to insert a compliment for their wives.

These wearables require Experience Analytics just as much as other Smart devices do. Smart glasses, for example, turn the whole world into augmented reality. That would raise all of the UX questions that brands have today about their websites and apps, which are so simple in comparison.

For Experience Analytics this will require everything that we've covered earlier here. It will also require insights into the accuracy of optical vision recognition.

Implants

I can't wait for smart implants to become available one day so that I can finally think of myself as "Smart." But, all kidding aside, digital implants are already here, for example, hearing aid implants and pacemakers can be adjusted digitally. Essentially, we will increasingly have a digital interface to ourselves.

Do you think Experience Analytics may be vital to lead to good outcomes? Heck, yeah. And when it's a matter of life and death, Experience Analytics will require a degree of robustness and quality assurance that is up to the level of medical standards.

Smart Cities

Smart people want a smart world around them. Already today, we can see glimpses of how cities will become increasingly intelligent. For example, think of traffic lights that sense whether there is a need to keep you waiting at a red light. Or think about security cameras where face recognition algorithms help with safety and law enforcement needs.

Even the great outdoors have their own Experience Analytics already in place today. Air quality reporting and weather forecasting are a type of Experience Analytics if you think about it. Who knows what else the future may hold. It's up to your imagination. For example, an intelligent road that detects and warns about ice and dangerous road conditions would be a great idea.

From Digital Channels to Digital Beings

Fast forward a bit further, and our kids—or theirs—are likely to see a shift from digital channels to digital beings. Just like we don't think of a car salesperson as a channel, we think of them as a person.

If these digital beings become so smart, why will they still require Experience Analytics to improve the experience of humans interacting with them? Well, don't you wish that the proverbial used car salesperson also underwent some experience-analytics and optimization?

In part, machine learning will automate the Experience Analytics mechanism for digital beings. The feedback they collect from their environment during interactions will automatically improve machine learning and optimization.

But even when AI becomes so good that it resembles human intelligence, we'll still need external Experience Analytics and optimization. At that point, we might shift from calling it analytics to calling it training or therapy. For instance, marriage counseling today could be considered a type of experience analysis and optimization, for humans. So, even we benefit from experience training and therapy. As we like to say sometimes, we're only human after all.

Privacy, Privacy, Privacy

If privacy assurances, controls, and laws are top of mind today, it will simply be unthinkable to get any analytics at all if privacy and digital trust cannot be assured. Nobody wants to live in an Orwellian world. But we do want to take advantage of what innovation has to offer. So along with an increasingly intelligent world, we'll want intelligent laws and regulations to go along. At the same time, we will depend on Experience Analytics as a mission-critical insight for this to be a good world.

For Experience Analytics this means a privacy-first design. Just like websites are designed mobile-first today, Experience Analytics needs to be privacy-first to be ready and acceptable for our digital future. That writing is already on the wall in the digital intelligence industry today. Browsers and regulations increasingly restrict even anonymous tracking cookies. The future of experience analytics is probably cookieless.

Anything That Can Be Done, Can Be Done Better

Murphy's law says that "anything that can go wrong will go wrong." That's one reason why Experience Analytics are mission-critical. But we can add another law to this too. Namely: "Anything that can be done can be done better." So, that's another reason why Experience Analytics are mission-critical for competing in the age of the customer experience.

Wherever there are opportunities and gaps with experiences on your digital channels today, hopefully, this book has provided you with the knowledge and practical recipes for catching them quickly.

For the digital future that is evolving so quickly in front of our eyes, hopefully, the C-SUITE mindset provides you with the right questions to ask of any experience using any Experience Analytics. Now, and in the future.

Our lives are increasingly digital. Thank you for studying this book and being a good steward of the experiences you are providing! Thank you for doing your part to make our world a better place.

Note

1 Robocop, 1987, www.imdb.com/title/tt0093870/

Table of C-Suites and Case Studies

C-SUITE Cheat Sheets

Here is a cheat sheet of the C-SUITE cheat sheets in the book. For the items marked as "see online", please visit https://ExperienceAnalytics.Live/CSUITE.

Topic	Page
C-SUITE method summary	108
Solve Marketing Acquisition Challenges	
Acquired traffic: Are we paying for the right (qualified) audience?	118
Reducing bounce rates on marketing landing pages	125
Improve SEO based on Google Core Web Vitals metrics	see online
Solve Brand Marketing and Content Challenges	
Is the content strategy working for engaging and persuading customers?	135
How to fit engaging experiences onto small screens by adjusting placement and layout of content?	143
Solve Ecommerce and Ebusiness Sales Challenges	
Nothing seems wrong, but how can we improve further?	156
Create more uplift from the campaigns, A/B tests, and new launches that we are working on	163
Proactively identify what puts customers off, regardless of whether it is due to errors, UX, performance, etc.	167
Solve Visual Merchandising Challenges	
Are Promotions effective for sales of the targeted Products?	174
Are there Products with opportunities or issues?	178
Fine tune pricing experiences towards market prices	see online
Solve Customer Feedback Management Challenges	
Improve the areas of the site and app that drive the most feedback	189
Increase actionability of feedback and prioritize what to improve	193

Topic	Page
Solve Operations, Triage, and Technical Performance Challenges	
Understand what's blocking customers from converting and quantify the business impact	201
Challenge Resolve customer service complaints (e.g. executive escalations)	206
Proactively identify the biggest areas of the site for improvement in regards to friction and frustrations	213
Solve Customer Experience, Service, Support Challenges	
Find and improve the self-service journeys that drive up contact volume	225
Increase customer success, satisfaction, and product usage by improving self-service help and documentation	229
Solve Customer Marketing Challenges	
Manage my video format content marketing assets based on their value for engaging and inspiring customers	236
Create more uplift from the customer campaigns that we are working on	244
Solve Product and UX/CX Challenges	
Letting customers guide better roadmap decisions and prioritization	258
Find and fix experience issues in (new) Product experiences to speed up release cycles and free up time for innovation	265
Solve Conversion Rate Optimization and Analytics Challenges	
Proactively find and eliminate bottlenecks for journey completion	274
Optimize Form Completions	282
Inform A/B testing roadmap with experience insights to create more uplift, more often	284
Understand customers and their wants and needs	288

Case Studies by Industry

For case studies marked "Online" in the tables below please refer to https://Expe
rienceAnalytics.Live/CaseStudies

Retail and Ecommerce

Create experiences that are more …	Challenges	Company	Topic	Page
Inspiring	Content placement	Beauty brand	Reduced bounce rates	Online
Inspiring	Content placement	Avon	Increased sales from the PLP	139
Inspiring	Content strategy, site redesign	GoPro	Increased mobile sales with a site redesign	133
Inspiring	Content strategy, site redesign, Mobile	L'Occitane En Provence	Increased mobile sales with a site redesign	130
Inspiring	Landing page optimization	Flash sales site	Increased ad conversion rates	Online
Inspiring	Pricing optimization	Home goods retailer	Adjusted prices to market	Online
Inspiring	Product placement	Home improvement retailer	Fine-tuned a promotion	171
Inspiring	Product placement	Castorama	Reduced abandonment due to out-of-stock products	175
Rewarding	Contextualize customer feedback	Beerwulf	Contextualized customer feedback	184
Rewarding	Findability	Beerwulf	Improved add-to-carts from the PLP	254
Rewarding	Findability	Lovehoney	Improved holiday campaign conversion	159
Rewarding	Mobile App	Sports retailer	Reduced app abandonment on the home screen	258
Rewarding	Mobile App, Findability, Inform A/B test	Retailer	Increased app sales revenue	Online

Create experiences that are more …	Challenges	Company	Topic	Page
Rewarding	Optimize content/ CTA	Pizza Hut	Improved the "Deals page" to drive uplift in revenue	156
Rewarding	Proactive innovation, Inform A/B test	Moss Bros	Identified a winning A/B test to increase mobile sales	149
Rewarding	Reduce distractions	Retailer	Optimized registration drive for the loyalty program	Online
Seamless	Customer feedback, find & fix friction	Big box retailer	Resolved the Mystery of the Blank Page	190
Seamless	Customer feedback, find & fix friction	Big box retailer	Resolved mysterious complaints about a gray screen	198
Seamless	Customer feedback, find & fix friction	Big box retailer	Resolved a mystery issue with promotion codes	200
Seamless	Find & fix friction	Top 20 retailer	Eliminated blockers in checkout	Online
Seamless	Find & fix friction	Department store	Increased loyalty sales	237
Seamless	Find & fix friction	Hobbycraft	Automatically identified and resolved a surprise UX issue in checkout	164
Seamless	UX	Luxury Fashion retailer	Improved their new gift packaging options post-launch	Online

Financial Services

Experiences that are more …	Challenges	Company	Topic	Page
Inspiring	Content placement	Credit card company	Increased account applications	136
Inspiring	Customer insights	Retail bank	Qualified acquired ad traffic	113
Inspiring	Marketing optimization	Retail bank	Financial services institution in the Netherlands launched their Next-Best-Action Engine	Online
Rewarding	Content optimization, self-service	Retail bank	Increased self-service success	220
Rewarding	Content strategy, site redesign	Leeds Building Society	Redesigned product pages and journeys	151
Rewarding	Content/CTA optimization	Insurance company	Right-channelled cases for third-party claims	222
Rewarding	Content/CTA optimization	Retail bank	Increased mobile app downloads	240
Seamless	Find & fix errors	The Conran Shop	Proactively resolved an error during checkout	206
Seamless	Form optimization	Insurance company	Automatically surfaced friction during applications	210
Seamless	Form optimization	Life insurance company	Improved customer service	Online
Seamless	Form optimization	Credit card company	Resolved friction during applications	280
Seamless	Performance	Fashion brand	Improved speed and sales on mobile	Online
Seamless	Resolve customer service issues	Wealth management	Resolved a spike in IT error alerts	Online

B2B

Create experiences that are more	Challenges	Company	Topic	Page
Inspiring	Qualify ad traffic	Software Company	Qualified traffic from ad campaigns	113
Inspiring	Content strategy, reduce bounces	Software Company	Improved landing page effectiveness	119
Rewarding	Content strategy, self-service	Software Company	Increased positive product ratings	226
Rewarding	Content/CTA optimization	Contentsquare	Improved landing page conversions	269

Travel and Transportation

Create experiences that are more	Challenges	Company	Topic	Page
Inspiring, Rewarding	Mobile App, Proactive innovation, customer insights	Transportation company	Tailor experiences to customer intent	295
Rewarding	Content/CTA optimization, strategy	Car rental company	Got buy-in for new mobile bookings strategy	285
Seamless	Find & fix struggle, resolve complaints	Ferry service	Identified and resolved CX issues during bookings	202
Seamless	Form optimization	Car rental company	Improved booking search form usability	274

Telecommunications

Create experiences that are more	Challenges	Company	Topic	Page
Inspiring	Content optimization, videos	Telecom company	Identified how to better engage customers with their videos	232
Inspiring	Customer Insight, Marketing Optimization	Telecom company	Improved retention marketing triggers based on digital behavior	Online
Seamless	Contextualize customer feedback, find & fix errors	Telecom company	Resolved the Mystery of Why Customers Aren't Finding What They are Looking for	Online

Other

Industry	Challenges	Company	Topic	Page
Automotive	Content/CTA optimization	Skoda	Increased test drive visits	262
Automotive	Customer insights	Auto manufacturer	Improved lead scoring and management	Online
Market place	Inform Product roadmap	Juniqe	Improved acquisition by reducing bounce rates	251
Media	Performance, SEO, Core Web Vitals	M6	Improved speed and SEO	Online

Index

1:1 marketing *see* customer marketing

A/B testing 29; benchmarks 30; challenges of 29, 98; C-SUITE 283–4; informing of 77, 99, 119, 138–9, 149, 156, 223, 238, 253, 264, 279; integration with 98
accessibility 84; auditing of 86
account application 210
acquisition source 113, 125
Adobe Analytics 27, 286
agile product release 19, 155, 196, 213, 256, 261–4; C-SUITE 265
analytics teams 266; challenges of 268; C-SUITE for conversion optimization 274; C-SUITE for informing A/B test strategy 284; mindmap of 267
API 35; errors 64, 198
API integration 103
application completion 210
application performance monitoring (APM) 35; challenges of 36, 197
app optimization *see* mobile app optimization
artificial intelligence (AI) 306; *see also* automated insights
attention heatmap 51
attractiveness rate 57, 120, 241, 252, 272
attribution 24
augmented reality 311
automated insights 44, 71
Avon 139

bargain hunting 178
Beerwulf 184, 254

behavioral data 40
blank rate 69, 279
blindspots 28
blockers 197
bounce rates 24; reducing of 118, 251; C-SUITE 125
brand marketing 127
brick and mortar experiences 4, 18, 32, 35, 46, 60, 92, 127, 130, 175, 177, 310
B2B lead gen optimization 269, 300
Buisson, L. 303
business case for experience 1, 16
business intelligence (BI) integration 103

call avoidance 220
call center 309; *see also* customer service
call to action optimization 29, 55, 157, 221, 264, 272
campaign optimization 155–9, 236; C-SUITE 163
Castorama 175
chatbots 306
checkout optimization 12, 26, 33, 42, 61–9, 164, 198, 206, 264, 310
Cherki, J. 121
churn risk *see* retention marketing
click distribution 131
click frustration 67, 71, 164, 271
click heatmap 52, 271
clickmap *see* click heatmap; click rate
click rate 57, 119, 134, 160, 176, 262, 271
competing on analytics 18, 313, foreword xi (*see also* analytics teams)

complaint handling *see* customer feedback management
The Conran Shop 206
contact center complaints *see* customer feedback management; customer service
content 12; zone 55
content optimization 127, 136–9, 232; challenges of 130; C-SUITE 143
Contentsquare.com 269
content strategy 130; C-SUITE 135
context 11
conversion rate 58; C-SUITE 274
conversion rate optimization (CRO) *see* analytics teams
conversion rate per click 121
conversion rate per hover 123
conversion tracking 26; challenges of 27
cookieless analytics 313
Core Web Vitals 82, 126; *see also* speed optimization
CRM (Customer Relationship Management) *see* customer marketing
cross-sell 285
C-SUITE method definition 108
CTA *see* call to action
cumulative layout shift (CLS) 82
customer 12
customer centricity 264; *see also* customer marketing
customer experience (CX) team *see* customer service
customer feedback management 181, 190, 195; C-SUITE for improving journeys leading up to feedback 189; C-SUITE for increasing actionability of 193; impact quantification 190; mindmap of 182
customer identifier *see* identifying individual customer sessions
customer insights 92, 284, 291; C-SUITE 288
customer loyalty 226, 237, 245; C-SUITE for self-help journeys 229
customer marketing 230, 236, 243, 291, 303; C-SUITE 244; integration 282; maturity model 301; mindmap of 231; use cases 297

customer onboarding 226, 232
customer satisfaction 93, 225; C-SUITE for self-help journeys 229
customer service 202, 217; challenges 219; C-SUITE for improving self-service 225; C-SUITE for service issues analysis 206; mindmap 218
CX *see* customer feedback management; customer service
CXL 110

data captured by experience analytics 40
data collection 41
data democratization 268
data relationships 244, 301
data science 291; integration with 103; *see also* customer marketing
Davenport, T. H. foreword 18, 95
democratizing data 268
DevOps team *see* Operations
dialog marketing *see* customer marketing
digital body language 92, 286, 292, 298, 302
digital analytics 22; integration with 96; team (*see* analytics team)
digital-first 2
digital intelligence and insights teams *see* analytics teams
digital intelligence ecosystem 22, 95
Document Object Model (DOM) 56
drill-down 63
drop rate 69, 277; *see also* form analysis
dynamic content 54

ecommerce/ebusiness 146; C-SUITE for experimentation 156; C-SUITE for optimization 163; mindmap 147
ecosystem 95
Eisenberg, B, 29
e-merchandising *see* merchandising
engagement metrics 57; scoring 75, 300
engagement rate 57
enterprise marketing management *see* customer marketing
error analysis 60, 63, 257; C-SUITE 265

escalation handling 197; *see also*
    session replay business impact
    quantification
event stream in session replay 62
event tracking 27; challenges of 28
existing customer business *see*
    customer marketing
exit rate 37, 141, 152, 161, 258–9;
    C-SUITE for reducing of 258
experience analysis 47
experience, defined 44; good
    experience 1, 75; inspiring 76;
    rewarding 77; seamless 16
experience economy 3
experience gap 148
experience metrics 56
experience scorecard 102
experimentation *see* A/B testing;
    analytics teams
Explainable AI 72
exposure rate 57, 99, 116, 140, 149,
    224, 241, 262, 271
exposure rate, heatmaps 115
exposure time 137, 153

fastback 72
feedback *see* customer feedback
    management; voice of customer
find and fix *see* error analysis;
    frustration scoring; struggle
    analysis; UX friction
first input delay (FID) 82
form analysis and optimization 68,
    210, 274, 280; funnel of 68, 275;
    C-SUITE 282
form validation errors 65, 210, 281
framework of experience insights 43
friction *see* error analysis; frustration
    scoring; struggle analysis; UX friction
frustration behaviors 71, 210
frustration scoring 71, 164, 210, 280;
    C-SUITE 265
full funnel optimization *see* whole-
    funnel optimization
functional errors 65
funnel report 26; challenges of 27

Gillmore, J. 3
Godin, S. 127
golden paths 141, 149, 160, 251
Google Analytics 24
GoPro 133

Heath, C. 20
heatmaps 51; challenges of 55;
    historical page backgrounds 53; live
    browsing 270; zone-based 55, 117,
    137, 140, 150–8, 222, 252, 260–3
Hobbycraft 164
home page/screen optimization 77,
    131, 203, 258, 271, 296
hover rate, heatmaps 115, 221
human digital experiences 295

identifying individual customer
    sessions 202, 243
impact quantification 63, 87, 177,
    191, 197, 200, 208, 279, 281;
    integration with voice of customer
    101
innovate 20, 250, 254
in-page analysis 51; *see also* heatmaps
in-store experiences *see* brick and
    mortar experiences
intent 114, 255, 292–5, 307; *see also*
    customer insights
interaction metrics 57

JavaScript errors 64, 206; *see also*
    error analysis
journey analysis 47, 127, 152, 160,
    185–91, 239, 254–9, 295; for
    chatbots 307; C-SUITE 274
Juniqe 251

Kaushik, A. 28
Kusmi Tea case study 64

landing page optimization *see*
    marketing acquisition; home page/
    screen optimization
largest contentful paint (LCP) 82
Laya, P. 110
lead management 300
Leeds Building Society 151
live browsing heatmap 270
live chat 294
L'Occitane En Provence 130
looping behavior 254
Lovehoney 159
loyalty *see* customer loyalty
luxury brands 127–9

mapping of page types 49
Margalit, L. 92

marketing acquisition 23, 27, 251, 269; business pressures 109; challenges of 24, 109; C-SUITE for qualifying traffic 118; mindmap 110; optimization challenges of 111
marketing attribution 24
marketplaces 129
match-back response attribution 297
McKinsey 2
mean time to resolution (MTTR) 196
merchandising 168; challenges of 171; C-SUITE for promotion effectiveness 174; mindmap 169; reports for 173
merchandising metrics 58
mindset see digital body language
mission control team see Operations
mobile app downloads 240
mobile app optimization 257–8, 295
mobile web optimization 136, 256, 275, 285
mobile site redesign 130, 133, 256
Moss Bros 149
mouse move heatmap 5; see also heatmaps
movie nights 62; see also session replay
multichannel marketing 292; integration with 103, 293 (see also customer marketing)

natural language processing 307
net promoter scoring (NPS) 93, 184, 226, 240
new release optimization see agile
next-best action 299

omnichannel marketing see customer marketing
operations team 194, 207–10; challenges of 197; C-SUITE for identifying root cause of blockers 201; C-SUITE for surfacing blockers 213; triage and impact quantification by 198, 200
organic traffic 111, 126
out of stock products 65, 175

page backgrounds 53
page structure 14
page types 49
paid traffic 109, 111
PDP see product detail page

peaks and potholes 19
Peppers, D. 301
performance 15
performance team see operations
permission to market see customer marketing
personalization 15, 32, 291; challenges of 33; integration with 98; informing 286, 295; intent-based 297, 302
personally identifiable information see PII
Peterson, E. 28, 100
PII 41, 292
Pine, B. J. 3
Pizza Hut A/B test 20, 156
placement optimization 14, 174; C-SUITE 178
PLP see product list page optimization
potholes and peaks 19
predictive analytics 299
price optimization 178
pricing 15
privacy 6, 41, 297, 301, 313
product analytics 250
product detail page redesign 149–151, 251
product displayed, pageviews, click rate, conversion rate 176
product-led growth 247
product list page optimization 159, 254, 284
products 14
products with opportunities and issues 173, 176; C-SUITE 178
product teams 247; challenges of 250; C-SUITE for roadmap prioritization 258; mindmap of 248
promotion code issues 200
promotion optimization 14, 157, 171, 285

qualifying acquired traffic 112, 118

"rage" clicks 58, 71; see also click frustration
real user monitoring (RUM) 79; advantages of 81
redesign see A/B testing; mobile site redesign; product detail page redesign

refill rate 69, 278; *see also* form
    analysis
registration 210, 231, 243, 247, 301
release management *see* agile
repeat business *see* customer
    marketing
response attribution 297
retention marketing 300
revenue attribution 58, 132; *see also*
    zone-based heatmaps
reverse journey analysis 184; *see also*
    journey analysis
right-channelling 223
roadmap prioritization 250; C-SUITE
    258 (*see* product teams)
Rogers, M. 301
root cause analysis *see* error analysis;
    frustration scoring; struggle
    analysis; UX friction
RUM *see* real user monitoring

SaaS (software as a service) 226;
    C-SUiTE for self-help journeys 229
Schwartz, T. 31
scoring 71, 164, 300; *see also*
    frustration scoring
scrolling heatmap 51; *see also*
    heatmaps and exposure rate
SDK 41
search engine optimization (SEO) 36,
    82, 126
segmentation 88, 93, 96, 199, 203,
    296; on existing customers 114; on
    marketing campaigns 113, 238
self-service journey completion 220,
    226; C-SUITE 225
sentiment analysis 307, 308, 309;
    see also digital body language; voice
    of customer
session replay 61, 66, 73, 87, 96, 164,
    192, 201, 208, 212, 278–81;
    business impact (*see* impact
    quantification); event stream of 62;
    integration with digital analytics 96;
    integration with voice of customer
    101, 193, 198–200
7 "Ps" 13
shortcut 63
side-by-side comparison 98
signals *see* personalization
skill gap 4
Skoda 262

smart devices 311
social media 111
speed optimization 78, 126, 213;
    impact of 82; metrics 81
store *see* brick and mortar
    experiences
sticker shock 178
strategy for competing on experience
    analytics foreword 1
struggle analysis 60, 67, 257, 273;
    C-SUITE 265; *see also* frustration
    scoring
Suárez, S. T. 251
sunburst diagram 48
support team *see* customer service
surveys *see* customer feedback
    management; voice of customer
synthetic monitoring 79; advantages
    of 81 (*see also* Core Web Vitals;
    speed optimization)

tag 41
tap rate 57
targeted marketing *see* customer
    marketing
technical teams *see* analytics teams;
    operations teams; product
    teams
time before first click 116, 158,
    277
traffic reports 25; challenges of 25
triage *see* operations teams
troubleshooting 20; *see also* error
    analysis; frustration scoring;
    struggle analysis; UX friction

unresponsive clicks 58; *see also*
    frustration scoring
upsell *see* customer marketing
user experience teams *see* product
    teams
user identifier 202, 243
UX friction 164, 203, 257, 273;
    C-SUITE 265 (*see* frustration
    scoring)
UX teams *see* product teams

video analysis and metrics 232;
    C-SUITE 236
video completion rate 234
visual merchandising *see*
    merchandising

VoC *see* voice of customer
voice assistants 307
voice of customer 33, 181, 190,
   212; challenges of 34; C-SUITE
   for improving journeys leading
   up to 189; C-SUITE for increasing
   actionability of 193; integration
   with 100, 186; mindmap for
   182
voice recognition 309

wearables 311
web analytics *see* digital analytics
web performance *see* speed
   optimization
whole-funnel insights 42
window shopping 253, 295, 298, 303
wisdom of the crowds 283

zone 55
zone-based heatmaps *see* heatmaps